Andrew Orr
The Gay Girl in Damascus Hoax

Transnational Queer Histories

Edited by
Bodie A. Ashton and Sabrina Mittermeier

Advisory Board

Volume 1

Andrew Orr

The Gay Girl in Damascus Hoax

Progressive Orientalism and the Arab Spring

DE GRUYTER
OLDENBOURG

ISBN 978-3-11-105657-9
e-ISBN (PDF) 978-3-11-105723-1
e-ISBN (EPUB) 978-3-11-105758-3
ISSN 2750-6096

Library of Congress Control Number: 2022950765

Bibliographic information published by the Deutsche Nationalbibliothek
The Deutsche Nationalbibliothek lists this publication in the Deutsche Nationalbibliografie;
detailed bibliographic data are available on the internet at http://dnb.dnb.de.

© 2023 Walter de Gruyter GmbH, Berlin/Boston
Cover image: iStock
Typesetting: Integra Software Services Pvt. Ltd
Printing and Binding: LSC Communications, United States

www.degruyter.com

For Sarah and Suzanne

Acknowledgements

This project has taken me far outside of my comfort zone as a historian of war, women, and politics. I am greatly indebted to a wide array of people for helping me decide to write this book and for improving it through their sage advice and support. I am grateful to my colleagues at Kansas State University, including Suzanne Orr, David Defries, Michael Krysko, Heather McCrea, Nadia Oweidat, and Phil Tiemeyer, who read drafts and discussed concepts I struggled with. I am indebted to the memory of Al Hamscher. It was a conversation with Al that convinced me to start writing this book. I wish he had lived to tell me what he thought of it. Marc DeVore has been especially stalwart in encouraging me to press forward with this project despite Covid-related setbacks. Nupur Chaudhuri and Sandra Dawson are two of my heroes, their capacity to be productive amid chaos is astounding and their encouragement helped launch this book.

I am grateful to the people and institutions that provided financial support for this project. I fear it will do little to enhance my school's research expenditure metrics, but the support I received was invaluable to helping me along the path to this book. That support included an Undergraduate Research Team Grant from Sam Houston State University which funded three undergraduate assistants (Angie Wood, Clayton Porter, and Walter Bauer) who helped me collect many of the internet metrics I used in this project. I was astounded SHSU gave me the grant after I resigned, but it helped me enormously and paid a portion of the students' tuition for the following year. I am also grateful to Tugrul Keskin and the Center for Global Studies at Shanghai University for providing support that allowed me to attend their 2018 Conference on Orientalism, Neo-orientalism and Post-Orientalism in African, Middle East, Latin American, Asian/Chinese Studies. The feedback I received from the diverse group of global scholars they brought together shaped my project. My conversations there led me to reimagine this project as a book instead of as an article.

This work reflects an incongruous combination of influences which have made up my education and experiences as a scholar. I see the influence of my undergraduate Government Department advisor at Claremont McKenna College, Harold "Bill" Rood. His realism and teaching focus on Nazi and Communist propaganda paid unexpected dividends when I began writing on the *Gay Girl in Damascus* hoax. I am also grateful to my Ph.D. advisor at Notre Dame, Thomas Kselman, whose focus on the social history of religion and how religious culture shaped identity in nineteenth-century France influenced my approach to this book. When combined with my own work on Communist propaganda, French imperialism, and gender in the French Army, these influences have informed my take on the *Gay Girl in Damascus* affair.

https://doi.org/10.1515/9783111057231-202

Finally, I am profoundly grateful to Rabea Rittgerodt and her team at De Gruyter. Her enthusiasm for this project and incredible efficiency have helped me drive this project forward and made me too embarrassed to miss her deadlines. Peer review is an inherently stressful process because it means opening oneself up to judgment, but I owe a debt of gratitude to this project's reviewers and series editors Sabrina Mittermeier and Bodie A. Ashton for their critical and productive advice. They were not afraid to point out weaknesses in my work and were generous in suggesting ways to improve it. I have tried to take their comments seriously and, although readers will judge for themselves whether my final product is useful, it is undoubtedly better for the experience of peer review.

Contents

Introduction: Orientalism and the Western Imagination

26 April 2011
Arraf Family Home,
Damascus, Syria

After midnight two armed men confronted Abdallah Arraf in the family's court-yard. The old man, who had recently moved home from the United States so he could die where he was born, knew they were there to arrest somebody. He was surprised though when they demanded he surrender his daughter Amina.

Amina, however, was not surprised. She had spent the last two months orga-nizing protests and proclaiming her opposition to the regime on her blog, *A Gay Girl in Damascus*. Not wanting to risk anybody else's life by trying to hide or es-cape, she went downstairs to face her fate. When she arrived, the men told her she was under arrest for participating in a Salafist plot. Her father interrupted, claiming it was ridiculous to arrest a woman who "doesn't even cover any more" for being an Islamist radical. He demanded to know how they could have read her defense of same-sex marriage or her argument that "there should be no reli-gion as religion of the state" and believe she was a religious extremist?

In response one of the men asked Abdallah, "Did she tell you that she likes to sleep with women . . . That she is one of those faggots who fucks little girls?" Abdal-lah, who already knew Amina was a lesbian, defiantly responded, "She is my daugh-ter and she is who she is and if you want her, you must take me as well." Angered, one militiaman grabbed Amina's breast, and threated that "Maybe if you were with a real man you'd stop this nonsense." Abdallah contemptuously asked, "Did the jackal sleep with the monkey before you were born?" After demanding and getting their names, he knew he had a chance because although they were Alawis, he knew their families. He recited details from their family' histories and explained that nothing they said would shake his love for his daughter, "she has done many things that, if I had been her, I would not have done. But she has never once stopped being my daughter and I will never once let you do any harm to her." He ordered them to leave and "tell the rest of your gang to leave her alone" because she was not their enemy. Instead of backing Assad's dictatorship out of fear, they should support Amina and democrats like her who "are the ones saying alawi, sunni, arabi, kurdi, duruzi, christian, everyone is the same and will be equal in the new Syria; they are the ones who, if the revolution comes, will be saving Your mother and your sisters."

Faced with Abdallah's outrage, the men apologized for disturbing the house and left. On her blog, Amina described how "everyone in the house was awake

https://doi.org/10.1515/9783111057231-001

now and had been watching from balconies and doorways and windows all around the courtyard . . . and everyone was cheering . . ." She gushed that "MY DAD had just defeated them! Not with weapons but with words" and that "My father is a hero; I always knew that . . . but now I am sure." Reason and acceptance had triumphed over violence and prejudice.[1]

Later that day Amina posted the story, which she called "My Father, the Hero" to *A Gay Girl in Damascus* and it spread across the world. Aided by Western journalists and activists who posted links to the blog, hundreds of thousands of people read the story. There was just one problem. Amina Arraf, the "gay girl of Damascus" was none of those things; she did not even exist. Amina and all the stories on *A Gay Girl in Damascus* were created by Thomas "Tom" MacMaster, a middle-aged male heterosexual American activist and graduate student who had recently moved not to Syria, but to Scotland.

The Arab Spring and *A Gay Girl in Damascus*

In late 2010 and early 2011 protestors filled the streets of many Arab countries. The protests soon became known in the West as the Arab Spring. In January 2011, protests in Tunisia convinced President Zine El Abidine Ben Ali to accept the end of his twenty-three-year reign and flee the country. Ben Ali's fall inspired people in other Middle Eastern countries to take to the streets. In January and February 2011 protests spread to Libya, Egypt, Bahrain, and Yemen. Protests in Egypt, and the threatened loss of American economic and military support, led the Egyptian Army to force President Hosni Mubarak to step down. The protest movements quickly acquired a checkered record. Tunisia democratized, but within two years the Egyptian Army reimposed a government resembling Mubarak's regime. The results were even worse in Libya and Yemen where the unravelling of the old regimes led to long and bloody civil wars. At first it seemed that Syrian dictator Bashar al-Assad would escape unscathed. Emulating Jordan's King Abdullah II, Assad promised reforms to head off protests. However, in February 2011 small protests slowly spread across Syria.

The Arab Spring captivated European and American observers. Western journalists, policy experts, activists, and academics debated what was happening,

---

1 Thomas MacMaster, "My Father, the Hero" *A Gay Girl in Damascus*, 26 April 2011. http://damascusgaygirl.blogspot.com. The blog has been taken down, but a facsimile of almost all of the blog is available from Minal Hajratwala's website http://www.minalhajratwala.com/wp-content/uploads/2011/06/damascusgaygirl.blogspot.com_.zip. Unless otherwise noted, all citations to the blog are to Hajratwala's facsimile.

what it meant, and how it would shape the region's future. It reminded many Westerners of the 1989 protests in Eastern Europe, but the development of the internet and social media meant that they could follow Arab activists directly on social media and had online forums where they could easily share and discuss news from the Middle East. Thomas "Tom" MacMaster was one Westerner inspired by the Arab Spring.

In early 2011, MacMaster was forty-years old and had recently moved from Atlanta to Scotland to begin graduate school in medieval history at the University of Edinburgh. MacMaster had been fascinated by the Middle East since he was a child. He had studied Arabic and visited the Middle East as a peace activist and student. After graduation he lived in Atlanta and campaigned for Palestinian rights and against the United States' wars in Afghanistan and Iraq. MacMaster felt validated by the Arab Spring. He saw the protests as proof of his belief that public opinion in the region was committed to a pluralist, democratic, and anti-capitalist agenda despite neoconservative claims that the dominant strain of Middle Eastern Islam was oppressive and dangerous. But MacMaster feared that Islamophobic and imperialist voices would trick Western public opinion into opposing the reform movements as he believed they had fooled Americans into supporting the invasion of Iraq in 2003.

In 2002 and 2003 MacMaster protested the Iraq War and spoke out against it in online forums. Frustrated with other users challenging his positions with what he viewed as ill-informed opinions he convinced himself that they would more readily accept his views on the Middle East and Islam if he were an Arab Muslim woman. Sometime in late 2002 or 2003, he created email accounts under the name "Amina Arraf" and began using them to post about controversial issues. Over the 2000s, MacMaster expanded the character, adding social media accounts on MySpace, dating sites, and Facebook. He even tried to blog as Amina briefly in 2007. The Arab Spring captivated MacMaster and on 19 February 2011, *A Gay Girl in Damascus*, a new blog MacMaster created in Amina's name, went live. Although MacMaster's previous attempt at blogging fell flat, *A Gay Girl in Damascus* quickly established an audience and caught American and British journalists' attention.

The revelation that the Syrian American "gay girl of Damascus" was a heterosexual white American man in Scotland led activists and journalists to ask how the hoax had succeeded. Most accounts focused on the inherent difficulty of proving identity in digital spaces and MacMaster's exploitation of people's assumptions that other people who had interacted with Amina online must have known that she was real. Although true, this ignored uncomfortable questions about why Western journalists, activists, and educated readers believed the stories MacMaster told as Amina instead of recognizing them as obvious fantasies.

Studying the Hoax, the Impostor, and the Audience

This project asks *why* MacMaster's sophisticated audience believed him. It explains the hoax's success by framing it as a political intervention and deploys historical methods of textual analysis and contextualization to study the hoax and MacMaster's audience's reactions. Understanding why so many people believed that Amina existed and accepted what MacMaster wrote in *A Gay Girl in Damascus* requires integrating Orientalism, progressive politics, and critical theory while paying close attention to who MacMaster was speaking to. All three factors functioned on conscious and unconscious levels to shape how MacMaster performed Amina and how his audience reacted to the performance.

Because MacMaster used Amina as a proxy for his own progressive politics, he rooted the character in American progressivism. When he then projected his persona into the Middle East and made her a lesbian woman, he relied on Orientalist tropes to sustain the illusion. Part of the reason MacMaster made Amina a lesbian Arab woman was because of his own attachment to liberating academic theory which emphasized the importance of listening to and challenging the Othering of marginalized people, including women, sexual minorities, and people of color. MacMaster's generally well-educated and progressive readers shared his theoretical deference to marginalized people, general social and political views, and were parts of the same culture which had Orientalized Arabs. The American tradition of strategic narcissism melded with the traditional Orientalist tactic of using the Middle East as a site to debate and define the West to allow MacMaster to use his imagining of the Arab Spring in Syria to validate Western, and especially American, progressive identity.

Although his hoax clearly reflected MacMaster's own emotional and psychological needs, it was also an attempt to persuade other Westerners to agree with him. MacMaster tried to build support for a policy of military non-intervention by shaping readers' views of Syria, Islam, and Syrian Revolution. However, MacMaster's intervention was fundamentally rooted in Western, and especially America, domestic politics. The posts on *A Gay Girl in Damascus*, including Amina's backstory, were designed to convince other progressive Westerners that the Syrian Revolution was culturally and politically progressive, which assured them that their own values were right and universal. MacMaster accomplished this by using the credibility Amina's carefully curated biography afforded him among educated progressive Westerners to create a fictitious approximation of Syria into which he projected his and his audience's hopes and beliefs. This process reinforced his readers' domestic politics and identities while leveraging them to affect their views of Islam, Syria, and the Arab Spring.

Academic scholarship shaped MacMaster's backstory for Amina. He even used examples pulled directly from scholarly works as plot points in Amina's life. MacMaster's biography for Amina combined eroticized and exoticized Orientalist tropes with progressive politics though his creation of a resistance identity that emphasized marginality to mark Amina as a truth teller. He presented Amina as a liberating agent by emphasizing her ability to cross boundaries, including the East-West boundary, the secular-religious boundary, and through her homosexuality, which in Orientalist tropes suggested an ability to cross gender boundaries. MacMaster exploited cultural homonormativity to use Amina's gender and homosexuality to present her as having been Othered but still be comfortable to middle class Western progressives. This allowed Amina to be marginalized while still closely resembling and not challenging his educated Western readers.

MacMaster's hoax distorted the intent while exploiting the form of the ideas he appropriated. Neither his actions nor those of the people who believed him negated the potential value of ideas he misused, but they do expose the continuing vulnerability of progressive ideas, even those rooted in indigeneity, critical studies, and other anti-imperialist and antiracist[2] critiques to the very concepts they were built to challenge. This emphasizes the need for scholars, especially white and Western scholars, to self-critically apply their critiques to their own ideas and be open to challenging their own *implicit* biases.

When *A Gay Girl in Damascus* was exposed as a fraud, most commentators reacted with shock and framed it as an extraordinary event. However, the following decade revealed that far from being unique, MacMaster's hoax formed part of a larger pattern of academic activists manipulating self-consciously liberating theory to craft fraudulent resistance identities for their own professional advantage and political validation. The steady stream of exposures has included graduate students, junior professors, and tenured senior professors. The forms of impersonation have varied from impostors, like MacMaster, impersonating marginalized people online to people passing in real life and building their careers and personal lives around their assumed identity. The consistent factor across these cases is the impostors' recognition and weaponization of the theoretical power attached to their appropriated identity.

---

2 Taking a cue from holocaust historians' use of antisemitism (as opposed to anti-Semitism) to represent the ideology of racial hatred toward Jews, this work differentiates between anti-racism and antiracism. It uses anti-racism to denoted general opposition to racism and antiracism to refer to an ideological commitment to challenge and root out systemic power structures that create and sustain racial hierarchies. Antiracists are thus anti-racists but not all anti-racists are antiracists.

This book does not claim to recover the voices MacMaster erased, nor does it seek to correct the record by identifying, explaining, and restoring each instance in which his ersatz Syria distorted reality. Instead, it studies the appropriated rendering as an artifice to explain how and why MacMaster was able to pass it off as reality for as long as he did; In other words, it studies the blog, its Western author, and its predominantly Western audience, not Syria. By turning its lens on the ideas that framed the Amina hoax, this book argues that egalitarian and academically infused ideas about racial and gender liberation in the global South are vulnerable to Orientalist understandings of people of color which complicate and truncate their ability to initiate truly liberating processes. In so doing, it responds to Robin DiAngelo's call for white people to speak to each other about the continuing role white racial privilege has in blinding them to the effects of their actions on people of color.[3]

Orientalism

Edward Said's 1978 book *Orientalism* has influenced scholars of many different fields. Said criticized the way Westerners studied and talked about the Middle East, Arabs, and Islam. He argued that European and American scholars, artists, politicians, and other opinionmakers used deceptive representations to turn their studies of the Middle East into processes for subordinating it to the West. Although rooted in literary theory and criticism, Said always infused his work with politics and history. He made it clear that Orientalism extended beyond the specific images being deployed and encompassed Westerners' appropriation of the Orient for their own purposes, regardless of their goal so long as their knowledge of the Orient remained rooted in a subordinating power relationship. He framed Orientalism as "a Western style for dominating, restructuring, and having authority over the Orient" which was reduced to "a place of romance, exotic beings, haunted memories and landscapes, remarkable experience."[4] Said focused his critique on "malicious generalization about Islam" but he rooted it "the idea of the West (and the United States, as its leader) as the standard for enlightened modernity."[5]

---

3 Robin DiAngelo, *White Fragility: Why it's so Hard for White People to Talk About Racism*, (Boston MA: Beacon Press, 2018).

4 Edward Said, *Orientalism* (New York: Vintage Books, 1979; reprint 1994), 1, 3.

5 Edward Said, *Covering Islam: How the Media and the Experts Determine How We See the Rest of the World* (New York: Vintage Books; 1981; 1997), xii, xxix, xliv; Edward Said, *Power, Politics, and Culture: Interviews with Edward W. Said* (New York: Vintage Books, 2002), 8.

Since Edward Said first presented his critique, scholars of Orientalism have been at the forefront of a movement in the academy that has incriminated the political, social, and cultural power mechanisms of the West. Orientalism is widely understood to be a tool of repressive forces and overcoming it has been an endeavor closely tied to progressive politics in the West. Noam Chomsky emphasized that Orientalism involves both Westerners' understandings of the non-Western world and their understanding of themselves. He framed Said's project as being "devoted to unravelling mythologies about ourselves and our interpretation of others, reshaping our perceptions of what the rest of the world is and what we are. The second is the harder task; nothing's harder than looking into a mirror."[6] Meyda Yeğenoğlu's feminist rendering of Orientalism provides this work with its central understanding of Orientalism. She emphasized that Orientalism is relational by operationally defining it as "the cultural representation of the West to *itself* by way of a detour through the other." Yeğenoğlu's conceptualization is especially well suited to this project because it locates Orientalism's power in its ability to "construct the very object it speaks about" and "produce a regime of truth about the other and thereby establish the identity and power of the subject that speaks about it."[7]

Scholars, including Said, have emphasized the centrality of sexuality to Western constructions of the Middle East and noted the role of sexuality and eroticization within the West's subordination of the Middle East.[8] Similarly Joan Scott has urged scholars to take unconscious processes that shape hierarchies of gender and power more seriously.[9] Reina Lewis argued Western representations of Middle Eastern women and sexuality, even when presented as an effort to liberate them, reinforce Western power over the Middle East.[10] While Rana Kabbani held that "to perceive the East as a sexual domain, and to perceive the East as a domain

---

6 Noam Chompsky in Maya Jaggi, "Out of the Shadows," *The Guardian* (11 September 1999) https://www.theguardian.com/books/1999/sep/11/2.

7 Meyda Yeğenoğlu, *Colonial Fantasies: Towards a feminist reading of Orientalism* (New York: Cambridge University Press, 1998).

8 Said, *Orientalism*, 188; Gayatri Chakravorty Spivak "Can the Subaltern Speak?" in Cary Nelson and Lawrence Grossberg eds *Marxism and the Interpretation of Culture* (Chicago: University of Illinois Press, 1988), 67; Rana Kabbani, *Europe's Myths of the Orient* (Bloomington: Indiana University Press, 1986), 10; Reina Lewis, *Gendering Orientalism: Race, Femininity and Representation* (Routledge: New York, 1995); Judith Butler, 'Explanation and Exoneration, or What We Can Hear' *Grey Room*, 7 (Spring 2002): 56–67; Lila Abu-Lughod, *Do Muslim Women Need Saving* (Cambridge MA: Harvard University Press, 2015).

9 Joan Wallach Scott, *The Fantasy of Feminist History* (Durham NC: Duke University Press, 2011), 1–4, 91–93, 116.

10 Lewis, *Gendering Orientalism*.

to be colonized, were complementary aspirations."[11] This project builds on Lila Abu-Lughod and Yeğenoğlu's insight that the eroticization of the Other is an inherent part of Orientalism and Yeğenoğlu's warning that within Orientalism "the discursive constitution of Otherness is achieved simultaneously through sexual as well as cultural modes of differentiation" even when this operates as a subconscious level.[12] It does this by using MacMaster's eroticization of Amina and journalists' uncritical acceptance and praise of it as a window into how they viewed the Middle East.

One way to do this is to follow Afsaneh Najmabadi's approach to studying gender and Middle Eastern politics by asking "what work did gender do" and "how did it perform cultural labor?"[13] This book turns Najmabadi's questions back upon Westerners, asking what cultural labor MacMaster's eroticization of Amina and focus on homosexuality performed as a way to understand how and why the rendering of the Middle East he created appealed to his audience. MacMaster's blog unintentionally validated Yeğenoğlu's work while twisting Pinar İlkkaracan's claim that gender and sexuality in the Middle East play out as a struggle between a progressive and liberating movement for autonomy and reactionaries seeking to regulate sex and women's bodies to buttress a decaying traditional order.[14]

The Privileged and the Marginalized

Critical scholars have highlighted privileged scholars' struggles to recognize the effects of their privilege. Gayatri Chakravorty Spivak and Gurminder K. Bhambra's work on the imperialist substructures of post-structuralist thought exposed the contradictions between Western thinkers' aim of freeing people from idea-based power structures while reproducing the very power structures they criticized. As Spivak showed in "Can the Subaltern Speak," poststructuralist critics felt able to speak in place of colonized or other "third world" peoples even as they critiqued the construction of value and knowledge structures that shifted economic and political power into the hands of the elites who created them.[15]

11 Kabbani, *Europe's Myths of the Orient*, 10.
12 Yeğenoğlu *Colonial Fantasies*, 1–2, 90–91; See also Lila Abu-Lughod, 'Review: "Orientalism" and Middle East Feminist Studies' *Feminist Studies* 27, No. 1 (Spring, 2001): 101–113.
13 Afsaneh Najmabadi, *Women and Mustaches and Men without Beards: Gender and Sexual Anxieties of Iranian Modernity* (Berkeley CA: University of California Press, 2005), 1.
14 Pinar İlkkaracan 'Women, Sexuality, and Social Change in the Middle East and the Maghreb' *Social Research* 69, no 3 (Fall 2002): 753–779.
15 Spivak, "Can the Subaltern Speak?" 289, 292–93; Gurminder K Bhambra "Postcolonial and decolonial dialogues," *Postcolonial Studies*, 17 no 2, (2014): 115–121.

Spivak, warned academics that their attempts to recover the voices and experiences of the marginalized can render the non-European world "transparent" by washing out the lived experience and perspectives of their subjects through imposing academics' own agenda on their subjects.[16]

More recently Robin DiAngelo's *White Fragility* exposed the inability of anti-racist and progressive white Americans (including antiracists) to fully accept that they remain supporters and beneficiaries of economic, social, and political systems that reinforce racial hierarchies even as they denounce racism.[17] She argued that white fragility, the defensive and emotional reactions of even anti-racist whites that protect them from being confronted with the full extent of their own racial power, leaves them unable to learn what life it really like for people of color. Their resulting ignorance of their own ignorance of the lives of people of color helps explain why so many Westerners, even those with bona fide experience with the Middle East, could not detect that Amina was a white male Westerner reading their own experiences back to them and why MacMaster himself was blind to the effects of his actions.

Critics of imperialism often challenge pernicious stereotypes of non-Western people that justify colonialism and other forms of domination, but their critiques can replace negative stereotypes with new ones that merely serve different political ends. Spivak called for scholars to destabilize imperial domination by "reversing, displacing, and seizing the apparatus of value-coding" which underwrites imperialism.[18] While focusing more closely on United States government policy, Judith Butler and Deepa Kumar have studied the ways academic and political knowledge production have shaped American policy. After the 11 September 2001 attacks, Butler warned that "frames of understanding violence emerge in tandem with the experience" and the only way to break the cycle of violence of which September 11th was a part was for Americans to reject imperialist frames that justified American military action in the Middle East. Butler urged scholars to be "open to narration that decenters us from our supremacy, in both its right and left wing form."[19] Middle East and LGBT+ studies scholars have challenged Western "liberationists," especially but not only neoconservatives, who have invoked LGBT+ oppression to justify Western intervention in the Middle East. Brad Epps called on scholars to confront the politicized fantasy of opposing "a permissive polysexual West" to a

---

16 Spivak "Can the Subaltern Speak," 67.
17 DiAngelo, *White Fragility*, 4–5.
18 Gayatri Chakravorty Spivak "Post-structuralism, Marginality, Postcoloniality and Value" in Peter Collier and Helga Geyer-Ryan eds *Literary Theory Today* (Cambridge: Polity Press, 1990), 28.
19 Butler, "Explanation and Exoneration," 56–64.

"repressive heteronormative Middle East."[20] Jasbir Puar warned that apparently positive depictions of gayness in the West have constructed a "national homonormativity" which is implicated in neoliberal capitalism and reinforces "the ascendency of whiteness." The resulting homonationalism justified American and/or Western imperialism through its juxtaposition with a terrorist and sexually disordered Islamic Other.[21]

Although most scholars of pinkwashing have focused on conservatives' opportunistic claims that Western intervention in the Middle East protects LGBT+ Middle Easterners, others including Jin Haritaworn, Tamsila Tauqir, and Esra Erdem have targeted progressive Western activists for equating Islam and homophobia in their domestic activism.[22] In a different context, Jane Naomi Iwamura's work questions the inherent value of recoding frames of understanding from negative to positive. Iwamura has studied Western romanticization of "exotic" cultures and religions and argued that superficially positive changes in how Westerners portray non-Western people and cultures "should not necessarily be taken as a sign of social progress."[23]

Feminist, queer, and post-colonial scholarship do not disavow the ability of the privileged to speak in support of the oppressed, but they problematize it and repudiate the privileged speaking *for* the oppressed.[24] MacMaster accepted the intellectual substructure of academic critical theory and activists' critiques of racial power, but he, like other academic impostors, balked at accepting the limitations they implied. By passing as Amina, MacMaster exploited the credibility he and many of his progressive readers and scholars gave to resistance identities. His hoax's success highlights Evren Savcı's warning that the dominance of the English language and American and British concepts in queer studies and activism creates a false sense of universality in scholars and activists' imaginations that

---

20 Brad Epps "Comparison, Competition, and Cross-Dressing: Cross-Cultural Analysis in a Contested World" in *Islamicate Sexualities: Translations across Temporal Geographies of Desire*, eds. Kathryn Babayan and Afsaneh Najmabadi (Cambridge MA: Harvard University Press, 2008), 114–160.

21 Jasbir Puar, *Terrorist Assemblages: Homonationalism in Queer Times* (Durham NC: Duke University Press, 2007). 1–3.

22 Jin Haritaworn, Tamsila Tauqir, and Esra Erdem "Gay Imperialism: Gender and Sexuality Discourse in the 'War on Terror.'" In *Out of Place: Interrogating Silences in Queerness/Raciality*, edited by Adi Kuntsman and Esperanza Miyake (York: Raw Nerve Books, 2008), 71–92.

23 Jane Naomi Iwamura, *Virtual Orientalism: Asian Religions and American Popular Culture* (New York: Oxford University Press, 2011), 8.

24 Lina Alcoff, "The Problem of Speaking for Others." *Cultural Critique* 5, no 20 (1991): 5–32; Trebilcot, "Dyke Methods" *Hypatia* 3 no. 2 (1988): 1; Said, "Representing the Colonized," *Critical Inquiry* 15 no. 2 (1989): 205–225.

erases differences in meaning and objectives and which unconsciously essential-izes language as a marker of distinct cultural groups.[25] This book uses historical methodologies as it primary tools of analysis, but joins postcolonial queer and Feminist theorists in exposing the contradictions in activists and scholars' subor-dination of the nuances of time, place, and modes of communication to ideologi-cally- and power-laden universalist assumptions.

A wide range of scholars including Jasbir Puar, Mari Ruti, Sara Ahmed, David Eng, Stephen Engel, and Timothy Lyle have criticized the whiteness of the LGBT+ voices highlighted by the media and the drive to assimilate Ameri-can LGBT+ identity into white middle class identity through the successful campaign to legalize same-sex marriage. Ahmed accepted that assimilation was understandably attractive to many middle-class white LGBT+ Americans but concluded that it was a morally mistaken stance. Ruti and Eng argued that the same-sex marriage debate involved the neo liberal state offering white LGBT+ Americans the chance for enhanced personal security in-exchange for breaking solidarity with people of color in America and victims of imperialism aboard.[26] The vehemence of theorists' critiques, however, showed that they were losing the political battle and LGBT+ Westerners and well-educated West-erners, including MacMaster and his audience, strongly supported marriage equality.

The whiteness of LGBT+ history and studies have shaped the way activists and progressive readers have understood what it means to be queer. David Halperin has shown that the centrality of white Western gay men in LGBT+ scholarship and media images has encouraged a form of perceived identity that helped fuel the *Gay Girl in Damascus* hoax. Halperin argues that Western gay white male tropes have highlighted the transgression of white middle class culture's sexual norms. This sexualizes gay men, and, by extension, other non-heterosexual people caught up in the power of the identity. This identity's celebration of "being naughty, disobedient, sinful, bad" made it an archetype for transgression. It also provided a foundation for MacMaster and his readers' construction and acceptance of Amina as well as

---

25 Evren Savcı, *Queer in Translation: Sexual Politics and Neoliberal Islam* (Durham NC: Duke University Press, 2021), 11–14.

26 Puar, *Terrorist Assemblages*; Mari Ruti, *The Ethics of Opting Out: Queer Theory's Defiant Subjects* (New York: Columbia University Press, 2017), 12–14; David Halperin, *What Do Gay Men Want? An Essay on Sex, Risk, and Subjectivity* (Ann Arbor: University of Michigan Press, 2007); Sara Ahmed, *The Promise of Happiness* (Durham NC; Duke University Press, 2010); David Eng, *The Feeling of Kinship Queer Liberalism and the Racialization of Intimacy* (Durham: Duke University Press, 2010); Stephen Engel and Timothy Lyle, *Disrupting Dignity: Rethinking Power and Progress in LGBTQ Lives* (Oxford: Oxford University Press, 2021), 223–262.

their mutual willingness to believe that her worldview and political identity could be understood through sex and sexuality.[27]

Scholarship exploring the lives of LGBT+ people of color in the West and in other parts of the world has expanded too slowly, though it as grown more rapidly recently. Scholars of LGBT+ people of color have emphasized that understandings of racial and sexual difference have often evolved in relation to each other and have long been inseparable. MacMaster built his hoax on the often-unnoticed assumption, which is rooted in scholarship, that people identified as being not-white and not-straight experienced ideologically similar forms of discrimination. As Laurie Marhoefer has argued, this tradition is often internally contradictory. Many of its most-cited proponents, including Siobhan Somerville and Valerie Rohy, sometimes present arguments that conflate racism and homophobia side-by-side with overarching claims that distance themselves from their own arguments or even outright contradict themselves in other parts of the same work.[28] MacMaster exploited popular perceptions of this equality in discrimination to impose the United States' political context on Syria. However, a robust body of scholarship has demonstrated that although racism and homophobia are related and often simultaneously constructed, being white and gay is a demonstrably distinct experience, which involves dramatically different levels of risk and access to protective alliances, than being a person of color, let alone a gay person of color. One unfortunate result of earlier assumptions, has been to encourage scholars, activists, and other politically engaged people to read supporters of LGBT+ rights, now and in the past, as presumptively part of an antiracist and egalitarian tradition.[29]

In recent years historians of LGBT+ history have expanded their studies beyond white Westerners. Marhoefer's exploration of the relationship between the gay German sexologist Magnus Hirschfeld and Li Shiu Tong, a gay Chinese man who was Hirschfeld's student in the early 1930s, broke new ground in showing the roles of people of color in the early American and European LGBT+ equality movement and revealed the centrality of racial ideas and concepts of empire within the movement.[30] Petrus Liu has explored the interrelationship of Marxism and queer

---

27 Halperin, *What Do Gay Men Want?* 57.
28 Laurie Marhoefer, *Racism and the Making of Gay Rights: A Sexologist, his Student, and the Empire of Queer Love* (Toronto, University of Toronto Press, 2022).16. Siobhan Somerville, "Scientific Racism and the Emergence of the Homosexual Body" *Journal of the History of Sexuality*, 5 no 2 (1994): 243–66; Siobhan Somerville, *Queering the Color Line: Race and the Invention of Homosexuality in American Culture* (Durham NC: Duke University Press, 2000); Valerie Rohy, *Anachronism and Its Others: Sexuality, Race, Temporality* (Albany, NY: SUNY Press, 2009).
29 Marhoefer, *Racism and the Making of Gay Rights*, 14–16.
30 Marhoefer, *Racism and the Making of Gay Rights*.

cultures in Taiwan and the People's Republic of China. Liu's work emphasizes the diversity of ways queer life and theories intersect and with economics, domestic politics, and international politics to argue that LGBT+ rights and queer studies need not be tied to liberalism or Euro-American cultural models whose proponents, including Eve Sedgwick, Michel Foucault, and Judith Butler, he believes have used the Othering of non-Western cultures (in his case China) as tools which allow them to conceptually delimit their Western-rooted theories so they can pass as universals.[31]

Scholars of political identity have distinguished between state-legitimated identities and resistance identities which are created by politically and socially marginalized people to challenge their status quo.[32] Resistance identities are culturally constructed around preexisting identifiers that are already implicated in a society's "terms of inclusion and exclusion."[33] Courtney Jung explained that resistance identities are formed when "the demands of excluded 'others' . . . arise to challenge the consensus thought from which they have been excluded and to renegotiate the terms of the incorporation." The resulting debate can transform the terms of inclusion and exclusion.[34] MacMaster tried to build a Syrian resistance identity for Amina, but his imposition of Western politics and social conflicts onto the character meant he built a Western insurgent and merely labelled her as a Syrian rebel, in the process overwriting the experiences, aspirations, and fears of real Syrians.

MacMaster's appropriation of Arab and lesbian identity reflected his engagement with and distortion of academic ideas. MacMaster's actions uncomfortably paralleled the ideas of critical media scholars like Deepa Kumar and he built on the work of Mary C. Walters and David Hollinger who argued that ethnicity in the United States is an elastic and adaptable concept. Hollinger went further, postulating an ability to cross ethnic identity boundaries through solidarity.[35] MacMaster had read Hollinger's *Postethnic America* before writing his blog. In addition to

31 Petrus Liu, *Marxism in the Two Chinas* (Durham NC: Duke University Press, 2015), 22–28.
32 Manuel Castells, *The Power of Identity.* (Oxford: Blackwell, 1997), 8.
33 Courtney Jung, *The Moral Force of Indigenous Politics: Critical Liberalism and the Zapatistas.* (New York: Cambridge University Press, 2008), 70–71. See also Anthony Marx, *Making Race and Nation: A Comparison of the United States, South Africa, and Brazil* (Cambridge, Cambridge University Press, 1998); Doug McAdam, John McCarthy, and Mayer Zald, *Comparative Perspectives on Social Movements: Political Opportunities, Mobilizing Structures, and Cultural Framings* (Cambridge, Cambridge University Press, 1996).
34 Jung, *Moral Force of Indigenous Politics*, 10–11, 234.
35 David Hollinger, *Postethnic America: Beyond Multiculturalism* (New York: Basic Books, 1995); Mary C. Walters, *Ethnic Options: Choosing Identities in America* (Berkeley CA: University of California Press, 1990).

assimilating some of Hollinger's arguments, he stole examples from Hollinger's life and reassigned them to Amina. MacMaster also stole examples from John Scagliotti's documentary *Coming Out in the Developing World*. This book argues that MacMaster's behavior went far beyond the forms of ethnic and racial choice Hollinger and Walters discussed and formed an extreme example of what Lisa Nakamura called "identity tourism." Nakamura explored internet users who experimented with race by playing other racial identities online. She concluded that far from breaking down barriers, it frequently reinforces stereotypes and helps people ignore the reality of racism by creating the fiction of a "post-racial" world.[36]

American Nationalism and Technological Determinism as Orientalism

This work understands readers, and especially journalists' reaction to the *Gay Girl in Damascus* hoax by combining scholarship on technological determinism, the ideology of American foreign policy, and the power of racial and cultural blinders to hinder privileged observers' understanding of the lives of the oppressed. Reading DiAngelo's critique of anti-racists white Westerners' inability to see their own privilege as an elaboration of Spivak and Bhambra's works places *A Gay Girl in Damascus* within a larger tradition of ideological nationalism that has subordinated non-Americans, especially people of color in the so-called Third World, to Americans' views of themselves.

Although rooted in different theory, Spivak and Bhambra's works resonate with the Realist political scientist Hans Morgenthau and psychologist Ethel Person's claim that American foreign policy has long been shaped, in their minds distorted, by Americans understanding international events through the lens of their own political, social, and ideological identities.[37] Similarly, Richard Feinberg's work warned policymakers of the dangers of American policy being hijacked by "an emotional public clamoring to project their sense of self onto the rest of the world."[38] Former U.S. National Security Advisor, U.S. Army general, and historian H.R. McMaster termed this "strategic narcissism" and argued that

---

36 Lisa Nakamura, "Cyberrace" *PMLA* 123 no 5, October 2008):1673–1682.
37 Hans Morgenthau and Ethel Person, "The Roots of Narcissism" *The Partisan Review*, (Summer 1978), 337–347.
38 Richard Feinberg, *The Intemperate Zone: The Third World Challenge to U.S. Foreign Policy* (New York: W. W. Norton & Company, 1983), 234.

it leads U.S. opinionmakers, including political, military, and academic leaders to assume that the world will converge toward America's path if given the opportunity.[39]

Initially journalists argued that social media use sparked the Arab protests and sustained their momentum. Over time scholars moderated these claims without denying that social media played a role in the movement. This trajectory mirrors long term trends in the history of communications technology. Merritt Roe Smith and Leo Marx as well as David Nye have explored the exaggerated the role scholars and commentators often initially ascribe to technological innovation in shaping history before ultimately placing it into a larger social context that debunks technological determinism.[40]

This work argues that MacMaster and his readers' technological determinism in 2011 masked deeper Eurocentric assumptions. In the context of the Arab Spring, technology-induced liberalization was supposed to include greater social solidarity, acceptance of difference, and the undermining of ethnic and gender hierarchies. It reflected Western technological determinists' hope for their own societies as well as their expectation that the Middle East would move toward that ideal. This marked Western progressivism as a universal truth and defined Middle Easterners as future Western progressives who only needed the right stimulus and opportunity to catch up along a common path. In so doing, ideological-technological determinists' inadvertently reasserted assimilationist justifications for colonialism in pre-World War I era and repackaged 1960s era Modernization Theory.[41] Critical scholars like Deepa Kumar have noted that Orientalism and Modernization Theory shared a "polarized view of the world" that contrasted and subordinated the East to the West despite using different methodological approaches.[42]

More recently, post-colonial queer theorists including Evren Savcı have critiqued the romanticization of Islam by Western critics of neoliberalism. She argued that "studying Islam, whenever it is addressed, as the subjected other in Western modernity" distorts scholars understanding of power structures in Muslim majority countries by, among other things, obscuring the importance of neoliberal economics

---

39 H.R. McMaster, *Battlegrounds: The Fight to Defend the Free World* (New York: Harper, 2020).
40 Merritt Roe Smith and Leo Marx, eds, *Does Technology Drive History? The Dilemma of Technological Determinism* (Cambridge MA: MIT Press, 1994); David Nye, *Technology Matters: Questions to Live With* (Cambridge MA: MIT Press, 2007).
41 Alice Conklin, *A Mission to Civilize: The Republican Idea of Empire in France and West Africa, 1895–1930* (Stanford: Stanford, University Press, 1997).
42 Deepa Kumar, *Islamophobia and the Politics of Empire* (Chicago: Haymarket Books, 2012), 39.

and other power-relationships. She has called for an unburdening of Islam from its assigned role as an alternative to political "modernity" and the imperial West.[43]

The dominant Western journalistic narrative of the Arab Spring as a social media induced revolution was rooted in pre-2011 scholarship and journalistic narratives. In 2008, Antony Loewenstein laid out the basic narrative that others used in 2010 and 2011 to explain the Arab Spring when he argued that blogs were opening new avenues for individual "citizen journalists" to spread information and engage in activism pressuring authoritarian governments to enact reforms throughout the world, but especially in the Middle East.[44] Most journalists echoed some part of this line and the American journalist Andy Carvin, who focused on reporting what Arab activists were saying on social media, emerged as the leading journalistic advocate that social media was central to the Arab Spring.[45]

Many journalists folded technological determinism into larger assumptions that the Arab Spring marked a natural step toward the Middle East converging with the West. These unexamined assumptions shaped how they understood and engaged with the Arab Spring and the *Gay Girl in Damascus* blog. In addition to longstanding Orientalist perspectives, journalists drew on free expression discourses rooted in the expansion of the internet in the 1990s. Early internet popularizers argued that the internet would democratize societies by allowing instantaneous person-to-person speech, making it impossible for governments, corporations, or even the established news media to control the transmission of ideas. This would shift the balance of power in favor of individuals and oppressed groups who could bypass establishment gatekeepers to speak directly to their fellow citizens. Scholars of life writing, including Gillian Whitlock, have critiqued popular Western assumptions that social media and other electronic communications transcend cultural differences and flatten hierarchies of power and privilege while recognizing the powerful effect such assumptions can have on Western readers.[46] The work magnifies Whitlock's critique.

Scholarly treatments of the Arab Spring have diversified journalists' narrative of the protests' origins. Ziad Majed and Juan Cole argued that the movement was generally pluralist, rooted in a youth rebellion, and facilitated by internet communication, but that the protestors also encompassed other groups with

---

43 Savcı, *Queer in Translation*, 2–4.

44 Antony Loewenstein, *The Blogging Revolution* (Melbourne: Melbourne University Publishing, 2008).

45 See Andy Carvin, *Distant Witness: Social Media, the Arab Spring, and a Journalism Revolution* (New York: CUNY Journalism Press, 2012).

46 Gillian Whitlock, *Soft Weapons: Autobiography in Transit* (Chicago: University of Chicago Press, 2006).

different goals, motivations, and systems of mobilization.[47] Rashid Khalidi, Axel Bruns, Tim Highfield and Jean Burgess agreed that social media helped facilitate the protests, but argued that "popular media narratives" exaggerated its centrality. Khalidi was an early voice challenging the media's technological determinism. He argued that the protest movements reflected long-term organizing efforts by "unions, women's groups, human rights activists, Islamists, intellectuals, campaigners for democracy, and many others" and that social media was thus only one of several enabling factors.[48] Hebatullah Selim's work on Salafi political organizing in Egypt since 2011 has shown that focusing on social media and internet presence made it easy to miss the strength and growth of Salafi political movements during and after the Arab Spring.[49]

Technological determinism, strategic narcissism, and Orientalism intertwined to shape how Westerners perceived the Arab Spring. Strategic narcissism and Orientalism worked together to allow journalists, activists, policy experts, and academics to subordinate the events of the Arab Spring to Western domestic politics. In the case of the *Gay Girl in Damascus* blog, MacMaster and his audience shared these common vulnerabilities, which helped MacMaster convince his audience to accept his performance of Amina and his analysis of the Syrian Revolution.

Progressive Orientalism

This project presents the concept of Progressive Orientalism to mark the unconscious contamination of what are meant to be liberating ideas with Orientalism and its components, including sexualization, exoticization, and Eurocentrism. In 2010 Graham Cassano presented a version of Progressive Orientalism when he argued that John Ford and Dudley Nichol's 1937 film "The Hurricane" was a critique of European imperialism but that "the energies for that critique come from a paradoxically 'progressive' orientalism that represents South Seas 'natives' as inher-

---

47 Ziad Majed, *Syrie: La revolution orpheline* (Sindbad/Actes sud L'Orient des livres, 2014), trans Fifi Abou Dib and Ziad Majed. Translated from *Sûriya al-thawra al-yatima* (Beruit: Sharq al-Kitab, 2013); Juan Cole, *The New Arabs: How the Millennial Generation is Changing the Middle East* (New York: Simon & Schuster, 2014).
48 Rashid Khalidi "Preliminary Historical Observations on the Arab Revolutions of 2011" in *Dawn of the Arab Uprisings: End of an Old Order?* eds Bassam Haddad, Rosie Bsheer, and Zaid Abu-Rish, (London: Pluto Press, 2012), 9–16.
49 Hebatullah Selim, "Religionizing Politics: Salafis and Social Change in Egypt," PhD Diss., (University of Birmingham, 2016).

ently wild and independent."[50] Assimilating Iwamura's conclusions, this work uses Progressive Orientalism ironically, positing that Orientalism infects and negates the otherwise anti-racist ideas with which it interacts.

This project partially models post-colonial queer theory's technique of reading multiple concepts into each other to expose insights that are not visible when examining only one of the factors. Examining the mechanics of MacMaster's impersonation of Amina and the concept of fraud that permeated it in tandem with Western – but especially American – Orientalism reveals a form of Progressive Orientalism. Progressive ideas (including antiracist, anti-imperialists, and egalitarian ideals) permeated the origins and form of MacMaster's hoax and distorted how he and his readers viewed the Middle East even as they leveraged their rendering of the Middle East to assert their own identity and advocate for progressive changes in their home countries.

Looking at the functioning of the impersonation as fraud or its Orientalism in isolation would obscure the process by which MacMaster and his audience reduced Syria and Syrians to tools to validate their own political and cultural identities. Seeing progressivism, Orientalism, and the impersonation together reveals insights that cannot be gleamed from focusing on the individual pieces in isolation. The result is a work that takes conceptual risks by bringing often conflicting ideas together to understand a multifaceted phenomenon through a deep inspection of a single example, in other words it is a history.

Postcolonial theorists including postcolonial feminist and queer theorists have led the way in revealing the distorting effects of Western critics of Western imperialism or globalism's use of Islam as a romanticized alternate model. This work's formulation of Progressive Orientalism is indebted to the work of post-colonial theorists,' including Evren Savcı, who have emphasized the unacknowledged universalist assumptions buried within the way Western scholars and activists have deployed queerness and Islam to critique globalism, Western security policy, and even critical scholars' approaches to understanding how Westerners interact with Islam.

Progressive Orientalism shares other forms of Orientalism's subordination of the East to the West, but often substitutes positive value coding. Traditional, Liberal (or Neoliberal), and Progressive Orientalism have different political objectives and worldviews, but they share a common relationship to the Middle East, which is why this project focuses on Orientalism as a relationship. Scholars argue

---

50 Graham Cassano, "'The Last of the World's Afflicted Race of Humans Who Believe in Freedom:' Race, Colonial Whiteness and Imperialism in John Ford and Dudley Nichols's The Hurricane (1937)" *Journal of American Studies* 44, 2010, 117–136.

that Traditional Orientalists present Arabs, Islam, and the Middle East negatively to justify Western domination of the region and to defend established power structures inside of Western society. They do this by using the threat of the Islamic, or other non-Western, Other to rally support for domestic power structures as well as Western domination of the non-Western world. Liberal Orientalism seeks to know the Middle East and diagnose its faults to justify Western reform projects that will transform and Westernize the Middle East in the name of liberating it. Progressive Orientalists seek to free the East from the West by positively coding the East, but still impose their own values on the Middle East to create an artificial East which they use to critique power structures in their own society.

Traditional and Liberal Orientalists produce knowledge about the Middle East to justify projects rooted in their domestic politics and interests, whether that is the explicit imperialism of classic colonial domination or the expansion of free trade, globalized economics, and international legal regimes that subordinate non-Western states to Western norms that characterize Liberal Orientalism. Progressive Orientalism codes the Middle East, Islam, and Arab cultures positively, thus avoiding the need to diagnose them. Instead, Progressive Orientalists use the positive coding of the Middle East to diagnose their own societies. However, the knowledge is still produced for Western observers' own domestic ideological purposes in ways that distorts their understanding of the Middle East by subordinating it to an external political project. In the process Progressive Orientalism's liberating and egalitarian impulses are rendered inert by its practitioners' inability to recognize the nature and effect of their own actions. In addition, Progressive Orientalists' tendency to overwrite the people and place they claim to be studying to fashion them into a tool with which to reshape their own society emphasizes that Progressive Orientalism is as much of a barrier to solidarity and understanding across cultures as other forms of Orientalism. Progressive Orientalism is thus closely related to the phenomenon of homonormativity in that both represent a projection of a middle-class left-of-center experiences and politics onto a group which Western progressives believed they are in solidarity with, but whose own views, experiences, and goals are easily overwritten in the minds of their would-be allies.

Although tied to different policies, all forms of Orientalism involve Westerners imposing convenient ideologically laden veneers on the East for the purpose of validating their domestic political identity and authority claims, thus reducing the East to a function of elite Westerners' needs. *The Gay Girl in Damascus* hoax provides a way to illustrate the form and harmful effects of Progressive Orientalism as well as scholars' susceptibility to it. It makes clear that Orientalism remains a pernicious form of marginalization, erasure, and exploitation even when superficially positive coding replaces explicitly negative coding.

Writing About the *Gay Girl in Damascus* Hoax

Scholarship and creative works on the Amina hoax have focused on the ambiguity of identity in digital communication. Kylie Cardell and Emma Maguire explored what the hoax meant for "reading and consuming life narratives in digital spaces" and the challenges of establishing authenticity in a digital forum. They also explored MacMaster's desire to claim the mantle of marginalization, which they identified as a sought-after marker of authenticity for both writers and "card carrying listeners" who consume life-writing as a form of engagement with social justice issues.[51] Julia Marie Smith studied the blog as an example of "problematic authorship" and focused on the role of mediating participants, especially journalists, who lent MacMaster's performance credibility by publicizing the blog, discussing Amina, and interacting with MacMaster posing as Amina.[52] Similarly, Omar El-Khairy's 2013 play *Sour Lips* focused on the blurred definition of reality online and imagined a digital Amina who evolved an independent will and turned against her creator. His work theorized that the collective and uncoordinated actions of commenters and readers shaped the blog's evolution.[53] Sophie Deraspe's documentary *Le Profil Amina* retold the story from the perspective of Sandra Bagaria, a lesbian woman from Montreal who had a five-month long online romantic relationship with MacMaster while he was posing as Amina. It explored the ambiguity of online identity and traced Bagaria's search to understand the hoax. It culminated in her confronting MacMaster after a panel at an academic conference.[54]

Kevin Young discussed *A Gay Girl in Damascus* as part of a larger study of hoaxes in American culture. He placed MacMaster in the context of American fraudsters who used exotic hoaxes to compensate for their own frustrated ambitions and analyzed the hoax itself in terms of archetypes including the travel liar and the Circassian beauty, which garners attention for the hoaxer by exploiting race and gender stereotypes through placing white women (in this case a half-white woman) in danger at the hands of non-white men.[55] Integrating Young's insights help explain the tactics MacMaster used to manipulate his audience, but

---

51 Kylie Cardell and Emma Maguire "Hoax Politics: Blogging, Betrayal, and the Intimate Public of a Gay Girl in Damascus" *Biography*, 38 (2) (Spring 2015), 208, 212–214.

52 Julia Marie Smith, "*A Gay Girl in Damascus*: A Multi-vocal Construction and Refutation of Authorial Ethos" in *Authorship Contested: Cultural Challenges to the Authentic, Autonomous Authors*, eds Amy E. Robillard and Ron Fortune (New York: Taylor & Francis, 2016), 21–39.

53 Omar El-Khairy, *Sour Lips* London, Oberon, 2013.

54 *Le Profil Amina*, Directed by Sophie Deraspe. Monteal: Esperamos and the National Film Board of Canada, 2015.

55 Kevin Young, *Bunk: The Rise of Hoaxes, Humbug, Plagiarists, Phonies, Post-Facts, and Fake News* (Graywolf Press, 2017).

this work contextualizes MacMaster's character within a contemporary political and academic frame which yields different insights than Young's work.

Grant Bollmer used the hoax to critique proponents of network citizenship's claim that greater information connectivity "will perfect political agency" by democratizing politics and culture. He warned against a libertarian ethos that fetishizes "connectivity and flow" over justice and thus misreads social movements by privileging means over ends especially in studies of blogging and other social media. Bollmer's inclination to read MacMaster's actions as symptoms of a larger problem was correct, and this project builds on his work by expanding the frame of reference beyond social media.[56]

Gordon Alley-Young applied Scholes's textual power method to argue that MacMaster's hoax was persuasive because he drew on pre-established texts and life stories. He found three main "sites of meaning" in MacMaster's work: Western fantasies of lesbian Muslim women, co-opting MENA (Middle East and North African) voices/identities, and the rise of the citizen journalist. Alley-Young focused on MacMaster's hoax within a journalistic frame including showing journalists and MacMaster were both vulnerable to the power of unacknowledged stereotypes which social media aggravated but did not create. Finally, he broke important new ground by framing MacMaster's fraud within an academic context by linking it to a phenomenon of fake articles being successfully submitted to academic publishers. This work expands on Alley-Young's insight but shifts its context from systemic vulnerabilities in publishing processes to ideological and cultural vulnerabilities rooted in concepts of identity.[57]

Academics, Activists, and Identity Appropriation

The *Gay Girl in Damascus* hoax existed at an intersection of culture, politics, activism, and the academy and needs to be understood as part of a larger phenomenon of academic misuse of liberating theory. The misuse of theory highlights a subset of academics' struggle to reconcile their lives and activism with the theory they espouse. Situating the *Gay Girl in Damascus* hoax within academic and ideological frameworks helps explain how and why the hoax worked and exposes the

---

56 Grant Bollmer, "Demanding Connectivity: The Performance of 'True' Identity and the Politics of Social Media" *JOMEC Journal*, 0 no 1 (June 2012): 1–12.

57 Gordon Alley-Young, "Co-opting Voice and Cultivating Fantasy: Contextualizing and critiquing the A Gay Girl in Damascus hoax blog" in *Ethic, Ethnocentrism and Social Science Research*, ed. Diya Sharma (New York: Routledge, 2021), 122–147.

Orientalist substructures that survive within self-consciously progressive and anti-racist Western thought.

In June 2011, most observers dismissed MacMaster's hoax as an unfortunate outlier that had lessons about the importance of verifying online sources, but little else. In retrospect though it fits into a larger pattern of privileged academic activists pretending to be oppressed people. Rachel Dolezal's exposure as a white woman living as a Black woman in 2015 sparked a discussion about identity appropriation that reframed MacMaster's hoax. Media coverage of Dolezal created a popular archetype for white people passing as people of color that made it easier for critics to gain traction when questioning a person's claimed identity, whether in person or online.

Most white academics who pass as marginalized people believe that systemic racism, sexism, colonialism, and homophobia have created durable hierarchies of power and exclusion that define access to wealth and power in the modern world and assigned greater weight to privileged people's speech. They further believe that the power structures of the modern life need to be amended and that one way to do this is for the privileged to decenter themselves to allow people from historically marginalized groups to have the space and platform to articulate critiques of their own oppression.

Ideological and personal motivations easily overlap for people whose conception of themselves includes their commitment to egalitarianism and antiracism. Impostors' behavior is a form of self-defense which they use to redirect their own attention from their complicity in the systems they decry. This provides a way for impostors to see themselves as fighters for justice without having to impose limits on themselves. However, their passing is inherently counterproductive because they obscure the voices they believe are critical to combating systemic discrimination.

Impostors reduce the identities they perform to instruments of their own self-validation. The assumed persona is a privileged Westerner cloaked in stereotypes. The stereotypes an impostor uses reveal a lot about the person who created the identity and why the impostor is seeking to pass. Impostors are more likely to convince other people their personas are real if the stereotypes are believable to the observers. A successful passing thus reveals commonalities in how the impostor and the audience construct the people and places that are part of the performance. Examples such as a *Gay Girl in Damascus* can thus reveal unacknowledged ideological and cultural baggage that survives within individuals' minds and groups' collective culture.

Sources, Challenges, and Structure

This work is essentially a biography of a woman who never existed, which poses certain challenges. Biographies typically start at the beginning of a person's life and proceed chronologically toward its end. However, Amina never existed, and her biography was not created in chronological order. This work could look back over the entire body of the hoax and present Amina's biography based on the fullest picture of material about the character, but that would obscure the hoax's evolution. Another option would be to narrate the hoax in order of events, beginning with MacMaster creating his character in the early 2000s and filling in details in the exact order they were revealed. That too comes with costs though, it would make it hard to piece together the final picture because it would be revealed in disjointed chunks. This work seeks a compromise that allows a coherent picture of the hoax to emerge while highlighting how it changed over time. It divides the hoax into periods which provide convenient points to analyze it as an ongoing process while allowing the analysis to sift the flood of evidence into a coherent narrative.

This book draws on journalists' accounts, memoirs, online discussion groups, social media posts, and period blogs as well as creative endeavors including a play and documentary film. However, its main source is *A Gay Girl in Damascus: An out Syrian lesbian's thoughts on life, the universe and so on . . .*, which it will refer to as *A Gay Girl in Damascus* throughout the text. MacMaster deleted the blog in June 2011 when investigators exposed his hoax, but copies of it remain. Most of the blog was preserved by Minal Hajratwala, an activist, journalist, and author who interacted with MacMaster while he was posing as Amina. Additionally, archived copies of individual pages of the blog survive thanks to Internet Archive's *Wayback Machine*. This book draws on interviews done with MacMaster both while he was posing as Amina and after his exposure. In both periods, it reads his words skeptically and pays close attention to how and why he says things. It also draws on interviews with people who were victims of the hoax and who investigated it. Reading their stories together made it possible to reconstruct a timeline that showed the growing problems MacMaster faced maintaining the hoax and the reasons why he made the decisions he did under pressure.

The topic and sources created special linguistic challenges. Amina Arraf does not and has never existed, but the blog and the media sources refer to the character regularly because the point of the hoax was to make it seem like she existed. This work refers to MacMaster as the author of all the material posted under Amina's name but analyzing MacMaster's propaganda requires describing the actions and thoughts he attributed to Amina. To avoid excessively confusing sentence structures this book treats the fictious people MacMaster created as characters he controlled, thus sentences like "MacMaster had Amina remember visiting . . ." or "MacMaster told Marsh that Amina believed . . ." It does not belabor the obvious point that all of Amina's family members, friends, and most of the people Mac-Master wrote that Amina met at protests were made up by him as part of sustaining the illusion that Amina and the fictionalized version of Syria she inhabited were real. The book manipulates naming conventions to help mark this. Academic works typically refer to people by their family name and this book follows that convention for real people but refers to MacMaster's characters by their first name. Thus, it will refer to MacMaster writing things, but to Amina, Rania, and Abdallah when discussing MacMaster's characters.

The first chapter focuses on MacMaster's construction of Amina, arguing that he used Orientalist tropes to create an avatar of American progressive political identity. Drawing on interviews with MacMaster and journalists' later investigations, it locates the hoax's origins in MacMaster's anti-Iraq War activism. The chapter explores Amina's evolution until late April 2011 when *A Gay Girl in Damascus* became a hit. It highlights Amina's Orientalist subtext and emphasizes Mac-Master's use of eroticized and exoticized tropes, often read onto Amina's body, to contextualize the Syrian Revolution as a validation of Western progressive politics. It demonstrates that MacMaster designed his blog to convince progressive Westerners that the Syrian Revolution was a multicultural movement that embraced gender, religious, ethnic, and sexual diversity. The chapter ends by analyzing "My Father, the Hero," which turned the blog into a viral success in the West by reading Western politics into Syria.

The second chapter examines the media's role in MacMaster's hoax during *A Gay Girl in Damascus*'s period of maximum success, late April to May 2011. It argues that journalists and other consumers of MacMaster's blog were central actors in the hoax. The chapter builds on MacMaster's exploitation of eroticized stories that used Amina's body and sexual life as sites to discuss Islamophobia, imperialism, LGBT+ rights, and ethnic diversity with his expanded audience. His audience's acceptance of a growing list of improbable and stereotyped events that repeatedly eroticized major political events and personal experiences provides an opportunity to show MacMaster's dependence on his audience's passive participation in his hoax. It finishes by exploring journalists and other social media users' engagement with the blog, paying special attention to how MacMaster's hoax shaped their coverage.

The third chapter studies MacMaster's failed attempt to end the hoax without being caught and the fallout of the hoax's revelation. It begins by reconstructing the pressures that led MacMaster to try to end the blog and the ways they shaped his performance of Amina before the final crisis. It places his exit strategy, pretending Syrian secret policemen kidnapped Amina, in the larger context of his political storytelling to reveal how he intended to end the story and show how Orientalist tropes influenced journalists and activists' reaction to the kidnappings. Drawing on media coverage and social media posts, the chapter argues that MacMaster's performance shaped its own coverage by convincing journalists that Amina was an important influencer of the revolution and even one of its leaders. It explores the Free Amina movement whose members wanted Amina released from prison and how it evolved into a search for the person behind the hoax.

The fourth chapter uses a study of academic hoaxes to delve deeper into the process of imposture and further interrogate Progressive Orientalism by placing Tom MacMaster and the *Gay Girl in Damascus* hoax into a comparative perspective with other academic impostors who have falsely claimed racial, ethnic, gender, and sexual identities other than their own. It refines the role of political ideology in identity appropriation and emphasizes the social violence inherent in this form of exploitation. The comparative perspective emphasizes the role of individual politics in motivating impostors and academic theory's decisive impact on the, often shifting, identities impostors choose to claim. The chapter concludes by delving deeper into the role of ideology in shaping Westerners' views of themselves and the world.

Chapter I
Crafting a Digital Heroine

Summer 1991
Arraf Family Home
Damascus, Syria

As Amina emerged onto the roof, her body recoiled from the Damascus heat and the call to prayer echoed in her ears, creating a waking dream. She saw three futures open before her. She could assimilate as a white American: declare herself "Amy, not Amina," forget "this stupid family and all their crazy fears and worries," and then "figure out this whole crazy sexuality thing" by either coming out or getting an "American boyfriend." A second road would make Amina "the rebel Arab girl." She could "smoke cigarettes in the cafes at night" and be "all intellectual and progressive" while trying to secularize and Westernize Arab culture. Or she could take a third path, the path of Islam on which she would know truth and sacrifice.

Struggling to choose when she was unsure who she really was, Amina walked forward to the edge of the roof. She looked down at the pavement and thought "here is the answer to all my troubles, so simple, so perfect, so sublime. . . reach out and fall, fall gently on the breeze, like an oakleaf tumbling from a tree." As Amina readied herself for the "leap into all embracing darkness" she felt a "great gripping hand" pull her back from the edge.

Lying on the roof for hours she saw thousands of birds circling above the city as the voices and sounds of Damascus merged. Finally, another call to prayer cut through her daze and she rose to her feet filled with hope and energy, shouting "Eshadu'an la illaha illalah! There is no God but God and Muhammad is the Messenger of God . . . God is Greater!"[1]

Introduction

The improbable rise and spectacular collapse of *A Gay Girl in Damascus* seemed to come out of nowhere to people watching the final phases of MacMaster's fraud, but the hoax began as a smalltime con by a frustrated peace activist in an obscure corner of the internet in the runup to the Second US-Iraq War. Tom

---

[1] Thomas MacMaster, "A Thousand Sighs: Part five, Heroes of the Return" *A Gay Girl in Damascus*, 21 March 2011.

https://doi.org/10.1515/9783111057231-002

MacMaster first created Amina Arraf as an online disguise in 2002 or 2003 to help him campaign against George W. Bush's plan to invade Iraq. He believed that his views would be better accepted if they appeared to come from an Arab Muslim woman. MacMaster's assumptions revealed the centrality of ideology in his decision making. He believed his relatively privileged background inhibited his ability to speak credibly on what it was like to be a victim of discrimination and to be a Middle Easterner facing American military intervention. However, instead of changing his behavior or arguments to reflect the limitations of his experience, he tried to change his perceived identity.

In early 2011 MacMaster rebranded Amina for a broader audience. He gave her political positions modeled on his own that would be popular with Western progressives in 2011. MacMaster used Amina's backstory, including her family and personal history, to make her embody the American progressive political coalition with which MacMaster identified. He assembled Amina to persuade people with views like his own that they should fully embrace the Arab Spring, the social revolutions that broke out in Tunisia in December 2010 and spread through the Middle East in early 2011. To make Amina more persuasive to Western progressives, MacMaster included a focus on LGBT+ rights and especially same-sex marriage in blog posts allegedly about the Arab Spring. LGBT+ issues' prominence in the blog reflected MacMaster's unconscious subordination of the Arab Spring to white middle-class American progressive identity.

MacMaster built Amina using a homonormative adaptation of his own biography and beliefs as a model, but Orientalism and his political goals shaped how he presented and used his character. He Orientalized and exoticized his character by conflating Amina with the history and geography of the Middle East. Doing so turned Amina into an allegory for MacMaster's, and his like-minded readers', own political and cultural views on Middle Eastern and American history, culture, and politics. He carefully packed in elements which implied that Amina was uniquely capable of crossing divides and building bridges between seemingly opposing groups because of her identity which reflected MacMaster's own hopes and his confidence that the Western progressive politics he modeled Amina on were universal truths.

This chapter explains why Amina was so believable to MacMaster's educated and politically progressive Western audience. Drawing on Orientalist tropes going as far back as Gustave Flaubert, MacMaster used sex and sexuality to define Amina and through her the Middle East. MacMaster presented Amina's recognition that she was attracted to women through heavily eroticized stories culminating in a graphic depiction of her first intimate experience. MacMaster's sex stories framed Amina's ambiguous relationship with American society and explained her conversion to a fundamentalist sect of Sunni Islam. Eroticizing Amina reduced major parts of the character's life, and thus the Middle East, to functions of her sexuality. Exploring the Middle East's political and cultural diversity through eroticism, including gay sex, is a traditional Orientalist tactic, which permeates Western society, making the hoax seem familiar and believable to MacMaster's audience. It emphasized MacMaster's rooting of Amina's authority in her identity and biography by appropriating concepts of marginality and tying her personal and family history to events and narratives with clear symbolic meaning to Westerners, especially American progressives.

A Frustrated Activist's Alter-Ego

MacMaster's background shaped how he constructed his character and behaved while passing as Amina. He built Amina by combining academic theory and progressive politics with elements of his childhood. His political engagement began early because his parents, who were active in peace and civil rights activism, often took their children with them to rallies. For example, a young MacMaster handed out origami doves in front of the Pentagon to commemorate the American atomic bombing of Hiroshima.[2] He rooted Amina's story in places he was familiar with, including the Shenandoah Valley and greater Atlanta and he made Amina Syrian, in part, because of his own connections to Syria.

While studying history at Atlanta's Emory University MacMaster traveled to Iraq in early January 1991, just before the First Gulf War began, as part of an antiwar student delegation that opposed the American-led coalition using force to expel Saddam Hussein's army from Kuwait. He later studied Arabic in Syria and Jordan. After graduation he remained in Atlanta, working as a book buyer, market researcher, and finally as an administrator and English as a Second Language teacher in a private school. MacMaster opposed the 2003 American invasion of Iraq and in the runup to the war he organized protests against CNN's coverage of the Middle East.[3] He remained engaged in peace activism throughout George W. Bush's administration, becoming co-director of Atlanta Palestine Solidarity, but expressed frustration that other members considered him too radical.[4]

---

2 Elizabeth Flock and Melissa Bell "'A Gay Girl in Damascus' comes clean," *Washington Post*, 12 June 2011. https://www.washingtonpost.com/blogs/blogpost/post/tom-MacMaster-the-man-be hind-a-gay-girl-in-damascus-i-didnt-expect-the-story-to-get-so-big/2011/06/13/AGhnHiSH_blog. html?utm_term=.b19b82dd2824.
3 Tom MacMaster, "Protesting the CNN Biased Coverage," *Al-Jazeerah*, July 9, 2002, http://www. aljazeerah.info/Media%20Watch/Protesting%20CNN%20for%20its%20biased%20coverage.html.
4 Flock and Bell "'A Gay Girl in Damascus' comes clean."

MacMaster's hoax grew out of the intersection of his political engagement, his hobbies, and the internet. He had a lively interest in history and politics and was fascinated by alternate history scenarios and science fiction. By the early–2000s, he frequented listservs and discussion groups focused on alternate history, science fiction, and Middle Eastern politics. However, when discussing the Second Iraq War, Bush's Middle Eastern policies, and the Israel-Palestine conflict, MacMaster "found that when I argued, debated and made points that I knew to be factually sound on issues relating to the Middle East by myself, I got pushback. I was prevented from [saying] what I wanted to say."[5] He speculated that readers would be more likely to believe an Arab woman arguing that Islam was friendly to women's and LGBT+ rights than a white culturally Christian man. At the height of his hoax, he described what he claimed were Amina's motivations, but which were transparently his own reasons for starting the hoax, writing that Amina was "deeply disturbed by the pervasive anti-Arab and anti-Muslim bias in both the genre [Science Fiction] and in fandom." He compared online Islamophobia to homophobia, writing that "it was harder to argue in such circles for equal rights for Arab Muslims than for LGBT people!"[6] Sometime in 2002 or 2003 he began creating accounts for an alter ego, "Amina Arraf." The Arabic name Amina has several meanings, one is trustworthy. MacMaster's first creation of Amina was an inefficient persuasive device. He crafted Amina within his own worldview but tried to use her to persuade conservative supporters of the Iraq War, who relied on different markers of credibility, to reverse their positions.

From its insignificant beginning to its flamboyant end the *Gay Girl in Damascus* affair was intrinsically rooted in digital media. The link went beyond merely playing out in digital media, its structure and existence were predicated on features of digital media. From his first creation of Amina, MacMaster used digital media as a screen behind which he could hide while performing Amina. The basic tactic predated digital media; women writers have long used male pen-names or gender-ambiguous contractions (such as publishing under their given names' initials) to hide their gender. However, digital technology allowed Mac-Master to create the appearance that Amina was an everyday woman living her life and responding spontaneously to events and other people.

Branding accounts as Amina's allowed MacMaster to present a superficial disguise that would require effort to penetrate. He did not use complicated encryption software or proxy servers to hide his location but relied on his audience accepting Amina was who and what she claimed to be. His audience could have

---

5 Flock and Bell "'A Gay Girl in Damascus' comes clean."
6 Thomas MacMaster, "Monsters and Critics and Trolls" *A Gay Girl in Damascus*, 8 May 2011.

investigated her and might have found holes in his presentation at any time, but it would have required time and effort to do and until Amina became a public figure, nobody he interacted with had an incentive to try to disprove Amina. Indeed, digital interactions routinely involve participants accepting that the people they engage with are who they say they are, or that it does not matter if they are not.

Posing as Amina in Yahoo!'s "alternate-history" group, MacMaster discussed what might have happened if the Ottoman Empire had quickly defeated the Greek Revolt in the 1820s or if Israel had withdrawn from the lands it conquered in 1967. MacMaster used Amina to argue that Islam was more open, tolerant, and progressive than he believed his audience thought and that violent and extremist minorities could only exercise power because of historically contingent events, often related to Western imperialism in the Middle East.[7]

MacMaster slowly filled out Amina's backstory to buttress his posts' credibility and maintain the illusion that Amina was a real person. He presented her as a politically progressive and devout Muslim woman living with discrimination in post–9/11 America. While posting as Amina, MacMaster established false friendships with other posters who thought they were communicating with their friend Amina. When a user asked for Amina's physical address so he could send her a card, MacMaster obliged and told members of the group they could send mail to "Amina Arraf & Ian Lazarus c/o Mr & Mrs Abdallah Arraf-Omari" and gave them his real address in Stone Mountain, a suburb of Atlanta.[8] Ian Lazarus was the name MacMaster was using for Amina's husband and was a stand-in for MacMaster himself. MacMaster eventually expanded his performance of Amina by opening accounts on MySpace and other sites, some of which remained accessible until the hoax's exposure in June 2011.[9]

In September 2007 MacMaster established a short-lived blog. He called it *Amina Arraf's Attempts At Art (and Alliteration)* and explained Amina would be posting a mix of autobiographical and fictional stories, but would not reveal which was which.[10] Writing under the account name "Damascus Girl," MacMaster

---

7 https://groups.yahoo.com/neo/groups/alternate-history/conversations/messages/24884; https://groups.yahoo.com/neo/groups/alternate-history/conversations/messages/20380.
8 Ali Abunimah, 'New evidence about Amina, the "Gay Girl in Damascus" hoax', *Electronic Intifada*, 12 June 2011. https://electronicintifada.net/comment/364.
9 Andy Carvin, *Distant Witness: Social Media, the Arab Spring, and a Journalism Revolution* (New York: CUNY Journalism Press, 2012), 202–3.
10 Thomas MacMaster, "This blog . . . what it is and what it is not" *Amina Arraf's Attempts At Art (and Alliteration)* at Internet Archive, retrieved 15 June 2019. https://web.archive.org/web/20110615060855/http://aminaarraf.blogspot.com/2007/09/this-blog-what-it-is-and-what-it-is-not.html. In June 2011 MacMaster deleted this blog as part of his effort to purge reference to Amina after journalists began investigating his hoax. However, copies of parts of it survive on Internet

revealed that Amina was writing a novel "A Thousand Sighs and a Sigh: An Arab American Education" that was "often but not always, the story of a young woman quite a bit like me."[11] A flurry of eleven posts in the last week of September was followed by nothing until a second wave in December, and then the blog ground to a halt. The blog's readership was so small that when MacMaster posted a poll, it got only one response.[12] The blog's rediscovery in June 2011 fueled doubts about *A Gay Girl in Damascus*'s veracity and Amina existence.

The Amina in *Amina Arraf's Attempts At Art (and Alliteration)* had a lot in common with the more developed Amina of *A Gay Girl in Damascus*, but there were major differences. *Amina Arraf's Attempts At Art (and Alliteration)* focused heavily on Amina's family history and life up until the seventh grade. The 2007 version of Amina was not gay; she was a "Damascus Girl" and not a "Gay Girl in Damascus." The blog contained a marriage trilogy that rewrote Amina's backstory to remove MacMaster's stand in, Ian Lazarus, as Amina's husband. Two posts chronicled her meeting and marrying her husband, now an Arab American man named Hisham. MacMaster described Amina meeting and falling in love with Hisham while he was courting her cousin Rania. MacMaster had Amina recall thinking he was "handsome, successful" and "everything you'd hope for; religious, funny, cute." Amina remembered lamenting that she would have to wait for "My Emir and, even then, I'd probably have to settle for someone less than perfect." A final installment explored their divorce in 2001, which resulted from Hisham's affair with a white Christian woman, and the fear Amina felt during the September 11th attacks.[13]

Although parts of the 2007 blog made clear Amina was attracted to men, other online activity showed MacMaster was already imagining making Amina gay. The blog contained a table of contents for a prospective book that included an unwritten section titled "Awakenings" that might have foreshadowed Amina

Archive (aka Way Back Machine). All references to the blog refer to the facsimile at *Internet Archive*.

11 Thomas MacMaster, "What I am Working on," *Amina Arraf's Attempts At Art (and Alliteration)*, 25 September 2007.,https://web.archive.org/web/20110615060928/http://aminaarraf.blogspot.com/2007/09/what-i-am-working-on.html.

12 Thomas MacMaster, "Rough Sketch of the Novel" *Amina Arraf's Attempts At Art (and Alliteration)*, 25 September 2007. https://web.archive.org/web/20110615063036/http://aminaarraf.blogspot.com/2007/09/rough-sketch-of-novel.html.

13 Thomas MacMaster, "A Thousand and One Sighs: 32 months earlier," *Amina Arraf's Attempts At Art (and Alliteration)*, 25 September 2007. https://web.archive.org/web/20110615060900/http://aminaarraf.blogspot.com/2007/09/thousand-and-one-sighs-32-months.html.

coming out as gay.[14] Also in 2007, MacMaster created a profile for Amina on a lesbian dating site. Using the Orientalist username "almondeyez," MacMaster described Amina as "the coolest, sexiest half-Arab SF [Science Fiction] loving geek girl you'll ever meet."[15]

While MacMaster was developing Amina he married Britta Froelicher, a Quaker peace activist he met through an internet dating site. In 2007, Froelicher was director of the American Friends Service Committee's Middle East Peace Education Program. Froelicher's job involved organizing academic and activist discussions about American imperialism in the Middle East and creating an independent Palestinian state. The two travelled in the Middle East together, including to Syria which later gave MacMaster a trove of images he could pass off as new pictures taken by Amina in 2011.[16] Froelicher and MacMaster's common academic and activist connections firmly anchored MacMaster in both communities that shaped his hoax and later caused some people to suspect Froelicher was behind the hoax.

In September 2010, MacMaster and Froelicher left Atlanta to attend graduate programs in Scotland. MacMaster studied Middle Eastern Studies and History at the University of Edinburgh while Froelicher started at the University of St. Andrews. Soon after arriving MacMaster joined Students for Justice for Palestine, a student group that supported Palestinian sovereignty and refugees' right of return.[17] He began a master's program in Middle Eastern Studies which he completed in the summer of 2011 by defending a thesis titled "News from the East: The Seventh Century Crises as Reflected in Western Sources." In it he explored Western Europeans' reactions to the Arab conquest of much of the Middle East, including Syria, from the Byzantine Empire. He focused on the often-inaccurate descriptions of Middle Eastern events provided by Western chroniclers who misunderstood or willfully manipulated news from the Middle East for their own purposes. Strikingly, MacMaster started his second blog while he was researching and writing his thesis meaning that he was engaged in a modern version of the process he was studying.[18]

---

14 Thomas MacMaster, "Chapters," *Amina Arraf's Attempts At Art (and Alliteration)* 15 December 2007. https://web.archive.org/web/20110615061842/http://aminaarraf.blogspot.com/2007/12/chapters.html.

15 Esler Addley and Nidaa Hassan, "Syria: Mystery surrounds 'Gay Girl in Damascus' blogger abduction," *The Guardian*, 8 June 2011. https://www.theguardian.com/world/2011/jun/08/syria-gay-girl-damascus-abduction.

16 Britta Froelicher, "Waging Peace in Atlanta," *Syria Comment*, 16 December 2008. https://www.joshualandis.com/blog/waging-peace-in-atlanta-by-britta-froelicher/.

17 Ali Abunimah, 'New evidence about Amina."

18 Thomas MacMaster, "News from the East: The seventh century crises as reflected in western sources" Master's Thesis, (University of Edinburgh, 2012) 3–5.

Amina 2.0: Progressive Avatar

As MacMaster was moving to Scotland he told Amina's contacts that she would be moving to Damascus in the fall of 2010. Although MacMaster tried to end his hoax, he returned to using Amina in December 2010 when anti-regime protests in Tunisia escalated into a revolution and protests spread to Egypt. MacMaster rebooted Amina to make her timelier and more compelling for his intended audience, people who generally agreed with him, but in his opinion, did not fully understand the Middle East. MacMaster identified his revamped Amina as someone whose cultural background and sexual orientation let her transcend the East-West divide to prove American progressivism was a universal force for good.

MacMaster was thrilled by the Arab Spring. He believed it would lead to a democratized Middle East free of foreign influence whose people accepted the region's diversity and looked to Islam and their own cultures instead of the West for their future. MacMaster resumed passing as Amina to advance his views by commenting on news stories and in online discussions about the Arab Spring and by engaging with Western and Middle Eastern activists and journalists through social media. In 2011, unlike in 2003, MacMaster used Amina to persuade people who were still forming their opinions about the Arab Spring. Because his audience in 2011 shared the ideological perspective inside of which he had crafted Amina's backstory, he was able to leverage Amina for maximum effect.

MacMaster used Amina to comment on leftwing sites, including *Lez Get Real*, which in 2011 specialized in LGBT+ news and lesbian blogs. He wrote long emails and comments objecting to aspects of *Lez Get Real*'s coverage. In early February he began an email to Linda Carbonell, the writer responsible for most of *Lez Get Real*'s Middle Eastern content, by identifying himself as a Syrian lesbian who lived in Damascus. He complained about a series of real and imagined factual errors in her coverage. He castigated her for not identifying opposition to Israeli aggression as one of the major factors driving the Arab Spring and praised Assad for his economic policies and willingness to allow more dissent in the previous decade. MacMaster deployed Amina's biography to pressure Carbonell to accept his analysis based on Amina's identity as a lesbian Arab woman. Chastened, Carbonell, who was not a Middle East expert, posted an apology "to the people of Syria and their President."[19] MacMaster's successful use of Amina's forged backstory to bully Carbonell reflected the social violence inherent in an impostor weaponizing other people's identity as well as Carbonell's own ignorance of the region she was covering.

---

19 Linda S. Carbonell, "Syria Protests Story Apology" *Lez Get Real*, 7 February 2011.

Lez Get Real's writers and managers' encouraged Amina to contribute to their site. On 15 February *Lez Get Real* featured a guest blog post from "Amina Abdallah" titled "'Halfway out of the Dark': On being a Gay Girl in Damascus." The post laid out Amina's basic biography and claimed that she was part of burgeoning lesbian sub-cultural in Damascus. MacMaster presented Syrian culture as generally friendly to LGBT+ rights and claimed that it was easier to be gay in Syria than in the United States.[20] Readers' positive reaction to the post and encouragement from people at *Lez Get Real* helped convince MacMaster to start a blog.

On 19 February 2011 MacMaster setup *A Gay Girl in Damascus: An out Syrian lesbian's thoughts on life, the universe and so on . . . .* His first post, signed "Amina A.," presented Amina as an elite outsider whose backstory read like a check list of progressive American causes and values. The post's title, "IS THIS DAWN OR DUSK? What can Arab LGBT people expect with the changes underway?" made clear that the blog's context would reflect its title. The two titles established Mac-Master's intention to write at the intersection of the Arab Spring, Arab culture, and LGBT+ life.[21] He became his own first subscriber by subscribing using an account under the name of Amina's fictitious cousin Rania. His second subscriber was Sandra Bagaria. Bagaria had encountered Amina when MacMaster was commenting on *Lez Get Real* posts and encouraged Amina to start her own blog.[22]

MacMaster uncritically supported the Arab Spring, using the blog's very first line to declare that "The winds of change are blowing hard through the Middle East." He explained that "it seems like a fresh wind of freedom is sweeping away the tired old dictatorships." MacMaster finished by asserting that many non-Muslims misunderstood Islam and that the political liberation would see the triumph of a form of Islam that embraced women's equality and the rights of sexual and religious minorities.[23]

The blog's early posts laid out a comprehensive backstory for Amina that focused on her experiences as a lesbian Arab American Muslim and rooted her credibility in her identity. MacMaster established Amina's personality and history through four long posts, all including variations of the phrase "A Thousand Sighs," that recycled material from MacMaster's first blog and focused on Amina's family history and childhood. MacMaster designed Amina's backstory to make her attractive to people like himself while giving him access to the moral credibility he attributed to

---

20 Thomas MacMacter (as Amina Abdallah) "'Halfway Out of the Dark': On Being a Gay Girl in Damascus" *Lez Get Real*, 15 February 2011.

21 Thomas MacMaster, "Is This Dawn or Dusk? What can Arab LGBT people expect with the changes underway?" *A Gay Girl in Damascus*, 19 February 2011.

22 Sandra Bagaria, *Le Profil Amina.*

23 MacMaster, "Is This Dawn or Dusk?"

marginalized people. He achieved this by projecting his own beliefs about Islam, Arabs, racism, and LGBT+ life into the character, making her attractive to progressive white Westerners who saw themselves as part of a diverse, progressive, and global community capable of showing solidarity across traditional political and social borders. Because MacMaster rooted Amina's credibility in her identity, he had to clearly establish her identity as part of introducing her to his audience.

The "Thousand Sighs" posts claimed Amina was born in October 1975 into a multiracial and multicultural family. Posing as Amina, MacMaster wrote she was born in Staunton, Virginia to Abdallah Ismail Arraf and Caroline McClure Arraf. Her father was a Syrian Muslim from a prominent Damascene family and her mother was from an old Virginia family which had begun arriving in America in 1730.[24] Amina was thus born a dual American and Syrian citizen and lived in both America and Syria for significant periods of her life. MacMaster presented her as an exemplar of social and racial progress and a living embodiment of the ability to be both American and global.[25]

MacMaster turned Amina's backstory into an allegorical lesson in Syrian and American history. He emphasized that Amina could join the Daughters of the American Revolution because one of her maternal ancestors fought at Yorktown, the battle that ensured American independence. He also gave her an illustrious paternal ancestor, Umar ibn al-Khaṭṭāb, the second Caliph and conqueror of Jerusalem. During the American Civil War, one of Amina's maternal ancestors served under General Thomas "Stonewall" Jackson in the Stonewall Brigade, creating an interesting allusion to Amina's own fight for LGBT+ rights because of the 1969 Stonewall Riot's centrality to the LGBT+ civil rights movement in the United States. Later Thomas Jackson McClure, named after General Jackson, married a Mennonite woman, further diversifying Amina's background.[26]

MacMaster had Amina remark that the first time she saw Old Order Mennonites in Virginia, she got excited because she thought they were Muslims, suggesting a desire by MacMaster to link Christian dissenters (and his own family's history) and Islam. MacMaster even wrote that Amina had attended Mennonite services for a time because of her friendship with an older Mennonite girl and remarked on how similar it was to attending mosque because men and women sat on separate sides of the church and the adult women covered their heads.[27]

---

24 Thomas MacMaster, "A Thousand Sighs, and a Sigh: An Arab American Education (part one)," *A Gay Girl in Damascus*, 22 February 2011.
25 Thomas MacMaster, "Halfway Out of the Dark," *A Gay Girl in Damascus* 19 February 2011.
26 MacMaster, "A Thousand Sighs, and a Sigh."
27 Thomas MacMaster "A Thousand Sighs: Part three Amina to Amy," *A Gay Girl in Damascus*, 1 March 2011.

MacMaster's claim that Amina mistook Mennonites for Muslims was an example of scholarship influencing his narrative. He adapted it from the preface to David Hollinger's 1995 book on race in American life, *Postethnic America*. In it, Hollinger, who was born in the Midwest, related that the first time he visited New York City his wife had to explain that the people he saw wearing plain black clothing were not, as he assumed, Amish or Old Order Mennonites, but Hasidic Jews.[28]

Amina's maternal family's more recent history highlighted popular progressive causes in 2011, including the antiwar movement and support for universal health care. Amina's eldest uncle Robert "Bucky" Lee McClure was an all-American teenager in the 1960s. He was a high school sports star who graduated from West Point and died in Vietnam. Rather than framing Bucky's death as a heroic sacrifice, MacMaster painted it as a meaningless waste fueled by Bucky's own excessive American patriotism because, "Uncle Buck got fragged. Apparently, the soldiers with him didn't really care for the all American Boy Scout." The death caused his father, Robert Lee McClure, to relapse into alcoholism and commit suicide, showing the self-destructive nature of militarism.[29] If anyone had checked they would have discovered that no Virginian of any rank with the last name McClure died in the Vietnam War.[30]

Amina's other maternal uncle's wife died after giving birth in Appalachia. MacMaster had Amina blame the American healthcare system, writing that her aunt would have lived if she had had access to the level of care available in a large city at the time. MacMaster thus connected Amina's American family to a second political battle that motivated American progressives in 2011. Bucky's death evoked the anti-war movement's struggle against the Afghan and Iraq Wars and Amina's aunt's death reflected the Obama Administrations' broadening of access to health care with the 2010 Affordable Care Act.[31]

MacMaster constructed Amina's father's biography to make his family a lesson in Syrian history. In addition to being a descendant of Umar I, her father's family had been aristocrats in Ottoman Syria. During World War I, her grandfather, Ismail Musa Bey, fought in the Ottoman Army before becoming an Arab nationalist because of his disgust with the Armenian Genocide. MacMaster made Amina's grandfather extraordinary and ordinary by giving him a common Syrian political trajectory – embracing Arab nationalism, while using his opposition to the Armenian Genocide to mark him as anti-racist. After the war, he was an

---

28 Hollinger, *Postethnic America*, ix.
29 MacMaster, "A Thousand Sighs, and a Sigh."
30 National Archives and Records Administration (NARA), Washington D.C. "U.S. Military Fatal Casualties of the Vietnam War for Home-State-of-Record: Virginia" https://www.archives.gov/files/research/military/vietnam-war/casualty-lists/va-alpha.pdf.
31 MacMaster, "A Thousand Sighs, and a Sigh."

advisor to King Faisal and supported the Great Syrian Revolt against the French before being elected to parliament after independence following World War II. Syria's post-independence turn toward Arab Socialism cost the family its wealth and lands, though the family home in Damascus remained.[32]

The three sons followed different paths. The eldest, Amr, became an army officer intent on liberating Palestine but was killed defending the Golan Heights against Israel during the 1967 War, meaning that, by an amazing coincidence, two of Amina's uncles died in different wars in the summer of 1967. This extremely unlikely overlap did not however cause journalists or other readers to question the blog's claims or Amina's authenticity after the character began receiving international attention. Amina's father Abdallah Arraf became a hydrological engineer after earning an M.A. at Virginia Polytechnic Institute (Virginia Tech). While working in Virginia, he meet Amina's mother Caroline McClure while she was a student. They married on January 1, 1973, and Amina was born in October 1975.[33]

MacMaster used Amina's Arab family's history to teach his audience about the Assad Regime's history of violence against Syrians. In 1976 security forces arrested Omar, Amina's second uncle for supporting the Muslim Brotherhood. As a result, Abdallah moved his family to Damascus to support his parents. MacMaster told his audience that Omar lost an eye to torture but survived because of a cousin who was high-up in the regime. In the winter of 1982, after Omar had been arrested and released again, the family fled to America.[34] In what was probably a joke aimed at his credulous audience, MacMaster wrote that the family "arrived (or returned depending on who was calling it) to Virginia on April Fool's Day, 1982."[35]

MacMaster's initial description of Amina's life in the United States was designed to make her a credible spokesperson about Islamophobia. Blog entries described teachers mispronouncing Amina's name, being demoted from first grade to kindergarten because of her initially limited knowledge of English, and how as a young girl she had wished she was not a Muslim so she would fit in better in Virginia.[36]

MacMaster used the 1991 Gulf War's effect on Amina's family to demonstrate his view of how American imperialism in the Middle East fed domestic racism. He claimed that Amina suffered anti-Arab discrimination because of the war, including being called a "rag head" and a "towel head." While attending a school dance a girl confronted Amina after she and her friends performed an Arab-

---

32 MacMaster, "A Thousand Sighs, and a Sigh."
33 MacMaster, "A Thousand Sighs, and a Sigh."
34 MacMaster, "A Thousand Sighs, and a Sigh."
35 MacMaster "A Thousand Sighs: Part three Amina to Amy."
36 MacMaster "A Thousand Sighs: Part three Amina to Amy."

inspired dance, asking Amina, "What are you, some kind of Iraqian [sic] terrorist or something?" The girl's use of "Iraqian" in place of Iraqi played to MacMaster's readers' prejudices by implying that their political opponents were both hateful and ignorant.[37]

MacMaster identified a group of allies who supported Amina and whose demographic background reflected the progressive political coalition in 2011 America: women, ethnic minorities, and progressive whites. He wrote that Amina's best friend Lori, who was white, repeatedly defended Amina against racist slurs, even when she herself was initially uncomfortable with parts of Amina's culture. Amina also had allies among her teachers. According to MacMaster's narrative, shortly after the war began, one teacher, Mr. Perez, asked Amina if anyone was giving her a hard time because of the war and promised to help her if they did because he knew "what it's like to have an odd name and be a little different."[38] The posts validated Western progressives' views of themselves as more intelligent, enlightened, and compassionate than their opponents, and framed their ideology as a worldwide force for good.

Lesbianism as Authenticity

MacMaster used Amina's sexual orientation to prove her honesty and authenticity as an oppressed person. In the blog's words, Amina was caught between Syria and the American South, neither of which were especially accepting of a young woman "struggling with what I considered inappropriate desires." MacMaster did more than identify Amina as a lesbian. By naming the blog *A Gay Girl in Damascus* he made sure that the first thing a reader learned about Amina was that she was a lesbian.

Passing as Amina, MacMaster eroticized her by filtering Amina's life and modern American and Middle Eastern history through Amina's sexual experiences. MacMaster' sex scenes resembled adolescent sexual fantasies, but also reflected the long-established Orientalist tactic of exploring the Middle East's diversity through sex. MacMaster repurposed traditional Orientalism to use Amina's body and sexuality as a metaphor for democracy and individual liberation. The salacious, symbol

---

37 Thomas MacMaster, 'A Thousand Sighs: Part four, First Loves' *A Gay Girl in Damascus*, 21 March 2011.
38 MacMaster, 'A Thousand Sighs: Part four, First Loves.'

laden, but poorly written sex scenes should have made readers suspicious, instead journalist readers praised Amina as "brutally honest" and "honest and reflective."[39]

MacMaster's stories about Amina's early romantic history revolved around Lori, Amina's best friend early in high school. He used their abortive romance as an allegory for democracy and personal liberation. The stories drew heavily on B-movie coming-of-age tropes. Seasoned journalists and activists accepted them because they played into more powerful Orientalist and progressive tropes. One post described their first kiss which resulted from Lori suggesting they kiss "as practice so we can make sure that we're doing it right." The entry claimed Amina fell asleep wondering "why would I want a boyfriend anyway if I had Lori to kiss?" After a school dance during which Lori confronted a girl for insulting Amina for being an Arab, the two briefly lamented that they had not kissed any boys, before Lori suggested practicing together again, whereupon MacMaster had Amina remember that she "just melted into her, my hero and my friend."[40]

The vignette encapsulated MacMaster's subconscious political project: validating progressive identity. It showed Amina, a woman of color from a disadvantaged culture, fawning over her anti-racist white savior for having supported her against xenophobic white racism. MacMaster and his heterosexual readers could not recognize the flatness of his depiction of Amina as a lesbian because they could not admit how limited their understanding of sexual minority's lives really was, despite their active desire to be allies.

MacMaster described Amina's first sexual experience as resulting from "practicing" with Lori. In formulaic and sometimes explicit terms, he wrote that "Lori had kissed down my neck and pulled off my shirt . . . and I'd done the same. And we kept pushing the boundaries farther, touching and kissing and holding each other." The post included a description of Amina giving Lori oral sex. Posing as Amina looking back on the event, MacMaster remarked that she and Lori had been lovers, "even if I couldn't have stated any of that clearly then." The story was an adolescent male fantasy, but MacMaster's readers accepted it as a lesbian coming-of-age story.[41]

---

39 Katherine Marsh "A Gay Girl in Damascus becomes a heroine of the Syrian revolt," *The Guardian*, 6 May 2011 https://www.theguardian.com/world/2011/may/06/gay-girl-damascus-syria-blog; Jenny Wilson, 'A Gay Girl in Damascus: Lesbian Blogger Becomes Syrian Hero', *Time*, 10 May 2011, http://newsfeed.time.com/2011/05/10/a-gay-girl-in-damascus-lesbian-blogger-becomes-syrian-hero/.

40 MacMaster, 'A Thousand Sighs: Part four, First Loves.'

41 MacMaster, 'A Thousand Sighs: Part four, First Loves.'; Paula Rust, "'Coming out' in the age of social constructionism: Sexual identity formation among lesbian and bisexual women," *Gender & Society*, Mar 1993, Vol.7(1), p.50–77.

MacMaster turned Amina and Lori's relationship into a parable about the damage of repressing sexuality. Drawing on the destructive but widely repeated trope that homophobia represents a persons' own repressed homosexuality, Mac-Master described Lori's fear of being homosexual turning her into a homophobe. MacMaster's Amina remembered that after having sex she told Lori she loved her, but instead of reciprocating, Lori pushed her away and cried. Unable to accept she was not heterosexual, Lori turned on Amina to excuse herself. When Amina next arrived at school other students called her a "lesbo" and a "dyke" because Lori had told people she was a lesbian. When Amina confronted her, Lori told her that "what you did to me" proved Amina was "sick."[42] MacMaster's story made having sex a pivotal moment in Amina's identity formation and personal liberation. Having sex made Amina realize she loved Lori and her declaration was an assertion of her autonomy. Lori's inability to accept and free herself led her to punish Amina, which caused Amina to retreat from her own liberation. Amina's struggle to accept her sexuality wrote Syrian's struggle for democracy onto her body.

Amina the Fundamentalist

MacMaster had Amina turn to religious fundamentalism to deny her attraction to women. MacMaster wrote that in the summer of 1991, at the end of the school year that included the Gulf War and Amina and Lori's intimate encounter, Amina became a fundamentalist Muslim when she and Rania visited Damascus while her family moved to Atlanta. MacMaster used Amina's conversion to convince his readers that Amina understood Islamic fundamentalism and so should be believed when she assured them it was less threatening than they assumed.

According to MacMaster's posts, before Amina went to Damascus she did not cover and had a blue streak in her hair. However, while in Damascus she was harassed by two drunk Saudi men driving a silver Mercedes who asked how much she would charge to have sex with them. After that she began wearing a headscarf when she left home. Rather than resenting the imposition, MacMaster reported that Amina found it liberating.[43] Amina then began attending fundamentalist women's prayer meetings. MacMaster implied that Amina's transition was facilitated by falling in love with Hind, a member of the group in her early twenties whom MacMaster described as "the most self-assured woman I'd ever

---

42 MacMaster, 'A Thousand Sighs: Part four, First Loves.'
43 MacMaster, 'A Thousand Sighs: Part four, First Loves.'

seen and quite possibly the most beautiful . . . dark eyes, clear skin, the kind of smile that made you utterly trust her and utterly melt."[44]

Writing as Amina, MacMaster claimed that she embraced her faith when she had a quasi-mystical experience on the roof of the family's home in Damascus. After being frightened by unexplained sounds and worrying that it was a jinn, a spirit, she heard the call to prayer and saw a series of roads open before her representing different life paths and identities she could choose: become "Amy, not Amina" by turning her back on Islam and Arab culture and assimilating into Christian America, become a secular Arab intellectual rebel, or fully embracing Islam. She also imagined jumping from the roof of the house, but felt a great hand hold her back. On that roof, MacMaster claimed, Amina embraced fundamentalist Islam.[45] MacMaster did not intend readers to take the story literally, but the supernatural experience further exoticized Amina by rooting her life in mysticism and thus conforming to Orientalist tropes about Middle Eastern mysticism.

After her conversion experience, Amina joined "the Sisterhood," a group that evoked the Muslim Brotherhood, and accepted Hind as her guide. Amina explained that the group was fundamentalist and devout, and that Westerners would consider its members to be Islamic extremists. The post concluded with Amina saying that at the time she had thought living a devout life would let her shed the "unnatural desires" that tempted her. However, she remained fascinated by Hind, imagining kissing her or having sex with her even as she was determined to "think myself straight."[46]

MacMaster's presented Amina's embrace of fundamentalist Islam through her sexuality. The centrality of Lori's rejection of Amina's love and Amina's attraction to Hind to Amina's conversion implied Amina's conversion was a function of her sexuality. Eroticizing Amina's religious conversion fit squarely within long-established Orientalist tropes which used sexuality as a metaphor through which to explore Arab culture and Islam. These tropes are so pervasive as to be almost invisible to most observers and their ubiquity made MacMaster's story seem familiar and thus believable to his readers. Because MacMaster equated sex and Amina's lesbianism with freedom, the conversion vignette implied that violent and culturally conservative versions of Islam were merely reactions against oppression; If Arabs and Muslims could live free from oppression in the Middle East and in the West, Islam would reemerge as a naturally tolerant religion. MacMaster would have bristled at the comparison, but his message resembled neoconservative regime-change advocates' belief

---

44 MacMaster, 'A Thousand Sighs: Part four, First Loves.'
45 MacMaster, 'A Thousand Sighs: Part four, First Loves.'
46 MacMaster, 'A Thousand Sighs: Part four, First Loves.'

that terrorist groups flourished because of discontent created by Middle Eastern dictatorships.[47]

The Arab Spring and LGBT+ Equality

Throughout the blog's run, MacMaster used Amina's body and sexuality as metaphors for democracy in the Middle East and the United States. MacMaster's first post laid down a bold prediction, "Our culture is changing; maybe not as fast as I'd like but I would expect within the decade that the first Pride march is held in Damascus and, not so long after that, that we gain full legal equality here."[48] Highlighting Amina's experiences as a Muslim lesbian woman, he argued that homosexuality was compatible with properly understood Islam. In his second post, MacMaster predicted that the Arab Spring would create a progressive egalitarian society because "a revolution is underway and all of us want to see it revolutionize every aspect of our societies, rethinking not just how the states are governed but also the role of women in these societies, the rights of sexual autonomy, and, yes, the right to marry who we love."[49] A 21 February post linked democracy with women's and LGBT+ liberation, explaining that "I'm also aware of the winds of freedom and change blowing from one end of the Arab world to the other. And I want that freedom wind to bring with it our liberation, not just as Arabs and as Syrians, but also as women and as lesbians."[50]

Forcing LGBT+ rights to the center of his analysis of the Arab Spring showed MacMaster believed the Middle East was evolving toward the same future progressive Westerners believed in. Support for LGBT+ rights was not a major factor in starting or sustaining the Arab Spring, but it dominated MacMaster's early blog posts. LGBT+ issues were central to MacMaster's coverage of the Arab Spring because he used the Arab Spring as a backdrop against which he performed American politics. The during the first month of his blog, he wrote about LGBT+ rights in almost every post other than those which only established Amina's backstory and he repeatedly touched on same-sex marriage.

MacMaster's audience was people like himself who saw LGBT+ equality as a critical issue and a major dividing line between themselves and their opponents. He used Amina to reassure progressives that Islam and the Arab Spring were

---

47 See Oz Hassan. "Bush's Freedom Agenda: Ideology and the Democratization of the Middle East." *Democracy and Security* 4, no. 3 (2008): 268–89. https://www.jstor.org/stable/48602627.
48 MacMaster, 'Halfway Out of the Dark.'.
49 MacMaster "Is This Dawn or Dusk?"
50 Thomas MacMaster, "Why I am doing this," *A Gay Girl in Damascus*, 21 February 2011.

naturally friendly to LGBT+ equality. This allowed him to use his readers' domestic politics to shape their view of the Arab Spring even as he used a stylized version of the Arab Spring to reinforce and validate his readers' domestic political identity. MacMaster used both cultural and theological arguments. He relied on what he claimed were Amina's personal experiences to prove his cultural point, opining that Arab culture was "far more at ease with homoeroticism than most western cultures" and that Amina felt safer showing affection to other women in public in Damascus than in the United States. He explained that gaining LGBT+ rights would be easier than most Westerners assumed and that "many of my own relatives are happier that I'm lesbian than if I were a sexually active unmarried heterosexual."[51]

According to the blog, shortly after arriving in Damascus, Amina discovered a semi-secret, but well-established lesbian community in Damascus that MacMaster used as a metaphor for the pro-democracy movement. It began after Amina "picked up on something" between the women in a hair salon. According to the post, after a long and coded conversation, she realized all the women there were gay and that she had found "an underground outpost of 'our kind.'" She soon discovered this salon was far from unique and began visiting a café where women discretely held hands. MacMaster explained that Syrian lesbians were "more furtive and repressed than in the USA or in Europe" but assured readers that was changing and that Amina now realized that even her old devotional group was "thick with repressed lesbianism" and that lesbians were "literally, everywhere."[52]

MacMaster presented an optimistic assessment of the prospects for LGBT+ equality in the Muslim world which made it easier for progressive Americans to see religious Muslims as allies. MacMaster challenged the assumption that Islam banned same-sex sex by reinterpreting a hadith that is often used to assert Islam's hostility to same-sex sex. MacMaster argued that Muhammad's condemnation of women having sex with women was based on the participants not being married to each other and not the nature of the sex act itself. He parsed the Prophet's declaration, which he attributed to the writings of the twelfth-century jurist and theologian Ibn Qudamah, but which is often attributed to other writers, that "If a woman has sexual relations with another woman, then they are both guilty of zina" by emphasizing the word "zina" (zina'). MacMaster argued that zina' referred to "sex outside of marriage," which implied the problem was the marital state of participants instead of the act itself.[53] MacMaster argued that because Sunni Islam did not have a formal priesthood, progressive religious scholars

---

51 MacMaster. 'Halfway Out of the Dark'.
52 MacMaster. 'Halfway Out of the Dark'.
53 Thomas MacMaster, "Islamic same-sex marriage? A contradiction in terms or an emerging reality?" *A Gay Girl in Damascus*, 20 February 2011.

could conduct valid marriages if the state would register them. That act would, he claimed, render same-sex sex between spouses entirely licit under a properly understood Sharia law.[54]

Through Amina, MacMaster reassured Western progressives that the Arab Spring was safe for LGBT+ people while fortifying his readers against any domestic retreat from marriage equality in the face of a conservative backlash. He argued that the Arab Spring was a manifestation of a progressive cultural shift that would bring down the region's dictatorships and usher in LGBT+ equality and democracy in the Middle East. By collapsing the three outcomes into each other, MacMaster made a supporter of one cause a partisan of all three. All opponents of the dictatorships thus became nascent democrats who, whether they knew it or not, would come to protect the rights of sexual minorities. In the process he forced the Arab Spring into the mold of the American progressive movement. MacMaster reinforced his claims by telling his audience that Amina was part of the Arab Spring because of, not despite, her sexual orientation.[55] By extension he framed American progressives' cultural and economic goals as an indivisible whole which had to be defended and advanced as a single unit.

MacMaster used Amina to try to persuade his Western readers to extend their support of the Arab Spring to include the Palestinian cause. He tied Amina's support for political liberation to LGBT+ rights and Palestinian nationalism. The linkage made it clear that the blog was a rebuttal to attacks on Muslim and Arab states' poor record on LGBT+ rights. Like MacMaster, many academics and activists believed these attacks were disingenuous and were designed to justify American and European intervention in the Middle East and to shield Israel from criticism of its occupation policies.[56] MacMaster had Amina assert that improving LGBT+ rights in the Middle East required the withdrawal of foreign forces, American and Israeli, by declaring that "our brothers and sisters in Iraq or Palestine, find themselves not just struggling for our dignity as a sexual minority nor just as women but also as human beings." He declared that "Queer Palestinians, like Afghan and Iraqi women" had "found their discourse co-opted" to "justify war and occupation." Masquerading as a lesbian Arab woman allowed MacMaster to tell his readers that gay activists in the Middle East wanted "their American brothers

---

54 Thomas MacMaster, "Islamic same-sex marriage? A contradiction in terms or an emerging reality?" *A Gay Girl in Damascus*, 20 February 2011.
55 MacMaster, "Why I am doing this."
56 Jasbir Puar "Citation and censure: Pinkwashing and the sexual politics of talking about Israel" in *The Imperial University: Academic Repression and Scholarly Dissent* ed. Piya Chatterjee and Sunaina Maira (Minneapolis: University of Minnesota Press, 2014), 281–298.

and sisters" to know that "if one actually cares about LGBT rights within Palestine, one should be working to end the occupation."[57]

Virtual Reality: Amina's Electronic Ecosystem

The most important reasons readers accepted *A Gay Girl in Damascus* and Amina as real was because MacMaster made them want to do so by making Amina and the blog reflections of his readers, but he also created a support system around Amina's accounts. MacMaster manufactured an electronic ecosystem that reassured people Amina was a real person. The blog featured pictures clearly identified as being of Amina. Readers who searched for Amina on Facebook found an account there under the name "Amina Arraf" that included more pictures of the woman from the blog. Amina's Facebook friends included accounts with names that matched family members mentioned in the blog. The most prominent of them was Rania Ismail, who the blog repeatedly identified as Amina's cousin and best friend. Rania's account contained pictures and material on its wall and frequently commented on Amina's posts. Over time MacMaster used Amina's Facebook account to make contacts with journalists and a veritable who's who of online Syrian activists. The ecosystem of accounts surrounding Amina's profile made it easier to believe Amina Arraf was a real person.

All the family and many of the early friends who appeared to exist online were fake accounts run by Tom MacMaster. He stole pictures for Amina and her family's profiles from other people's social media accounts. In the 2000s MacMaster had relied on pictures of famous Arab activists as avatars for Amina, but by 2011 he had found pictures he could pass off as Amina. He stole the pictures from the Facebook account of Jelena Lecic, a Croatian woman living in London. Lecic was not an Arab, but MacMaster felt she had the right look for Amina, dark hair and eyes, and light olive skin. MacMaster passed off pictures of Lecic in Paris as pictures of Amina in Damascus. Using pictures of a Croatian woman in Paris to represent an Arab woman in Damascus was an obvious illustration of Meyda Yeğenoğlu's concept of Orientalism as the West exploring itself using the Middle East as a backdrop.[58]

---

57 MacMaster "Is This Dawn or Dusk?"
58 'Syrian mystery of Amina Arraf: "A gay girl in Damascus"' *BBC News* http://www.bbc.co.uk/news/world-middle-east-13719131.

Exploiting Marginality

Amina's biography emphasized markers of her marginality and line crossing that were familiar to MacMaster's Western readership, including gender, religion, ethnicity, and dual citizenship, but he especially emphasized her sexuality. MacMaster later acknowledged that he intentionally presented her as marginalized but elite because 'there is a certain orientalism, where we in the West tend to pay more attention to people that are like us, people we can relate to" and that "someone marginalized is more interesting."[59] Amina's biography marked her as authentically Syrian and American but marginalized in both countries. As a Sunni Arab she represented Syria's majority population and as a descendant of early American settlers, she was quintessentially American. From MacMaster's readers' perspectives, the factors that made her an authentic Syrian marginalized her in the United States, and her gender and sexuality marginalized her in both countries.[60] MacMaster's carefully curated biography commodified marginality, reducing it to a theoretical marker that could be claimed by checking just the right set of demographic boxes without having to engage with a real history of disenfranchisement, violence, or expropriation.

Amina could speak about being a racial and religious minority in the United States from personal experience. That was something MacMaster and the majority of even his American readers could not do. By assigning his own views and much of his own background to an Arab American woman, he could lead readers to the same conclusions he himself had reached, that Islamophobia was a new form of racism which should be fought as aggressively as more traditional forms of American racism. Amina could also speak about her experience of homophobia in America and make comparisons to life in the Middle East which allowed MacMaster to cite Amina's personal experience to confront pinkwashing. The cumulative effect of MacMaster's performance of Amina was to assure readers that their support for LGBT+ rights at home and opposition to neoconservative interventions in the Middle East put them on the right side of history and grouped them with Abolitionists and early civil rights leaders. It was an attractive vision; all one had to do to be a hero was to agree with Amina and MacMaster's progressive

59 Elizabeth Flock and Melissa Bell, "Tom MacMaster, the man behind 'A Gay Girl in Damascus:' 'I didn't expect the story to get so big'" *Washington Post*, 12 June 2011. https://www.washington post.com/blogs/blogpost/post/tom-macmaster-the-man-behind-a-gay-girl-in-damascus-i-didnt-ex pect-the-story-to-get-so-big/2011/06/13/AGhnHiSH_blog.html.
60 MacMaster "Apology to Readers" *A Gay Girl in Damascus*, 13 June 2011. Accessed via https:// web.archive.org/web/20110613161818/http://damascusgaygirl.blogspot.com.

readers agreed with most of what MacMaster wrote in Amina's name before they even encountered his hoax.

Amina's Opportunity: The Syrian Revolution Begins

On 15 March 2011 the first major protest broke out in Damascus. The speed of events surprised observers and it took MacMaster four days to be ready to deal with the movement. By the morning of 19 March, it was clear that the situation in Syria was serious. The day before protests had broken out in Daraa, a city on the Jordanian border. Daraa was a flash point because of climate-related stress. A drought in Syria had created water shortages in Daraa while the city was hosting refugees from northern Syria where the drought had been even more severe. The local police tried to preempt major protests by arresting anyone who they thought was a threat, including a group of fifteen students they accused of writing anti-regime graffiti on walls, including the phrase "the people want the fall of the regime," which had become an emblem of the Arab Spring. On 18 March, the police responded to a protest demanding the students' release by opening fire on the crowd, killing several people. The Daraa massacre galvanized the protest movement and drew MacMaster's attention.[61]

The Syrian Revolution spread quickly through late March and early April. Initially Assad tried to balance repression and timely concessions to defuse the crisis, but that tactic failed. Violence flared early in several places and Assad's refusal to make fundamental concessions that would end his dictatorship combined with protestors escalating demands made an effective compromise elusive. By the middle of April, the cycle of protest, repression, and more protests was well-established, and the regime resorted to increasingly brutal repression to stay in power. Initially, many Syrians and Western sympathizers expected the Syrian Revolution to follow the example of the Tunisian and Egyptian Revolutions. Western journalists clamored to tell the story but faced major challenges. Many journalists could not get into the country and most of the first-hand accounts were in Arabic, which limited how many Western journalists could understand them. Journalists thus searched for accessible sources, and *A Gay Girl in Damascus* emerged as a convenient source for some western journalists, especially those who liked its hopeful and progressive message.

---

61 Hugh Macleod, "Syria: How it all began," *Public Radio International*, 23 April 2011. https://www.pri.org/stories/2011-04-23/syria-how-it-all-began.

On 19 March, MacMaster laid out the editorial line he stuck to for the rest of the blog's life. He praised the protest movement, insisting it was a religiously, ethnically, and ideologically diverse effort to peacefully usher in a tolerant democratic society. To establish Amina's credibility MacMaster referenced news reports, blogs, social media posts, and internet videos that buttressed his claims, including linking videos in his blog entries. The Syrian Revolution came at a fortuitous moment for MacMaster. His blog was already established, and he had expanded Amina's profile before the crisis began in Damascus, which put him in a good position to articulate his vision of what events in Syria meant and Amina's pre-revolution paper trail made journalists and other readers less likely to question her existence. As news coverage of the Syrian Revolution drove traffic to *A Gay Girl in Damascus*, MacMaster used it to argue that the revolution was progressive, and its victory was inevitable. Both claims reflected the unacknowledged power of MacMaster's performance of his progressive Western identity.

Emboldened by the beginning of uprising, MacMaster claimed that Amina was an organizer and well-connected to senior protest leaders by placing Amina into verifiable events. He placed her in meetings that included leaders known to the international press, but he was studiously vague about her role in the meetings. Readers could choose to believe Amina was an important leader or that she was a merely present to listen to others debate. The ambiguity allowed him to imply Amina was a leader while retaining an escape route if accounts of meetings she allegedly attended emerged. In one post, Amina revealed to readers that the regime was trying to intimidate activists and that, "activists (including this writer) had visits from the security services and experienced preventive detention."[62]

"Peaceful!" and Diverse

MacMaster's string of protest updates, all gleaned from public sources, served to spread information about the protest movement and shape how readers viewed the movement. His posts provided a stream of specific information to his Western readership which was often more detailed than they were passively encountering on mainstream news sites. However, spreading information was only MacMaster's hook to get his audience's attention. He molded events in Syria to make the revolution and his readers' reaction to it fit his own beliefs.

---

62 Thomas MacMaster, "Syrians moving beyond fear?" A *Gay Girl in Damascus*, 22 March 2011; MacMaster "Has the Revolution begun?"

The Arab Spring was controversial in the West. Although most journalists and everyday observers hoped the movements succeeded in democratizing the region, skeptical experts warned the protests could spiral into civil wars or allow religious radicals to seize power. Beginning in his first report on a protest in Damascus, MacMaster emphasized protestors' commitment to peaceful change. Writing on 19 March he claimed Amina had attended a "relatively small (around two to three hundred)" person protest outside the Ministry of Interior to demand the release of political prisoners. MacMaster quoted the groups' slogans: "God, Syria, Freedom!" and "Peaceful!"[63] On 2 April, Amina assured readers that although the protest movement was anti-regime, it was not hostile to the regime's supporters, "I believe, all of us, whether for a more democratic Syria or supporters of the regime want some of the same things: a better, stronger, more prosperous Syria and a united one."[64] In a direct appropriation of rhetoric from the May 1968 Paris student uprising, MacMaster had Amina declare "a free, prosperous, democratic and open Syria is not just possible but is mandatory!"[65]

On 22 March MacMaster celebrated, what he claimed was, the movement's intercommunal alliance, saying that protests included "Christians, Muslims, Druze, Alawis, Arabs, Kurds, everyone."[66] Two days later he told readers that the protestors were actively working to avoid sectarianism because and "the idea of sectarianism returning terrifies everyone."[67] On 2 April, MacMaster had Amina report that a gathering of activist leaders included "liberals, democrats, Arab and Syrian nationalists, members of Muslim brotherhood, even some communists and disillusioned Baathists!"[68] Amina explained that the movement was uniting the Sunni Arab majority with minorities because "we are struggling for freedom, dignity, and democracy for all of us."[69]

MacMaster reassured his readers that the Syrian Revolution was not a danger to women's rights by claiming its leaders were primarily women. He acknowledged that "the demonstrators were largely younger men," but insisted that "women, both covered and uncovered" were there and that "the organizing, though, has been largely spearheaded by women."[70] When describing the individual protests Amina highlighted women's presence and roles. Doing so emphasized

---

63 MacMaster, "Has the Revolution begun?"
64 MacMaster, Frday [Sic]."
65 Thomas MacMaster, "After the Speech," A *Gay Girl in Damascus*, 31 March 2011.
66 MacMaster, "Syrians moving beyond fear?"
67 Thomas MacMaster, "What a time to be alive!" A *Gay Girl in Damascus*, 19 April 2011.
68 MacMaster, Frday [Sic]."
69 MacMaster, "Damascus Dispatch: Another Day in the Revolution."
70 MacMaster, "Has the Revolution begun?"

the breadth of the movement and reassured progressive readers that Syrian women supported the protests. In the process, MacMaster made women's bodies proxies for the protest movement's religious balance. Emphasizing the presence of both covered and uncovered women signaled to readers that the movement contained strong currents of secular Syrians and that more religiously conservative protesters were willing to cooperate with secular uncovered women, implying that Islamist elements in the movement were relatively moderate.

Using women's bodies to map the Syrian Revolution gave MacMaster a way to shape his audience's reactions. Westerners often used women's bodies as the sites for cultural and political battles. Those battles, including abortion and healthcare as well as Muslim women covering in public, were well-established and formed part of MacMaster's Western readers' political formation. These issues have enormous personal stakes for individuals but are also symbolic battles involving contested visions of individual rights, equality, and identity. MacMaster's readers were seeped in this context, and because he aimed his blog at Western progressives, they shared a common, if sometimes subconscious, understanding of the symbols in their Western context. Thus, when MacMaster used women's bodies as proxies for the revolution and marked them as central to the protest movement, he was playing on symbols that invoked solidarity from progressive Westerners. His readers were accustomed to identifying with causes that self-consciously championed women's bodily autonomy and social and political equality, so MacMaster's description of the Syrian protest movement clearly signaled to them that they should support the protestors.

As part of reassuring his Western audience that Islam was compatible with progressive values, MacMaster asserted that Islam respected women's reproductive freedom. To do so he integrated his own historical research into the blog by claiming that Amina had been "looking over one of the earliest English works of canon law, the Penitentials of Theodore of Tarsus [*Paenitentiale Theodori*]" and had been struck by its position on abortion. MacMaster did not explain why Amina would be taking time out from her busy life to read seventh-century Christian theology, though he later revealed that she had been accepted to a doctoral program in history. After telling readers that Theodore's text said that ending a pregnancy was only a sin after the fortieth day after conception, MacMaster glibly explained that was also the "'Islamic rule' as well. Up to 40 days, perfectly legal, no harm no foul."[71] MacMaster's digression into the theology of abortion signaled progressives that they should see religious Muslims as natural allies, even on social issues.

---

71 MacMaster, "Abortion, Islam and the Catholic Church," A *Gay Girl in Damascus*, 21 March 2011.

The Alawis were problem for MacMaster because they did not conform to his vision of how Syrian politics should work. Alawis made up roughly eleven percent of Syria's population in 2011 and MacMaster believed they should support democratizing Syria because that would be the best way to protect minority rights over the long term. However, the ruling Assad family were Alawis and commanded staunch support from fellow Alawis and other minority groups, except for the Kurds. In addition, many Alawis feared that a revolution would bring a radical Sunni government to power which might target them because some Sunni clerics taught that the Alawis were heretics or apostates.[72]

MacMaster repeatedly promised that the protest movement was not anti-Alawi and predicted that Alawis would abandon the regime. He trumpeted any sign of Alawi support. A 19 March post celebrated reports of "a large and peaceful protest for democracy in Baniyas, a Mediterranean port in the very heart of the Alawi dominated area."[73] Later posts passed along reports MacMaster found of protests in Alawi areas or relied on Amina claiming to have seen a large Alawi presence at the protests MacMaster pretended she attended.

The Alawis were merely the most obvious examples of a larger problem for MacMaster. His political norms and identity were rooted in his American political context in which racial and religious minorities usually aligned with progressive whites in the Democratic Party against social and economic conservatives in the Republican Party which drew most of its support from the white majority. However, in Syria the Sunni Arab majority had long been kept on the political periphery and, except for the Kurds, religious and ethnic minorities aligned with the regime. MacMaster's rhetoric reflected his personal political commitment to respecting minority groups, but in Syria the majority ethnic group had been on the losing side of state power and violence and so a democratization movement could easily become a threat to minorities. MacMaster worked to convince himself and his readers that Syrian minorities were supporting the protest movements because it allowed him to align the Syrian Revolution with his, and his readers, political experiences.

---

72 Yvette Talhamy, "The Fatwas and the Nusayri/Alawis of Syria" *Middle Eastern Studies* 46 no 2 (2010): 175–194.
73 MacMaster, "Has the Revolution begun?" 19 March 2011; "The Revolution Spreads?"

Refighting the Iraq War: Syrian Non-Intervention

From the very beginning of the crisis in Syria, Western politicians and commentators discussed the danger of a civil war or a wholesale massacre of dissidents. Protests in Libya had quickly degenerated into civil war when Muammar Gaddafi ordered police and troops to fire on dissidents and units in Benghazi rebelled. The British, French, and American governments responded with air strikes to stop government troops from massacring dissidents in Benghazi. As violence in Syria grew, so too did debates about how Western powers should respond to the regime's attacks on protestors. MacMaster used the blog to argue against any form of American or European intervention.

MacMaster argued that Western intervention would doom the Syrian Revolution. On 22 March he warned that the regime was claiming that "the protests are inspired by Israel, by al Qaeda, by the Western Powers, by the Islamic Brotherhood, by the Palestinians, by the Saudis . . . but the people are not believing that." The passage assured readers that the protests were organic but warned that if foreign governments tried to control events in Syria, it would play into Assad's hands. While impersonating a Syrian, MacMaster argued that Western governments needed to break the cycle of colonial domination by resisting the temptation to intervene and allow Syrians to shape their own destiny.[74]

As the regime ramped up its repression in late March, more Western, but especially American, voices called for armed action against Assad. The debate internally divided the left and the right. Zaid Majed framed the leftwing European and American debate as reflecting progressives' opposition to the invasions of Iraq and Afghanistan, fear of political Islam, and opposition to imperialism trumping their humanitarian impulse to support pro-democracy movements.[75] MacMaster's opposition to intervention fit within Majed's overall argument, though MacMaster saw Syrian Islamism as a pluralistic and tolerant movement. MacMaster's response was rooted in his opposition to the Iraq War. He focused his ire on leaders he viewed as neoconservative war hawks, including Senators John McCain, Jon Kyl, and Joseph Lieberman. On 31 March Amina condemned Kyl and Lieberman who MacMaster claimed were "calling for American freedom bombs to flatten us."[76]

MacMaster's anti-imperialism and opposition to neoconservatism and neoliberalism shaped his opposition to intervention, rooting it firmly in Anglo-American progressive politics. Before the Syrian Revolution began, MacMaster used Amina to

---

74 MacMaster, "Syrians moving beyond fear?"
75 Majed, *Syrie*, 151–56.
76 MacMaster, "After the Speech."

take a nuanced position on Assad, calling for liberalization while praising the regime for its economic and political independence from the United States and Western Europe. After the revolution began MacMaster became increasingly critical of the regime, except when discussing Western intervention. When arguing against intervention, MacMaster continued praising Assad for keeping Syria outside of the Western-dominated neo liberal global economy.[77]

On April 25 MacMaster used Amina to rhetorically speak directly to Obama, challenging the administration. In a post titled "Thanks, but no thanks, Mr. Obama," he cited a *Wall Street Journal* article to warn that the administration was considering a range of ways to intervene in Syria. MacMaster was skeptical of sanctions effectiveness but focused on denouncing military intervention. He had Amina object to the idea that the Americans should "take a more 'active' role" in defending the protestors, including imposing a no-fly zone or invading. MacMaster warned Western readers that foreign powers wanted to "steal the revolution and subvert it into the old channels of colonial dominance." He assured his intended audience, which was skeptical of intervention, that Amina, and other Syrian activists, agreed with them. He had Amina promise them that Syrians did not "want foreign 'help' when it comes to bringing democracy to our beloved Syria" because activists knew that those offers only reflected imperial powers' self-interest.[78]

MacMaster concluded by appealing to Obama, though he certainly would not be reading the post. MacMaster implored "If, Mr. Obama, your fine words about democracy and freedom are to prove true, you will not offer us the poisoned cup of assistance." He appealed for him to "let us find our own path to freedom" and to "stand aside and let us choose for the first time in decades the kind of government that we, the Syrian people, want." He begged him not to "send bombs to rain on our cities, nor kill our misguided brothers" and to restrain America's Israeli and Saudi allies which he feared would intervene.[79] Although officially aimed at Obama, MacMaster was appealing for his fellow Western progressives to oppose military action as they had opposed the Iraq War. His appeal used the crisis in Syria to validate his reader's opposition to the Iraq War by placing rebranded anti-Iraq War arguments into the mouth of a Syrian activist.

---

77 MacMaster, "Syrians moving beyond fear?"

78 Thomas MacMaster, "Thanks, but no Thanks, Mr. Obama," *A Gay Girl in Damascus*, 25 April 2011.

79 MacMaster, "Thanks, but no Thanks, Mr. Obama."

My Father the Hero: Going Viral

By late-April 2011, *A Gay Girl in Damascus* was a modest success. It was not a major source of news, but it had acquired a respectable reader base without MacMaster's fraud being exposed. However, on 26 April 2011, MacMaster achieved a break-out success for his blog when he reported that early that morning two men from the Assad regime's security forces had barged into the Arraf family's compound in Damascus to arrest Amina. He opened in a matter-of-fact tone, telling readers "We had a visit from the security services" in the middle of the night. The men's accents revealed they were "straight from a village in the Jebel Ansariya[h]." Jebel Ansariyah is the western mountainous region of Syria and the most Allawi part of Syria, making it a bedrock of Assad's support. MacMaster was implying that urbane Amina was being confronted by a stereotype of a poorly educational and ignorant rural extremist, a Syrianized version of the conservative rural Southerners MacMaster had used as foils for Amina when he was setting his story in the United States.[80]

MacMaster claimed that Amina's father risked his own life and freedom to protect her. After the armed men claimed Amina was part of a Salafist plot Abdallah mocked them in an extended monologue:

> 'Look at her: can't you see that that is ridiculous? She doesn't even cover any more . . .
> When was the last time you heard a wahhabi, or even someone from the brotherhood say
> that wearing hijab is the woman's choice only?'
> he pauses, they don't say anything.
> "I did not think so," he goes on. "When was the last time you saw one of those write that
> there should be no religion as religion of the state?"
> Again nothing.
> "When was the last time you saw them saying that the gays should be allowed the right to
> marry, a man to a man or a woman to a woman?"
> Nothing.
> "And when you say nothing, you show," he says, "that you have no reason to take my
> daughter."[81]

The men then confronted Abdallah with his daughter's lesbianism:

> Did she tell you that she likes to sleep with women?" he grins, pure poison, feeling like he
> has made a hit. "That she is one of those faggots who fucks little girls?" (the Arabic he used
> is far cruder . . . you get the idea)
> My dad glances at me. I nod; we understand each other.
> "She is my daughter," he says and I can see the anger growing in his eyes, "and she is who
> she is and if you want her, you must take me as well."

---

80 MacMaster, "My Father the Hero."
81 MacMaster, "My Father the Hero."

Abdallah's response infuriated the invaders who responded with homophobic attacks and by threatening to rape Amina. One of them swore at him, saying "Stupid city-fuckers . . . All you rich pansies are the same. No wonder she ends up fucking girls . . ." Then he grabbed Amina's breast and said that if she were "with a real man . . . you'd stop this nonsense and lies; maybe we should show you now and let your pansy father watch so he understands how real men are."[82]

Amina's miraculously self-composed father intervened again, shaming the men. He identified one man's father as an officer and told him he knew his mother and grandmother. Then he asked how his family would react if they saw what he was doing. He finished by chastising them and telling them that rather than arresting Amina, they "should be heaping praises on her and on people like her" who wanted equality and justice for all and that "if the revolution comes, [they] will be saving Your mother and your sisters." Finally, he demanded they leave and tell their community that "people like her are the best friends the Alawi could ever have."[83]

MacMaster's Amina described her anxiety waiting for them to respond because "they would either smack him down and beat him, rape me, and take us both away . . . or . . ." they would leave. Then one apologized and the pair left. After they left, household began applauding Abdallah. This dramatic scene was pure fiction, but it fooled journalists and Western activists. In real life, Amina's father would have joined her on the list of disappeared dissidents. Instead, in MacMaster's appropriated, Orientalized, and fictionized Syria, Amina praised her father, writing 'My father is a hero; I always knew that . . . but now I am sure . . . MY DAD had just defeated them! Not with weapons but with words."[84]

The scene was a textbook example of Meyda Yeğenoğlu's rendering of Orientalism. It was set in the Middle East, but it was about MacMaster and his Western progressive audience's political identities. The militiamen represented two different Others MacMaster defined himself and his readers against. On the simplest level they represented the entire Assad regime and its supporters, but they were also a caricature of the American social conservatives MacMaster had spent his life campaigning against. MacMaster's text marked them as rural through speaking with a distinctive rural regional accent and by calling Amina and her father "stupid city-fuckers." The militiamen represented rural Southern white men and functioned as general proxies for cultural conservatives.[85] Their homophobic rhetoric, rape threats, and groping emphasized their brutality, hostility to cultural

82 MacMaster, "My Father the Hero."
83 MacMaster, "My Father the Hero."
84 MacMaster, "My Father the Hero."
85 MacMaster, "My Father the Hero."

differences, and lack of respect for women, all traits that American progressives associated with their conservative opponents. The scene was a wish fulfillment fantasy for progressives. Abdallah did not just win the argument; he utterly humiliated his reactionary opponents through his intelligence, acceptance of Amina's sexuality, and affirmation of the dignity of ethnic, sexual, and religious minorities.

The scene ended with the triumph of an alliance of progressive men and women over corrupt, rural, violent men. Amina's father's ostentatious acceptance of her sexuality and his effective nonviolent response to the attempt to arrest and, potentially, rape and murder his daughter appealed to MacMaster and his progressive Western audience by showing their values triumphing over their opponents. Abdallah's monologue showcased the power of intersectionality through its integration of the rights of sexual, ethnic, and religious minorities. The fact that it was a straight man who did this validated straight cis male progressives' view of themselves as heroic participants in women, racial minorities, and LGBT+ people's struggle for equality.

Just as MacMaster had stolen from David Hollinger's life when building Amina's backstory, he also borrowed heavily from Dilcia Molina's life to pad out "My Father the Hero." Molina told her story in John Scagliotti's 2003 documentary film *Coming Out in the Developing World*. In the film, Molina described the repercussions of her participation in Honduras's first Pride Parade. On 7 November 2001 armed men burst into her home looking for her. Their leader yelled out "Where is this bull dyke? Where is the bitch? We are going to rape her . . ."[86] The parallels between Molina's family's experiences and MacMaster's tale were significant. In both, armed men burst into a lesbian activist's home brandishing weapons and threatened to rape her as punishment and to correct her behavior. The two groups of men, one terrifyingly real and one mercifully imaginary, also had much in common. Their coarse speech marked them as stereotypically lower class even as their violent threats revealed their hatred of people they viewed as different.

"My Father is a Hero" drew Western media and activist attention to *A Gay Girl in Damascus*. The blog post went viral, spreading through Western activist networks on Twitter and Facebook. Within days the number of subscribers to the blog quintupled and the number of views exploded.[87] His readers shared the story aggressively and Western journalists began reporting about it. The blog was doubly useful for journalists, not only did it reflect their own values, but it also

---

86 *Coming Out in the Developing World* directed by John Scagliotti (2003, cited in Christopher Pullen, *Gay Identity, New Storytelling and the Media* (New York, Palgrave Macmillan, 2009), 203–4.
87 Bagaria, *Le Profil Amina*.

provided a first-hand English account of an attempt to arrest an activist, which was something that they struggled to be able to report. Journalists' engagement with the blog drove even more traffic to the blog. By early June 2011 "My Father the Hero" alone had accumulated 430,000 views and more people had read about it on new sites or seen excerpts in other forums.[88]

MacMaster sugar coated the suffocating power of the regime's repression. Writing in her diary shortly after MacMaster's breakout post, Samar Yazbek, a real Syrian writer and dissident, described the dark and increasingly frightening reality facing Syrian activists:

> The cities of Syria are under siege. Water and electricity have been intentionally cut off for two days, and now there is a growing threat of humanitarian disaster. People began sending calls for help on behalf of children who might die of starvation. That all started yesterday, even as reports about the use of live ammunition against the people were still ringing in my ears.[89]

The regime's violence went beyond impersonal collective punishment and indiscriminate shooting. Security forces could not find Yazbek, so they tracked her electronically. After hacking into her Facebook account, they deleted comments and posts and left messages threatening to kill her daughter if she continued organizing and publicizing protests. MacMaster's fictional Amina had a father who could shame the regime's agents into submission, but for real activists like Yazbek, life in Syria was increasingly dangerous and their activism was putting their friends and families' lives on the line. Yazbek lamented her increasing feeling of powerlessness in the face of the regime's crackdown, ironically at the very moment that Amina was becoming a darling of the Western press because of a fabricated a story that claimed to show that acceptance, faith, and courage were all Syrians needed to defeat the regime.[90]

Conclusion

Establishing Amina as a character and laying out her backstory, values, and identity before the Syrian Revolution began put MacMaster in a position to quickly expand the blog's profile. Leveraging Amina's backstory and the contacts he built

---

88 Liz Sly, 'Syrian American blogger is detained in central Damascus' *Washington Post*, 8 June 2011. https://www.washingtonpost.com/world/middle-east/gay-girl-in-damascus-blogger-detained/2011/06/07/AGOTmQLH_story.html?utm_term=.e22706a39594.

89 Samar Yazbek, *A Woman in the crossfire: Diaries of the Syrian Revolution*, trans. Max Weiss (Haus Publishing: London, 2012), 38.

90 Yazbek, *A Woman in the crossfire*, 39.

up using Amina, MacMaster tried to make *A Gay Girl in Damascus* a source of information on the revolution, but until 26 April, it remained a peripheral outlet. "My Father the Hero" however changed the blog's profile. Overnight it became an important source of information.

MacMaster exploited his readers' Orientalism to build up his character when he first introduced Amina in *A Gay Girl in Damascus*, and he kept leaning on Orientalism as the blog and the character developed. He uses several tactics, including conflating Amina with the region's history and geography and explaining Amina and the region through sexuality. Orientalizing Amina and Syria helped MacMaster's audience accept his performance of Amina and her message.

From the beginning, MacMaster inserted progressive politics into his character and the blog in ways that exposed progressivism's vulnerability to Orientalism. That combination became increasingly prominent during the Syrian Revolution. Amina's identity reflected progressive Americans' view of themselves, which made Amina's take on the Arab Spring and the Syrian Revolution especially easy to swallow since MacMaster was effectively telling American, and British, audiences that the Syrian revolutionaries believed in the same things they did. Not only did Amina's Orientalized backstory and identity not clash with her progressive persona, but they also reinforced each other, showing that Orientalism can exist even within self-consciously egalitarian and liberating ideas.

MacMaster's Progressive Orientalism allowed him to use the Arab Spring to reinforce his readers domestic political identity. Subordinating Syrians to American, and more broadly Western, progressives' political identity allowed MacMaster to use the Syrian Revolution and the Arab Spring to reinforce and celebrate his and his readers' commitment to their common domestic political movements. MacMaster showed the primacy of his domestic focus when he falsified events in Syria to make the Syria Revolution conform to American political identity. To the extent that *A Gay Girl in Damascus* strengthened MacMaster's readers' commitment to the Arab Spring, it did so by substituting a reflection of Western progressives' own desires for the real revolution going on in Syria.

Chapter II
Amina and the Media

Damascus, 2 May 2011

Amina was engrossed in a political discussion with friends and fellow activists in a Damascus café when Sandra Bagaria emailed her asking why nobody was answering the home phone number Amina had given her. After tracking her father down by phone, he told Amina the police had come to arrest her again and "This time, there's nothing I can do. Go somewhere and don't tell me where you are. Be safe. I love you."

Suddenly, Amina was homeless and on the run. Any encounter with security forces could land her in jail, where she could be raped, tortured, or killed. But she had another problem, her main weapon against the regime, the laptop she used to blog, was still in her home. Amina returned home wearing a niqab to find the door guarded by police, so she snuck into the house through a secret entrance and retrieved the precious laptop.

After reaching safely, Amina posted to her blog, promising her readers "The revolution will succeed and we will rise above sectarianism, despotism, sexism, and all the dead weight of these years of bitterness, of division and partition, of oppression and of tyranny. We will be free!"[1]

Introduction

"My Father, the Hero" turned *A Gay Girl in Damascus* into a sensation and gave Tom MacMaster the chance to exploit his hoax on a far larger scale than he could have realistically imaged when he started the blog. It also came with risks because his propaganda would be tested on a much bigger and potentially less forgiving stage. However, rather than back away from the blog or moderate his posts, MacMaster intensified his engagement and deepened his eroticization of Amina. Both in the blog and via interviews, all of which he conducted via text or email, he claimed Amina was trying to affect change in Syria. As he did so, he spoke directly to Western readers and explicitly endorsed progressive American and British activists' calls for nonintervention.

---

1 Thomas MacMaster, "Gone underground," *A Gay Girl in Damascus*, 4 May2011.

https://doi.org/10.1515/9783111057231-003

Before the blog made it big, MacMaster had been speaking to a limited audience of activists with occasional minor interest from journalists, but after the blog went viral, he had the chance to influence major news outlets and through them to affect public opinion. MacMaster took advantage of his expanded stage to present versions of Syria and the United States as he imaged and desired them to be. While writing about Syria, he overwrote the real revolution with a story about a Westernized progressive movement. MacMaster used his pseudo-Syria to critique American society by constructing a version of the United States that validated American progressives' sense of themselves and urged them to remake American society in the image of their own ideas and values. The result appropriated racial and religious discrimination in the United States, rewriting it let progressives escape reflecting on their own place in racially defined hierarchies and cast MacMaster's domestic opponents as an ignorant baying mob.

Far from challenging his propagandized versions of America and Syria, American and British journalists as well as activist bloggers in both countries embraced Amina and *A Gay Girl in Damascus* as provocative truthtellers. They hailed Amina as an inspirational leader shaping the Syrian Revolution. Western journalists magnified MacMaster's message by using Amina as proof that the electronically mediated free exchange of ideas and expression of individual identity would make the Middle East a tolerant and egalitarian society that reflected Western progressive values. Journalists' magnification of MacMaster's voice showed the power of Progressive Orientalism and its potential utility to progressive elites. The blog also highlights problematic assumptions about the universal efficiency of the politics of visibility.

A Gay Girl in Damascus, Journalists, and Technological Determinism

Following MacMaster's "My Father the Hero" post, interest in *A Gay Girl in Damascus* exploded. MacMaster's followers shared the post and brought it to the attention of journalists who reported about it and shared it themselves. Rather than reacting skeptically to the blog's outlandish claims, ordinary Western readers and journalists accepted Amina's backstory and journalists clamored to include Amina's perspectives in their reporting. Several reached out to the person they believed was Amina and integrated her into their coverage through interviews and drawing information from the blog. Journalists' coverage often used *A Gay Girl in Damascus* to argue that social media was causing or catalyzing demands for political change in the Middle East. Their coverage melded technological determinism and strategic narcissism by assuming technological change was naturally leading to a more culturally inclusive and politically pluralist future that was in-line with progressive Westerners' hopes for their own countries.

Western journalists' previous experience with Middle Eastern stories prepared them to believe that Amina Arraf and *A Gay Girl in Damascus* were real. Since the mid–2000s, technology had diversified how journalists gathered information and led many to trust blogs as sources of information. As Antony Loewenstein showed in 2008, journalists had begun drawing on Middle Eastern blogs during the Iraq War to integrate Iraqi perspectives into their reporting and had become used to relying on information and perspectives from people they viewed as a combination of informants and private journalists. Many Western journalists treated blogs and other forms of social media as a corrective to government-controlled sources of information that dominated early coverage of the Iraq War.[2]

MacMaster built his blog and his presentation of Amina based on his contact with the same material that journalists had consumed. He benefited from the trust the bloggers he emulated had built among journalists and activists. The 2011 version of Amina resembled the Tunisian blogger Lina Ben Mhenni, whose blog *A Tunisian Girl /* بنيّة تونسية was a major force in the Tunisian Revolution (December 2010 – January 2011). A linguist, she blogged in Arabic, English, and French and was a conduit for information inside of Tunisia and to the West. *A Tunisian Girl* was well-known to journalists and the trust Ben Mhenni had earned encouraged them to accept MacMaster's fraud. Despite the similarities to Ben Mhenni's blog, there were critical differences which journalists and activists ignored. Most obviously, Ben Mhenni blogged in languages which were widely used inside Tunisia, Arabic and French, as well as English, making it reasonable to believe her blog could reach enough people in Tunisia to be influential.

A Gay Girl in Damascus reflected features of Ben Mhenni's blog, including the title and its engagement with her country's revolution. MacMaster's call for free debate and the breaking down of social and political barriers echoed Ben Mhenni who had declared "I am a free electron, and I want to remain one" and that "all the world's dictators fear the web, the Net." During and immediately after the Tunisian Revolution Ben Mhenni emphasized the power of the internet to cause social change by spreading information and encouraging solidarity among otherwise separated people. Ben Mhenni argued that "nothing will change if information does now flow, if the truth does not spread, if we do not connect to each other." She prophesized that the interconnected world of social media would create "a world

---

2 Lowenstein, *Blogging Revolution*, 8–17.

without leaders where everyone can participate in decision making, where each person can have an effect on reality."[3]

There were also examples of English blogs in the Middle East which helped reassure journalists that MacMaster's blog could be real. MacMaster aimed his blog at the same audience as the English-language blog *Baghdad Burning*. Riverbend, the blog's anonymous author, who identified herself as a young Iraqi woman, was active between 2003 and 2007. The blog was popular with journalists who drew on it to understand the war in Iraq from an Iraqi perspective, without having to go to Iraq, learn Arabic, or earn the trust of Iraqi civilians. *Baghdad Burning* was popular enough to influence coverage of the Iraq War and win Riverbend blogging awards.[4] *A Gay Girl in Damascus* was also reminiscent of *In Iraq, sex is like snow*, a blog written by an anonymous Iraqi man (Caesar) who identified himself as an Iraqi refugee in Syria after the American invasion of Iraq. Caesar mixed sex and politics and challenged the virginity double-standard in Arab culture.[5]

A Gay Girl in Damascus also borrowed credibility from Syrian websites and social media accounts. Before the revolution there had been a dramatic growth of opposition websites and free media emerging on the internet. In early 2010, Salam Kawakibi surveyed the internet scene in Syria and reported that young Syrians were increasingly using the internet to bypass official censorship.[6] Moreover, Shereen El Feki has shown that in 2011, blogs had a reputation for truth telling and many Arab activists believed they were the most accurate expression of Arab youth opinion.[7] *NPR* journalist Andy Carvin spoke for many when he celebrated Middle Eastern bloggers for laying the groundwork for the Arab Spring, writing that "From the earliest Arab political bloggers to the citizen journalists of the 2009 Iran election protests, they blazed a trail that foretold the methods used to help organize the Arab Spring."[8]

Communicating with journalists was dangerous for MacMaster because they wanted direct access to Amina that he could not give. He could neither meet journalists in Syria nor speak to them using video conference software or on the phone because he could not simulate Amina's existence if he had to reveal his

3 Lina Ben Mhenni, *Tunisian Girl: Blogueuse pour un printemps arabe* (Barcelona: Indigène éditions, 2011), 3, 30–1.
4 Riverbend, *Baghdad Burning*, https://riverbendblog.blogspot.com/.
5 Caesar, *In Iraq, sex is like snow* http://pentra.blogspot.com/.
6 Salam Kawakibi, 'Les médias privés en Syrie,' *Maghreb-Machrek*, 203 (2010): 70–71.
7 Shereen El Feki, *Sex and the Citadel: Intimate Life in a Changing Arab World*, (New York: Anchor Books: 2014), 97.
8 Carvin, *Distant Witness*, xiv.

face or voice. MacMaster had advantages which helped him maintain the illusion that Amina existed despite journalists' desire to speak with her. Long term budget cuts in news organizations and the Syrian government's attempt to hamstring coverage within Syria made it hard even for major outlets to operate effectively inside the country. Most new organizations either did not have permanent physical presence in Syria or their correspondents were known to the Syrian government. Reporters in Syria had to assume that the secret police were tracking everything they did which limited who they could safely interview. This meant that most Western reporters would not credibly ask Amina to meet them and if they did, MacMaster could easily justify demurring. When journalists asked to call or video conference, MacMaster explained that Amina feared her phone was not secure and that she struggled to find reliable and secure internet access that would safely support a video conversation, Instead, Amina offered to answer questions either through email or text messaging. Some journalists declined, but others accepted MacMaster's terms.

However, *The Guardian* had a reporter, writing under the pseudonym Katherine Marsh, who appeared to be able to operate surreptitiously inside Syria. Marsh emailed MacMaster, believing she was communicating with Amina, asking to conduct a face-to-face interview in a public place in Damascus.[9] MacMaster agreed to Marsh's request because he could not easily justify why Amina would be unable or unwilling to meet her. MacMaster sent Marsh what he claimed was a recent picture of Amina so she could recognize her when they met. However, the picture was just another image stolen from Jelena Lecic. In the meantime, they began the interview via email to reduce how long they would have to be together in public. Obviously, Amina never appeared. Instead MacMaster emailed Marsh that Amina had aborted the meeting when she saw security agents nearby. The next day, he emailed Marsh again, telling her that Amina could not meet because she was going into hiding.[10] That same day he posted on the blog that Amina was going into hiding because the police had made a second attempt to arrest her which failed only because she was at a café when the police raided her home.[11] That post reflected both Marsh's attempts to meet Amina and Sandra Bagaria's persistent attempts to speak directly to Amina. Together they forced MacMaster to alter his performance of Amina to keep Amina's refusal to meet or speak to real people from raising questions about whether she was real.

---

9 Carvin, *Distant Witness*, 198–99.
10 Carvin, *Distant Witness*, 198–99.
11 Thomas MacMaster, "Gone underground" *A Gay Girl in Damascus*, 4 May 2011.

MacMaster used Amina going on the run to his advantage. The police hunting for Amina was proof that she was an important activist. That in turn made MacMaster's claims about the movement's composition and progressive aims more credible to Western media outlets. Amina's life on the run made for dramatic reading, helping to keep readers coming back to the blog to make sure that Amina and her father were still safe. Each time they did, readers consumed more of MacMaster's propaganda. Amina's life on the run provided drama and moments of cloak-and-dagger suspense. When he revealed Amina had to go into hiding, MacMaster described her infiltration of her family home. According to the blog, Amina risked her life to retrieve her clothes, contact lenses, and her primary weapon against the Assad Regime – her laptop computer.[12]

MacMaster exoticized Amina's return to and escape from her family's home. He told readers that the police were guarding the front door, so Amina snuck in using one of the ancient house's innumerable secret entrances. He explained that there were so many secret ways in and out that even the family did not know all of them. The secret entrances framed the house as a metaphor for the Orient, an exotic place of mystery with more secrets than Westerners could understand.[13]

MacMaster added exoticism and drama to Amina's story by having her cover as a disguise. He had teased Amina covering before with comments about the usefulness of face coverings as a defense against tear gas. When Amina went on the run, the aggressively out "Damascus Gay Girl" went from being extremely open about her body and sexuality to covering herself from head to toe, obscuring her body and identity.[14] That symbolic capture emphasized the repressive nature of Assad's crackdown. It also drew an analogy, as it had in Amina's backstory, to being closeted. Coming out had freed Amina emotionally and spiritually and led her to stop covering after 2001, but now political repression was metaphorically forcing her back into confinement. Only by freeing Syria could Amina free herself.

On 8 May, MacMaster posted an update "aimed at my friends and family who I know are reading this." It assured them that "I haven't been arrested (obviously)" and that she was still in Damascus. She had found a fairly safe place to stay and reunited with her father, who was "as feisty as ever."[15] Three days later, in the provocatively titled post "Hopefully not a Final Post," MacMaster wrote about Amina having to change her location once again, and offered hope that the new hideout would have better internet access.[16]

---

12 Thomas MacMaster, "Gone underground" *A Gay Girl in Damascus*, 4 May 2011.
13 Thomas MacMaster, "Gone underground" *A Gay Girl in Damascus*, 4 May 2011.
14 Thomas MacMaster, "Gone underground" *A Gay Girl in Damascus*, 4 May 2011.
15 Thomas MacMaster, "Reunion," *A Gay Girl in Damascus*, 8 May 2011.
16 Thomas MacMaster, "Hopefully not a Final Post," *A Gay Girl in Damascus*, 11 May 2011.

On 18 May 2011, MacMaster claimed Amina had escaped an attempt to flush her out of hiding using a honeytrap, an espionage term for using sex or the promise of sex to entrap a potential source. In a post titled "Honey trap?" he included a color cartoon of a topless woman with bee stripes kneeling beside a honey pot. MacMaster described Amina receiving an email from "my beloved's account" (Sandra Bagaria) telling Amina she had arrived in Damascus and was in a specific room at a hotel. Although realizing it was extraordinarily unlikely, he reported Amina nevertheless "found myself hopelessly longing for my lover's touch" and was tempted but responded with personal questions that the person controlling the account got wrong, exposing it as a secret police operation.[17] In other words, MacMaster taunted his readers that Amina survived because, unlike them, she was alert to the danger of being hoaxed.

Despite Amina being on the run, MacMaster continued to correspond with journalists. Posing as Amina, MacMaster repeated his message that the Arab Spring was a technology-driven progressive revolution to a range of Western media outlets including the *Guardian*, *Washington Post*, *CNN*, *Time*, and *Jezebel*.[18] Each journalist who quoted, interviewed, or reported about Amina made it easier for readers, activists, and other journalists to believe MacMaster's hoax.[19] Journalists who reported on Amina and *A Gay Girl in Damascus* reinforced MacMaster's characterization by focusing on Amina's sexuality. Katherine Marsh, a pseudonym used by a *Guardian* reporter in Syria, began her first article about Amina by recapitulating Amina's biography to establish her identity-based authority. She called her the "unlikely hero of revolt in a conservative country" while describing Amina as "female, gay and half-American' in her first sentence. Marsh praised Amina and explained that 'the blend of humour and frankness, frivolity and political nous comes from an upbringing that straddles Syria and the US." She quoted MacMaster, posing as Amina, as saying "I'm the ultimate outsider" and that "my views are heavily informed by being both a member of a small marginal minority as an Arab Muslim in America and as a part of a majority as a Sunni in Syria, and of course as a woman and as a sexual minority."[20] MacMaster's answer exposed his self-conscious appropriation of the moral authority which academic and activist thought has given to marginalized peoples as a means to validate his blog and lend credence to his views. Marsh's decision to

---

17 Thomas MacMaster "Honey Trap?" *A Gay Girl in Damascus*, 18 May 2011.
18 Duncan Fyfe 'Hoaxed: The Disappearance of Amina Arraf, a gay girl in Damascus' *The Kernel*, 29 May 2016. http://kernelmag.dailydot.com/issue-sections/headline-story/16738/amina-arraf-a-gay-girl-in-damascus-hoax/.
19 Smith, '*A Gay Girl in Damascus*'.
20 Marsh 'A Gay Girl in Damascus."

emphasize it, and the *Guardian* editors' decision to print it, suggested that they shared MacMaster's overall perspective.

Marsh rooted Amina's authenticity in the blog's eroticism, remarking that Amina and *A Gay Girl in Damascus* were "brutally honest, poking at subjects long considered taboo in Arab culture." Those taboos were about sex and sexuality, and Amina's "poking" at them involved posts which "vividly describe falling for other women." Marsh did not explicitly say Amina was believable because she talked about her life through sex, but Marsh had read the blog, found Amina credible, and praised her challenging of taboos, without raising any concerns about the eroticization of Amina's life story or the conflating of Amina's sexual orientation and sexual history with freedom and progress. MacMaster reinforced Marsh's perception and framed the blog as unfiltered, writing to her that "blogging is, for me, a way of being fearless." He also explained that Amina talked openly about being gay and explicitly about her sex life as a gay woman because "I believe that if I can be 'out' in so many ways, others can take my example and join the movement."[21]

Journalists' focus on Amina's apparent willingness to expose her sex life reflected the influence of what Grant Bollmer has called "networked citizenship." Bollmer cast MacMaster's fraud as part of a larger shift to "the belief that liberation comes from the 'complete' revelation of self, fully connecting to the totality of the network." Amina's revelations then became a central part of her credibility because it validated her networked citizenship.[22] Amina's public performance of a lesbian identity reflected MacMaster and his audience's assumptions that the politics of visibility worked and that individual examples were politically powerful.

Journalists' eagerly presented Amina as a leader in the Syrian Revolution despite lacking any evidence suggesting she was important to events in Syria beyond the blog's claims. Marsh told readers Amina was a force within the Syrian opposition, writing that Amina "is capturing the imagination of the Syrian opposition with a blog that has shot to prominence as the protest movement struggles in the face of a brutal government crackdown." Marsh presented Amina as a committed activist who was determined to build a free, democratic, and tolerant Syria. She described Amina being on the run from the secret police and "moving from house to house with a bag of belongings" while updating her blog and working toward a revolution that she hoped "will bring more freedoms, both sexual and political." Nowhere in Marsh's article did she present any evidence that Syrian protestors or opposition media were reading Amina's blog or even knew who she was.[23]

---

21 Marsh 'A Gay Girl in Damascus."
22 Grant Bollmer, "Demanding Connectivity: The Performance of 'True' Identity and the Politics of Social Media" *JOMEC Journal*, 0 No 1 (June 2012): 2.
23 Marsh "A Gay Girl in Damascus."

In a 10 May article, *Time* magazine's Jenny Wilson extensively quoted from *A Gay Girl in Damascus* and claimed that "inspiring the Syrian protest movement is an honest and reflective voice of the revolution: a half-American citizen journalist who, in illustrating her country's plight, risks death herself." Wilson bought into the hoax, but also partially emulated MacMaster by declaring that Amina was a journalist and that she was shaping the revolution. Wilson thus used Amina to give her own profession credit for turning the revolt into a progressive revolution, despite presenting no evidence that people in Syria knew anything about Amina or the English-language blog. A more accurate description would have been that Wilson, Marsh, and other educated Western observers felt a cultural kinship with Amina. They accepted MacMaster's invitation to project their feelings onto a semi-fictionalized Syria to place Amina, and thus themselves, at the center of the drama. Like Marsh, Wilson did more than look past the most unbelievable parts of the blog, she used them as evidence for Amina's importance and credibility. She quoted Amina's father's exchange with the men sent to arrest his daughter in "My Father, the Hero" and presented it as inspirational.[24]

Although most of the media attention came from English-language publications, the hoax penetrated other media as well. *Le Monde* added credibility to MacMaster's hoax by quoting translations from his blog on its Arab Spring-themed blog after "My Father, the Hero.[25] On 30 April 2011, the French newspaper *Le Journal du Dimanche*, reprinted a French translation of part of "My Father, the Hero" under the byline "Amina Abdallah."[26] MacMaster reposted the entire article on *A Gay Girl in Damascus* on 1 May to emphasize to readers' how broadly the blog was being read.[27] In an interview with *CBS News* journalist Shira Lazar, MacMaster, posing as Amina via text, claimed that the blog's success had been a huge surprise because "I assumed my readership was countable on single hand." Feeding the media narrative that Amina was a leader in the democracy movement and that her, English-language, blog was influential inside of Syria, MacMaster told Lazar that Amina had "begun to be called 'Damascus Gay Girl' by friends in

---

24 Wilson, "A Gay Girl in Damascus."
25 'La communauté internationale doit-elle intervenir en Syrie?' *M Blogs*, 26 April 2011. http://printempsarabe.blog.lemonde.fr/2011/04/26/la-communaute-internationale-doit-elle-intervenir-en-syrie.
26 Amina Abdullah [Thomas MacMaster], "Syrie: 'On a reçu la visite des services de sécurité la nuit dernière'" *Le Journal du Dimanche*, 30 April 2011. https://www.lejdd.fr/International/Moyen-Orient/Les-manifestations-continuent-en-Syrie–306563-3250538.
27 MacMaster, "'On a reçu la visite des services de sécurité la nuit dernière'" 1 May 2011.

the protest movement" and had received nothing but support from gay and straight fellow protestors.[28]

Journalists, activists, and bloggers who interacted with MacMaster posing as Amina followed the blog for information about Amina's life on the run. At *Lez Get Real*, Managing Editor Linda Carbonell continued to update readers about Amina. On 30 April she referred to Amina as "Our Girl in Damascus" in the title of a post and told readers that she and the *Lez Get Real* staff were constantly worried about Amina's safety. To manage their fears, they had an understanding that "all sentences beginning with the word 'Amina' must be followed with 'she's alive and at liberty.'" For emphasis she wrote, "Seriously, we live in terror of the day we don't hear from her." Carbonell explained why Amina had become *Lez Get Real's* unofficial correspondent, "It's her country and only she can tell us what is going on." Carbonell welcomed wider interest in Amina and her story, but worried that it would "jeopardize her safety by drawing even more attention to her."[29]

A week later Carbonell continued her fawning coverage, declaring that Amina "is the face and voice of the new Middle East" and that "She is the path to peace that has eluded the world for so long." Carbonell also predicted that Syria's progressive rebels would "in time, treat Barack Obama the way people in South America treat Bill Clinton – as a man who understood that all people have a right to find their own way to liberty and freedom." Carbonell not only accepted MacMaster's backstory for Amina, she embraced and built upon his projection of their common progressive politics into the world, claiming that Middle Easterners and Latin Americans would look to American politicians Carbonell supported, and thus she herself, as saviors.[30] Carbonell's hyperbole underscored the persuasive power Amina's biography could have on an engaged but poorly prepared progressive observer. The dubious claim that South Americans saw Bill Clinton as their savior also emphasized Carbonell's projection of her political identity onto people living in other places.

Journalists' reports formed a feedback loop in which each new report relied on previous reports for credibility while providing support for the next report. The cumulative weight of reports created a powerful presumption that the person so many reporters were writing about and had interviewed existed and mattered. The stories even influenced Sandra Bagaria. Bagaria was a lesbian woman living in Quebec who followed the Arab Spring and encountered MacMaster posing as Amina online. The two had Facebook chat conversations and evolved into an online

28 Shira Lazar "'A Gay Girl in Damascus' bravely blogs and builds online following from Syria," *CBS News*, 6 May 2011. https://www.cbsnews.com/news/a-gay-girl-in-damascus-bravely-blogs-and-builds-online-following-from-syria/.
29 Linda S. Carbonell, "Our Girl in Damascus" *Lez Get Real*, 30 April 2011.
30 Linda S. Carbonell, Amina Alive and Protesting," *Lez Get Real*, 6 May 2011.

romantic relationship. MacMaster put off direct contact with Bagaria by telling her Amina could not get Skype to work and had other connectivity problems because of the revolution. Bagaria found the claims plausible but suspicious until the *Guardian* ran Marsh's interview. After MacMaster's hoax was exposed, Bagaria explained that the story had erased her nagging doubts because she thought, "Okay, the *Guardian* met her, so of course she exists. Why should I keep on doubting?"[31] Bagaria made her claims as part of a documentary filmed a year after the hoax collapsed, so it is possible her collaborators' focus on the *Guardian* interview influenced Bagaria's memory, but in April and early May 2011 it was widely assumed that Marsh had met Amina in person.

MacMaster framed the Syrian Revolution as growing out of technologically mediated connectivity which allowed Syrian dissidents to spread information and quickly organize electronically. His analysis celebrated things journalists valued: the free flow of information and spreading truth outside of government channels. This analysis was far from unique to MacMaster, it was one of the most widely endorsed assumptions about the Arab Spring among popular Western commentators and so met little resistance. At its core, the claim that the Arab Spring was enabled by the internet made social media central to the outcome. MacMaster and other technological determinists assumed that technology was the spark for the revolution and that it was pushing toward a progressive revolution without explaining why social media was more likely to reward a progressive instead of a fundamentalist or ethno-nationalist movement.

The Social Violence of Impersonation

MacMaster used his success to intervene in Western debates about the Syrian Revolution, even when doing so required him to contradict real Syrians. In the process he provided a vivid illustration of the power of positionality; speaking in the guise of a person with a different cultural background, gender, and sexual orientation allowed him to credibly make claims that would have been easily dismissed if readers had known they were being written by a straight white cis-male American activist in Scotland. Without the forged authority of being Amina, journalists would not have cared what MacMaster believed, let alone given him an international platform.

MacMaster leveraged Amina's positionality to shout down people from the background he was assuming who did not think or behave how he wanted them

---

31 Kira Brekke, "'Gay Girl in Damascus' Hoax Highlights Failure to Vet Sources" *HuffPost*, 30 July 2015 www.huffpost.com/entry/a-gay-girl-in-damascus-media_n_55ba51e0e4b0af35367a81a7.

to. On 27 May 2001, *CNN*'s Catriona Davies posted an article asking, "Will gays be "sacrificial lambs" in [sic] Arab Spring?" Davies surveyed the state of LGBT+ rights in the Middle East and warned the Arab Spring could usher in a new wave of state-sanctioned anti-gay violence. She quoted an academic specialist in Islamic law, queer Middle Eastern journalists, NGO reports, and "Amina Abdullah." The report's overall tone was gloomy and most of the voices Davies presented warned of the potential dangers that queer Middle Easterners faced.[32]

In Davies's report Sami Hamwi, a pseudonym used by a gay Syrian journalist warned that the Arab Spring could lead to violence against sexual minorities. He explained that "I am very scared now. I can think of a million things they can do to me if I was ever arrested or investigated." Hamwi warned that the "death penalty is the Islamic punishment for gay men" and that "a more open society regarding sexuality needs years, if not decades, of work after Syrians get the freedom they aspire to." Davies also quoted Haider Ala Hamoudi, a professor specializing in Middle Eastern and Islamic law at the University of Pittsburgh School of Law who writes on sex and Sharia law. Hamoudi acknowledged that "it's not black and white" and that there are a wide range of interpretations of Islamic law but argued that it was "commonly accepted that the foundational sacred sources (the Quran and the Sunnah) ban homosexuality" and that despite some dissenting opinions "the dominant standing pretty clearly condemns homosexuality."[33]

Responding as Amina in an email interview, MacMaster assured *CNN*'s readers that the situation was hopeful. Instead of creating new dangers for LGBT+ Syrians, the Syrian Revolution would liberate them. Citing Amina's fabricated personal experience, MacMaster swore that the revolution's embrace of diversity was liberalizing Syria at a breathtaking pace, "A whole lot of long time changes are coming suddenly bubbling to the surface and views towards women, gay people and minorities are rapidly changing." Syria, he claimed, was experiencing a "sea change" as participation in the protest movement allowed people to overcome social, cultural, and religious barriers. MacMaster claimed that despite *A Gay Girl in Damascus*'s overt discussion of lesbianism and Islam, reactions to the blog had been "almost entirely positive" and that "I have received no criticism from Islamic sources" instead, "they've been entirely positive." He attributed this to the revolution transforming social life, "suddenly people are working together, regardless of their other views, to achieve a single goal: a free Syria."[34]

32 Catriona Davis, 'Will Gays be "sacrificial lambs" in Arab Spring', *CNN*, 27 May 2011, updated 13 June 2013. www.cnn.com/2011/WORLD/meast/05/27/gay.rights.arab.spring/.
33 Davis, 'Will Gays be "sacrificial lambs" in Arab Spring?'
34 Davis, 'Will Gays be "sacrificial lambs" in Arab Spring?'

MacMaster lacked the self-awareness to see that he was imposing his own hopes and view of Islam on events in Syria instead of analyzing the evidence that existed. Because his analysis was a projection of his own identity onto Syria, he was especially sensitive to being challenged. MacMaster lashed out at Davies for challenging his claims. He condemned the article, and the other people quoted in it, for making "an argument against freedom" and for pinkwashing Assad. MacMaster declared that Davies, Hamwi, and the others were perpetrating "the sort of pinkwashing that the enemies of Arab freedom have come to rely on increasingly in recent years." MacMaster lumped Hamwi and Davies together with "the advocates of war, occupation, dispossession, and apartheid," who used claims that they needed to protect sexual minorities to convince Westerners that "the primitive sand-people don't deserve anything other than killing by the enlightened children of the West."[35]

MacMaster drew from Amina's faked personal experience to claim that she was freer in Syria than in the West. He wrote that "having lived in both worlds" Amina had never experienced anti-gay discrimination or violence in the Middle East and that she "never once encountered any problem here on account of my sexuality that I would not have encountered were I straight as an arrow." However, life had been much worse in the United States because of Islamophobia, "I have had dung thrown at me in America for wearing a hijab, been attacked and struck by strangers for being an Arab." He closed by arguing that pinkwashing reflected "a fundamental hatred of democracy" and that the pinkwashers opposed the Arab Spring and supported dictators with bad records on gay rights because of "the aid they gave to states bent on apartheid and imperialism" [Israel and the United States]. Amina assured readers that having "sat and drunk tea and coffee" with the Muslim Brotherhood's clerics, "I fear them no more than I fear anyone else" and that she would not "let myself be used as propaganda for the enemies of democracy." Amina, so MacMaster told his Western audience, did "not want personal freedom if it comes at the cost of the oppression of millions. Freedom is merely privilege extended unless enjoyed by all."[36] Neither MacMaster nor his readers noticed that he fell back on a critique of Western societies to defend his analysis of what was happening in Syria. His rhetorical tactic revealed the truth that MacMaster created Amina to intervene in American politics at least as much as to comment on the Middle East.

After MacMaster's fraud collapsed, Sami Hamwi responded to his attacks. He warned that MacMaster's fictionalized version of LGBT+ life in Syria was far off

---

35 Thomas MacMaster, "Pinkwahsing Assad?" *A Gay Girl in Damascus*, 27 May 2011.
36 Thomas MacMaster, "Pinkwahsing Assad?"

target and that MacMaster's fraud "has cast a dark shadow over the credibility of LGBT bloggers in the Middle East." He believed that in addition to lying about the discrimination LGBT+ Syrians and other Arabs faced, MacMaster had hurt democracy advocates and put real sexual minorities at risk. Hamwi explained that "this has given the Syrian regime a new target which won't need any PR to gain the people's backing." He warned that "they are already homophobic and think of us as sinners, sick and liars" and went on to complain that the fraud meant that it would be harder to speak behind a shield of anonymity, "to be credible or to be safe is what he added to our struggle."[37]

Media coverage gave MacMaster the ability to influence other activists and bloggers who often reacted to media reports. The London-based blogger Sara Yasin, who blogged at *Muslimah Media Watch*, a transnational blog run by and aimed at Muslim women, readily accepted MacMaster's lead. Writing on 31 May, Yasin referenced Amina's sexually explicit posts and praised her for "creating more opportunities for conversations about homosexuality in Muslim and Arab contexts." Drawing on academic-derived theory, she praised Amina because "she recognizes her position" and "acknowledges her privilege."[38]

Yasin backed MacMaster's allegation that *CNN* was pinkwashing opposition to the Arab Spring by publishing Hamwi's comments and not accepting Amina's claims at face value. Yasin approvingly echoed MacMaster's claim that pinkwashing was used as "justification for genocide by the ranting bleach-blond buffoon in the Dutch parliament [Geert Wilders] and as a reason for reviving the worst of the Third Reich by neo-fascists across Europe and America." She repeated his claims that it reflected rightwing Westerners' belief that "the primitive sand-people don't deserve anything other than killing by the enlightened children of the West."[39] Unwittingly, Yasin joined MacMaster's central project, reducing the Middle East to a backdrop against which he, and she, could assert their political identities and the superiority of their ideology over their domestic political opponents.

Overcoming Fear, Embracing Diversity

"My Father, the Hero" connected with MacMaster's overwhelmingly Western and Anglophone audience by showing a courageous progressive man standing up for

---

37 Sami Hamwi [pseudonym] 'What life is really like for gay Syrians', *Pink News*, 16 June 2011. https://www.pinknews.co.uk/2011/06/16/comment-what-life-is-really-like-for-gay-syrians/.
38 Sara Yasin 'A Gay Girl in Damascus Tells it Like it is' *Musilmah Media Watch*, 31 May 2011, http://www.muslimahmediawatch.org/2011/05/31/a-gay-girl-in-damascus-tells-it-like-it-is/.
39 Yasin 'A Gay Girl in Damascus Tells it Like it is.'

his lesbian daughter. The day after "My Father, the Hero," MacMaster wrote about the need to overcome fear. He explained that until the Arab Spring, Syrians had been too afraid to challenge Assad and demand democracy, but things were now changing and "the movement we stopped being afraid, the earth shook."[40]

The specter of the sectarian violence during the Iraq War hung over MacMaster's analysis. His claim that Syria's groups were historically accepting of each other was necessary to reassure his Western audience that Assad's fall would not trigger the sectarian violence that emerged in Iraq, another diverse country, after an American-led force overthrew Saddam Hussein's regime. According to MacMaster the explosion of political activism in Syria was ensuring that civil war would not happen. The experience of the protest struggle was bringing people together and strengthening civil society by dissolving the artificial barriers that had separated Syrians.[41]

MacMaster used the combination of friendly comments on the blog, concocted emails, and fabricated firsthand experiences as evidence for his claims that Syrian Islamists respected gender, ethnic, religious, and sexual diversity. According to him, Islamist groups in Syria were among the most "modern" and moderate in the region. He claimed that the revolution was bringing all of Syria's diverse groups together in a "spirit of togetherness and unity" that precluded the religious bigotry, sectarian score-settling, or gender or sexual violence that some Western commentators' feared, and which eventually occurred.[42]

Throughout the blog, MacMaster emphasized the unifying role of Islam and its ability to invoke solidarity within diversity. On 1 June he posted a defense of Islam against what he characterized as misinformed and Orientalist commentators. Distinguishing between "their Islam and ours" he critiqued popular Western assumptions about Islam that he believed underwrote military intervention, regime change, support for Israel, and a lack concern for Muslim lives. He claimed Amina had "seen lots of talk" claiming Islam was hostile to homosexuality, democracy, human rights, and feminism but "that never comes from actual Muslims." MacMaster offered up an interpretation of Islam that celebrated diversity, embodied gender equality, and created unity within difference. He wrote that Amina's Islam "was diverse and beautiful." She remembered "Eid prayers in America where immigrants from a hundred lands, children of immigrants, converts and reverts" prayed together. It was a religion created to celebrate diversity, because "God has made us into nations so that we might learn from one another."

---

40 Thomas MacMaster, "Beyond Fear," *A Gay Girl in Damascus*, 27 April 2011.
41 Thomas MacMaster, "Martyrs' Day," *A Gay Girl in Damascus*, 6 May 2011.
42 Thomas MacMaster, "An Observation and an Insight" *A Gay Girl in Damascus*, 10 May 2011.

He wrote about Amina "sitting at the feet of the Sheikha (our Islam has sheikhas as well as sheikhs!) as she explained it was perfectly natural to desire other women."[43]

Relying on the dualist tropes which underwrote the entire blog, MacMaster opposed "our Islam" to an Orientalized fantasy of Islam. Building on Katerina Dalacoura and Joseph A. Boone's arguments that Westerners have used the Middle East as a venue for discussing homosexuality, MacMaster claimed that "Their Islam" was a foil for Westerners changing views of themselves. When European elites viewed homosexuality as a sign of lax morality, they associated it with Islam to define Islam as "sensual" and "too feminine" but, after Western elite began seeing themselves as "anti-sexist and gay friendly" they rewrote Islam as homophobic and misogynistic. He denied that these Western views had any connection to real-world Islam because they merely reflected Westerners defining themselves against Islam. In a beautifully ironic passage, MacMaster condemned the subordination of Islam and the Middle East to Western identity formation as representing "the worst aspect of orientalism and 'othering'" and a "fantasy masquerading as reality."[44]

Reading the post ironically makes it extremely perceptive because MacMaster's analysis hit home against both Traditional and Progressive Orientalism. Just as Traditional Orientalists have used distorted renderings of Islam as foils against which they constructed an imaginary image of their own society, MacMaster and his readers used Islam to define a vision of their society. Turning Islam into a proxy for Western progressivism reinforced his readers' support for the Arab Spring, encouraged them to support the Palestinian cause, and validated their domestic political identity.

MacMaster emphasized the revolution's ability to liberate marginalized groups. The blog critiqued the failures of the Ba'ath Party's rule, arguing that the party had begun with noble goals, including "independence and the greatness of the nation" but had failed because it forgot that "real change doesn't come from above, it comes from below." This time, MacMaster assured his readers, Syrians would not try to "take a short cut" because using force and state power to modernize "always fails." The Ba'ath Party's shortcuts, he argued in an analysis that implicitly conflated Assad and George W. Bush, led to leaders "frog marching people and shooting those who object" in the name of creating "a modern, free democratic society" from the top-down.[45]

---

43 Thomas MacMaster, "Their Islam and Ours" *A Gay Girl in Damascus*, 1 June 2011.
44 Katerina Dalacoura, "Homosexuality as cultural battleground in the Middle East: culture and postcolonial international theory" *Third World Quarterly*, 35 no 7, (2014): 1290–1306; Joseph A. Boone, *The Homoerotics of Orientalism* (New York: Columbia University Press, 2014).
45 Thomas MacMaster, "Why Emma Fled" *A Gay Girl in Damascus*, 10 May 2011.

Victory through Peace

MacMaster's version of the Syrian Revolution was resolutely nonviolent, in part to answer critics in the West who predicted it would lead to a civil war. He assured readers "we aren't planting bombs and doing assassination" and "that is why we will win."[46] On 5 June, he wrote that Amina was traveling around the country visiting protest groups in different regions, urging them to stick to the nonviolent program in the face of a minority who wanted to answer violence with violence. Instead, Amina believed that "you fight fire with water, not with fire." Blog posts revealed that Amina was telling other protestors that the only way to change Syria was by being better than the regime, asking "If we take power by killing and torturing, if we make summary justice and examples of Them, how are we different?" MacMaster claimed Amina was urging dissidents to "put out the blind hatreds of sectarianism not with sectarianism of our own but with love and with solidarity."[47]

Amina's revolution was progressive, patriotic, and non-violent. The increasingly popular blog explicitly opposed Western intervention in Syria as counterproductive and imperialist. By the middle of May 2011, American and Western European leaders were debating intervention in the face of Assad's increasingly murderous attempts to retain power. MacMaster hammered away against the idea of any repeat of the American or European interventions in Iraq and Libya. On 13 May he ridiculed advocates of a "Libyan style" Western intervention. Wrongly questioning whether Western powers had the necessarily bases to launch successful air attacks, he warned that any such intervention would guarantee Assad's survival because it would be transparently pro-Israeli. Explaining that "the long struggle for independence is still too real" for Syrians to accept any Western intervention, MacMaster had Amina declare that "if a foreign army invaded, I'd gladly fight and die to defend Syria, even if it meant to defend Assad!"[48]

Although he opposed any European or American initiative against Assad, Mac-Master hoped Turkey might be able to broker a compromise. MacMaster praised Erdoğan's Turkish government for abandoning the Kemalist legacy of "struggling to be accepted as 'European' by a club that would never accept a Muslim country" and instead embracing its Muslim identity. He lauded it as a "working, though not perfect, democracy" and saw in Erdoğan's Justice and Development Party an Islamic party what "didn't reject modernity or progress."[49]

46 Thomas MacMaster, "This is no 1982: A History Lesson," *A Gay Girl in Damascus*, 11 May 2011.
47 Thomas MacMaster, 'Another Day in Damascus' *A Gay Girl in Damascus*, 5 June 2011.
48 Thomas MacMaster, "Talkin' Turkey About Intervention" *A Gay Girl in Damascus* 13 May 2011.
49 MacMaster, "Talkin' Turkey About Intervention."

According to MacMaster's Amina, Turkey's democratization and rejection of Kemalism had made it a model for Arabs seeking to assert their democratic rights and escape from Western neocolonialism. He hoped the Turkish government would be able to use its growing economic influence, and what he claimed was popular respect for Erdoğan's model, to pressure Assad into opening a national dialogue. If negotiations failed, Turkey was the only country "remotely capable" of intervening and "being greeted by flowers and not by IEDs."[50]

With global media outlets suddenly paying attention to *A Gay Girl in Damascus* after "My Father, the Hero," MacMaster sought to shape readers and journalists' expectations about what would come after the revolution. Claiming that "I cannot speak for everyone in Syria but I can speak for what I want and what those I'm in touch with want" he laid out what he claimed were their hopes and goals: They wanted a democratically elected and accountable government that was bound by the rule of law. They hoped for a cross-class government and "a Syria that is truly secular, where neither one region dictates to the rest nor does a philosophy against religion reign." He also made clear it would be a feminist Syria, "where the half of us who are women can progress" and where women were neither pressured to cover nor discouraged from doing so. Breaking down the regime's artificial sectarian barriers would end Assad's crony capitalism and allow a more dynamic economy in which "good ideas . . . not political connections" would "fuel economic growth." He admitted that the new Syria would take work but believed it would be able to "welcome back our lost provinces," suggesting that democratization would allow Syria to reclaim the Golan Heights from Israel and absorb Lebanon.[51]

MacMaster predicted that a democratic Syria would transform the region in a kind of domino theory. The advent of a democratic government in Syria would, MacMaster prophesied, spark a revolution in Iraq that would sweep away the "thieves" and "sectarian warlords" in Baghdad. Lebanon would abandon the idea of a "western facing Lebanon, severed from the Arab nation" and embrace a larger Arab identity by unifying with Syria.[52]

MacMaster prophesized what he viewed as the decolonization of the Middle East. He blamed Western powers for the "minority regimes" in power and imagined a democratic wave sweeping away the regimes and many of the countries themselves. "All these states" which he claimed came about "from drinking bouts of Churchill and his peers" would "vanish when the last of these puppets goes."

---

50 MacMaster, "Talkin' Turkey About Intervention."
51 Thomas MacMaster, "After Assad Goes: 1: Inside Syria" *A Gay Girl in Damascus*, 20 May 2011.
52 Thomas MacMaster, "After Assad Goes: 2: Beyond Our Borders" *A Gay Girl in Damascus*, 21 May 2011.

The last domino to fall would be Israel itself when a Palestinian state would emerge from the regional revolution. He warned his Western readers that they should mistrust any American or Iranian initiative because their interests were tied into the colonial regime which dominated the region.[53]

The MacMaster's academically informed use of colonialism as a lens through which to analyze the contemporary Middle East produced something akin to a Manifest Destiny for a diverse democratic Syria. He imaged that a democratic Syria would inspire Arabs and even non-Arabs in the Middle East and would create a bottom-up momentum for transformative political change. That change would not just involve the overthrow of specific regimes, it would lead to the unification of peoples. As he put it in a post on the power of Syrian federalism, "a Syria where minorities prosper and both they and majorities enjoy full democratic freedom will make the partitions of last century look like a bad idea to more and more." That change would redraw the map of the Middle East, creating a greater Arab state.[54] MacMaster's new Middle East would be resolutely socially and economically egalitarian and free for foreign domination. It also held out the hope that solidarity in diversity would lead to social change in Western countries that would end discrimination and transform economic and political hierarchies.

Using Sex to Tell Stories

MacMaster could have reacted to *A Gay Girl in Damascus*'s growing popularity by backing away from his eroticization of Amina and the Middle East, but instead he reinforced his use erotic stories and poems to build Amina's credibility and character. The risks of relying on eroticism to validate his character and advance his narrative were smaller in February and March 2011 when his audience was smaller. The expanded audience made it more likely that somebody would challenge Mac-Master's improbable stories and expose his fraud. It also increased the price of being caught. When only a handful of people subscribed to the blog, exposure would have had little long-term effect on MacMaster. However, after attracting media and activists' attention, exposure risked painful long-term consequences. Exposure would damage his career because the resulting stories would immortalize his fraud. However, rather than responding suspiciously, his growing audience of

---

53 MacMaster, "After Assad Goes: 2: Beyond Our Borders."
54 Thomas MacMaster, "Federalism: A Short Proposal for Our Future," *A Gay Girl in Damascus*, 23 May 2011.

Western readers, including journalists and activists cited his eroticized stories as evidence of Amina's authenticity.

MacMaster's eroticization of Amina and the Syrian Revolution was not subtle. The very day he claimed militiamen tried to arrest Amina, MacMaster posted a batch of erotic poetry on the blog. One poem, "M'amoure et moi (elle sait)" [My love and I (she knows)] described two women making love and emphasized their sameness. The lovers both had dark hair and eyes, which in the context of the blog suggested they were Arab. The poem meditated on sexual desire, creating a parallel to the Syrian people's desire for freedom and ended with the lovers' common desire leading them to "become one," making the poem an allegory for MacMaster's version of the Syrian Revolution. The poem's invocation of sameness used lesbian sex and orgasm to symbolize Syria overcoming the oppression and divisions that preoccupied much of the blog.[55]

Another post, which described a recent relationship of Amina's also used her body and sex life to explore Middle Eastern politics. Titled "A Syrian Romance," it chronicled Amina's relationship with a Druze professor who MacMaster told readers Amina would refer to as Zina.[56] The name Zina came with layered meanings. Zina is a common Arabic name which can mean beautiful or strong. Using Zina also helped dedicated readers feel like they were becoming experts in the Middle East and Islam because an earlier post had explained the theological meaning of "zina," (zina') illicit sex, when arguing same-sex sex was only forbidden in Islam if it occurred outside of marriage.[57] Finally, the name had a popular culture resonance for Americans of MacMaster's age, especially fans of fantasy television, because Zina is pronounced identically to Lucy Lawless's character Xena from the 1997–2001 series *Xena: Warrior Princess*, who many viewers believed was in a lesbian relationship with her companion Gabrielle.[58]

MacMaster used Zina to argue that Syria was more tolerant of homosexuality and religious diversity than he thought his readers assumed. The post described Amina and Zina meeting at a university event in Damascus and becoming close friends. Making them both Western-educated elites helped his educated Western readers identify with the couple. The attraction broke into the open during a phone call while Amina was visiting Britain. When Amina returned to Damascus,

---

55 Thomas MacMaster, "M'amoure et moi (elle sait)," *A Gay Girl in Damascus*, 26 April 2011.
56 MacMaster, "A Syrian Romance," *A Gay Girl in Damascus*, 28 April 2011.
57 MacMaster, "Islamic same-sex marriage?"
58 Helen Caudill "Tall, Dark, and Dangerous: Xena, the Quest, and the Wielding of Sexual Violence in *Xena* On-Line Fan Fiction" in *Athena's Daughters: Television's New Women Warriors*, edited by Frances Early and Kathleen Kennedy (Syracuse University Press: Syracuse NY, 2003), 27–39.

Zina met her at the airport and "we are kissing in the airport itself, barely making it back to her apartment dressed . . . and, well, you can guess the rest . . ." The post described meeting Zina's family, who knew she was gay, and how they accepted Amina despite her not being Druze. Zina's family's acceptance of their same-sex and intercultural relationship was meant to convince readers that Amina's family's acceptance of sexual, ethnic, and religious diversity was not an aberration.[59]

The post chronicled Amina and Zina's deepening relationship. MacMaster wrote about a vacation Amina and Zina took to a cosmopolitan Egyptian resort, and had Amina celebrate that "we can be 'out' at Sharm al Sheik and model our bikinis and such . . . life is good as we come back to Damascus. We are pretty lesbians in love."[60] The visit to Sharm El Sheik, a well-known Egyptian resort on the Red Sea, implied that the acceptance of public same-sex relationships varied throughout the region. MacMaster's refence to modeling bikinis and "pretty lesbians in love" was neither subtle nor well-written, but it tapped into Orientalist tropes of using women's bodies and sexuality to map the Middle East for Western readers, a fact which helped MacMaster's readers accept his story even as he railed against Orientalists' history of eroticizing the Middle East.

Zina and Amina eventually broke up over the revolution; Zina supported the Assad Regime because she feared a Sunni government would threaten minorities like her and usher in a radical Islamic state. MacMaster put history and Islamophobia at the center of their breakup. Zina feared that "they would cut our throats if they could" and when Amina asked who she meant, she said "the Muslim brothers, all Muslims, really . . ." Then they began "arguing about what happened in 1982, 1976, 1973, 1967, 1963, 1961 . . . and so on . . . ugly things that we have avoided all the months we have been together." MacMaster closed the post on a hopeful note, claiming that Zina was warming to the protest movement.[61] MacMaster postulated a primordial historical conflict which is a traditional Orientalist trope for describing the Middle East and channeled the conflict into a sexual relationship, which is the Orientalist trope *par excellence*. MacMaster's final note that Zina was reconsidering her support for Assad held out the hope that the progressive movement embodied in the Arab Spring could allow Syrians to transcend their history by embracing the same set of values he and other Western progressives used to defined themselves. Without explicitly saying it, MacMaster made his message clear: Progressivism would save Syria and it could save America too.

---

59 MacMaster, "A Syrian Romance."
60 MacMaster, "A Syrian Romance."
61 MacMaster, "A Syrian Romance."

Eroticizing 9/11: An Alternate Path

MacMaster's Orientalist blend of progressive subtext and explicit eroticism reached its zenith in the posts describing Amina's relationship with Katy. According to Mac-Master's story, Katy was Amina's first official girlfriend and the woman who prompted her to accept that she was a lesbian. Their love story began as just a vague statement to fill out Amina's backstory. In a post on the first day of the blog, MacMaster wrote that "I came out just before my twenty-sixth birthday, first to my-self, then to the woman I had fallen for. I was liberated at last from my fear." That placed Amina's coming out in the fall of 2001 but was otherwise vague.[62] After "My Father, the Hero," MacMaster tied Amina's coming out to the September 11th attacks.

The story evolved over several posts between 2 May and 11 May, but from 2 May MacMaster tied Amina's coming out story to terrorism and Islamophobia, turning it into a celebration of the affirming and liberating power of accepting oneself and the triumph of acceptance over hate, solidly progressive themes. The first post set the stage by emphasizing Amina's shock at the September 11 attacks and her fear of racist violence. MacMaster gave the second installment the pro-vocative title "Thanks to Bin Laden . . ." Written days after American SEALS as-sassinated the Al-Qaeda leader, he criticized the assassination and Americans' celebration of it. MacMaster then tied the 11 September attacks to Amina accept-ing that she was a lesbian. Saying the fear Amina felt on 11 September caused her to slip and do "the one thing I was terrified of: I kissed a girl . . . and came out . . . so, thanks Bin Laden for that . . ."[63]

On 11 May he finished by narrating Amina's coming out as a clumsy seduction that sexualized Amina and the September 11th attacks. The scene relied on readers' active suspension of disbelief to accept an adolescent sex story was a real adult re-lationship. MacMaster began with Amina remembering feeling like a failure on the morning of 11 September 2001 because her husband Hisham had recently left her for a blonde Christian woman. Seeing the footage of planes crashing into the World Trade Center distracted and terrified Amina who realized that either "my people" had done it, or "we'll be blamed for it anyway." MacMaster claimed Amina knew immediately that "it's going to get bad, fast" and expected the U.S. government would begin mass arrests and deportations of Arabs and Muslims. She feared that "there'll be riots, I'm sure, Kristallnacht again, only this time we'll be the Jews."[64]

---

62 MacMaster, "Halfway Out of The Dark."
63 Thomas MacMaster, "Thanks to Bin Laden . . ." *A Gay Girl in Damascus*, 8 May 2011.
64 Thomas MacMaster, "September," *A Gay Girl in Damascus*, 2 May 2011.

Amina's panic only subsided when Katy, her only close friend in Chicago, offered to come over that evening. According to the post, "for the first time today, I'm not obsessing about the news."[65] First they shared a bottle of wine and watched *The Princess Bride*. After seeing that Amina had hurt her shoulder, Katy offered her a massage, noting that Amina was "incredibly tight" and that despite having worked as a masseuse, she had never "seen anyone knottier" than Amina. The massage session moved to the bedroom and required Amina to disrobe. In the middle of the massage Katy told Amina she was gay, causing Amina to jokingly ask why "you've never ever even tried making a pass at me!" To which Katy retorted "I've got you sprawled under me naked right now" and then admitted that "I've had this huge, enormous crush on you for the longest time." Amina responded that she too had a crush on Katy and then "next thing, I know, I kiss her . . ." after which he described them having sex.[66]

MacMaster made it clear that the sex itself was liberating in a physical and psychological sense and marked Amina escaping from fear of her own lesbianism and Islamophobia. After a session that lasted "hours, actual hours" and involved "kissing and touching each other and having the most intense orgasms and such," Amina and Katy fell "asleep entangled in each other's arms and I can't quite tell where Katy ends and Amina begins." He had Amina end the story, claiming that "as I fall asleep, I realize that, for the first time in a long time, I'm not afraid" The next morning MacMaster made sure to have Amina reassure Katy that she did not regret anything because she had made an affirmative decision to accept her sexuality.[67]

Amina's coming out story emphasized the liberating power of accepting identity. It was a progressive story in which fear of discrimination and violence caused Amina both psychological and physical trauma in ways legible to critical race and sexuality studies. Amina feared other people's bigotry toward her, and so feared accepting that she was gay. The solution was for her to accept herself and to find validation from Katy, a woman from a different culture. The emotional release of sex with Katy, and the acceptance of herself that went with it, was so great that it allowed Amina to emerge from 11 September 2001 less afraid than she had been when it began. MacMaster exploited his Orientalized eroticization of Amina to present an alternate path he suggested America should have taken in the wake of the attacks, embracing solidarity and equality across

---

65 MacMaster, "September."
66 Thomas MacMaster, "Coming Out: part one???" *A Gay Girl in Damascus*, 11 May 2011.
67 MacMaster, "Coming Out: part one???" *A Gay Girl in Damascus*, 11 May 2011.

religious and cultural lines instead of using force to impose American security upon the Middle East and repress diversity at home.

Retelling the September 11th attacks through Amina's body and sexuality fit easily with MacMaster's overall approach. In the tradition of Gustave Flaubert, Jean-Léon Gérôme, and Benjamin Disraeli, MacMaster made Arab women's bodies symbols of the Middle East and then turned his objects back on his subjects by using them to argue for changes in his own society's culture and government policies. MacMaster used a post about Amina and Katy's growing relationship to argue that Islamophobia was pervasive in the United States, juxtaposing Amina's fear of racist attacks with her joy at being in a relationship with Katy. He had Amina remember that although "I was actually with someone I was crazy about and I was actually having the kind of sex I had imagined" she was fearful of the coming war and worried that "there'd be a lynch mob looking for Muslims."[68]

True to his tactic of having Amina and her family personify his political narrative, MacMaster claimed the FBI wrongly arrested Amina's brother for being a terrorist because of racial profiling. MacMaster explained that Amina's brother Amr had done nothing wrong, but he had been taking "flying classes at Bristow Field and he was born in Damascus and he was an Arab Muslim and some of the 9/11 hijackers had visited there" so the FBI had detained and questions him for days.[69]

In MacMaster's hands, the American government's response to 9/11 became a reflection of the Assad regime's secret police state and rural or Southern whites resembled sectarian militiamen. He wrote that Amina wanted to visit her parents after the attacks, but "especially after what had happened with Amr" Amina was too afraid to fly because she "had visions of disappearing into some dark cell." Instead of flying, Amina and Katy decided to drive from Chicago to Atlanta, although even that frightened Amina because it meant driving through conservative rural areas. She instructed Katy to call her Amy and wore a baseball cap instead of a hijab because she had feared "being stopped in some remote place in southern Indiana getting gas while big guys howled for my blood."[70]

MacMaster's rendering of America Othered Americans whom he disliked, conservative Southern and rural whites, reducing them to flat foils he used to emphasize his and his reader's superiority. MacMaster's intended his parable to be antiracist and it was superficially anti-racist, but its unreality rendered it impotent as a response to the kind of structural racism based on deeply engrained

---

68 Thomas MacMaster, "Coming Out: Part Two," *A Gay Girl in Damascus*, 19 May 2011.
69 MacMaster, "Coming Out: Part Two."
70 MacMaster, "Coming Out: Part Two."

privilege and stereotypes that antiracism aims to destabilize. Far from forcing educated middle or upper-class Americans to confront their own complicity in racism, his image of rural men baying for Amina's blood reassured MacMaster's readers that they were different from, and superior to, the dehumanized conservative rural and Southern racists he cast as their domestic political opponents.

Conclusion

By early June 2011, MacMaster's hoax was remarkably successful. Since February he had established his blog, built an accepted backstory for Amina, and learned how to connect with his target audience, people generally like him: educated Western progressives. Initially, MacMaster had only limited opportunities to influence public opinion, either directly or indirectly, but that changed after the viral success of "My Father, the Hero." The post received hundreds of thousands of direct views and influenced many more people indirectly through media reports. By May 2011, MacMaster was able to insinuate his views into global media outlets' coverage of the Syrian Revolution.

MacMaster's propaganda worked by making his objects, his audience, complicit in his hoax. By operating inside of established Orientalist tropes, he made his material seem familiar to his audience, which made it easier for them to believe it without inquiring too closely about its details. His messages were also well tailored to his audience. Instead of trying to convince people with different ideologies to jettison their views, MacMaster focused on people like himself, allowing him to operate within their shared ideological and cultural framework. He drew on shared ideas, images, and values to lead his audience of allies toward his preferred positions: military nonintervention, enthusiastic support for the revolution, and support for the Palestinian cause abroad while reinforcing the drive for a more progressive America at home.

Far from objecting to MacMaster's tactics, journalists enabled him by giving him a platform. Interacting with journalists posed risks for MacMaster. On his blog he could control the environment, but interviews, even ones conducted by text or email, forced him to respond to questions from savvy independent actors who had the time, money, and ability to dig into Amina's backstory if they suspected something was amiss. His message and how he presented it proved popular with journalists who repeated his claims, magnifying their effects. Journalists and social media commentators praised both his erotic posts – which they read as showing Amina's bravery and authenticity – and MacMaster's explicit use of academically derived liberating theories encapsulating the concept of the Other, including critical approaches to race and sexuality. He wielded them effectively enough to convince his Western audience that Amina was an honest and even influential participant in the Arab Spring. MacMaster misused liberating theories – including the concept of pinkwashing –to displace and silence Middle Easterners, including LGBT+ Arabs, whose views did not accord with what MacMaster's own beliefs. As a result, he divided critical theory from its progressive underpinnings, seeking antiracist and inclusive policies through a process of silencing and displacement that was antithetical to his goals.

A close reading of *A Gay Girl in Damascus* and press reports about it shows the power of the assumptions MacMaster and the journalists reporting on his blog shared. Journalists easily accepted MacMaster's technological determinism, which was widespread in the Western media and among Western commentators on the Middle East more generally. Journalists and activists believed MacMaster's implicit and explicit claims that social media was facilitating the liberalization of the Syrian Revolution and society for the same reasons they did not question Amina's existence and backstory; they validated their own values and identities.

Chapter III
The Scandal

Damascus, 6 June 2011

A little after 6:00 pm Amina and a friend walked into a bus station in Damascus's Abbassiyyin square to meet a member of the Local Coordinating Committee. As Amina recognized her contact, a group of young men attacked her. She fought for her life, striking one man before they covered her mouth and forced her into the waiting red Dacia Logan.

Two hours later Amina's cousin, Rania, sat in Atlanta typing out the message she had long feared she would have to post on *A Gay Girl in Damascus*. The entry, which Rania posted using Amina's "Amina A." username, informed readers about the kidnapping and bespeeched anyone with information to contact Abdallah, Amina's father. Like Amina, Abdallah had been in hiding, but the venerable patriarch risked arrest by returning to the family home to organize the effort to save his daughter.[1]

Amina's friends, readers, and the journalists who used her blog in their reporting, rallied to demand her release. The *BBC*, *CNN*, and *Al Jazeera* all picked up the story. By 7 June, the Free Amina Arraf Facebook page had over 10,000 members and activists were tweeting #FreeAmina.[2] Because the blog identified Amina as a dual American-Syrian citizen, journalists asked the State Department what it, and Secretary of State Hilary Rodham Clinton, were doing to help Amina.[3] Meanwhile, the already popular blog was flooded with new visitors drawn by the press coverage and social media campaign. By kidnapping Amina, the Assad regime was making her the international face of the Syrian Revolution and, at least as far as the Western media was concerned, the most important Arab woman in the world.

Introduction

By early June 2011, Tom MacMaster knew he risked being exposed by his own success. Posing as Amina had allowed him to influence Western newspapers, television

---

1 Thomas MacMaster, "Amina," *A Gay Girl in Damascus*, 6 June 2011.
2 Muna Khan, "Desperately Seeking Amina Arraf," *Al Arabiya News*, June 8, 2011, http://english. alarabiya.net/articles/2011/06/08/152470.html. In 2013 #FreeAmina became associated with the Tunisian activists Amina Tyler who was arrested for posting a nude picture of herself on Facebook.
3 Sonja Zekri, "Tall Tales from the Desert," *Qantara.de*, http://en.qantara.de/content/journalism-from-the-middle-east-tall-tales-from-the-desert.

https://doi.org/10.1515/9783111057231-004

networks, and online media which never would have cared what an obscure American activist thought about the Syrian Revolution. MacMaster's hoax was never successful enough to control Western public opinion or dominate the Western media, but while people believed Amina was real, MacMaster had a metaphorical seat at the table. His success vividly illustrated the power of positionality in elite Western discourse and its potential to be coopted by unscrupulous actors.

Unfortunately for MacMaster, the more success he had pretending to be Amina, the harder it became to sustain the illusion that Amina existed. The blog's growing visibility caused him to interact with more people while posing as Amina, increasing his influence and the risk of exposure. MacMaster needed to convince the people he interacted with that they were communicating with Amina, despite his inability to engage with them in person, through video, or in a phone conversation. All these limits became even more challenging as journalists continued asking to interview Amina.

MacMaster needed a way to end the blog and justify Amina backing away from her connections without exposing his fraud. His solution was as over-the-top as much of the Amina's biography, a traumatic kidnapping that would lead to her escape or expulsion from Syria, justifying her being cut off from the latest information about Syria and retiring from social media to recover from her trauma. However, MacMaster could not simulate the family, professional, and friendship networks, nor the paper trail, that journalists and government officials expected a real person with Amina's background would have. MacMaster's hoax began unravelling as soon as the first critical investigations began and within days journalists and activists had traced it back to him, showing that the hoax had always relied on his readers' unconscious complicity. Strikingly, even as his illusion collapsed, the blog continued to shape how journalists and activists behaved, exposing the abiding influence of Orientalism on Western perceptions of the Middle East.

Hunting Amina: Real People and Pretend Secret Police

Making connections to real people fueled MacMaster's hoax, but it was also a vulnerability because those people could expose him if they grew suspicious enough to demand evidence of Amina's existence that MacMaster could not fabricate. While passing as Amina MacMaster had communicated with a lot of people online, Sandra Bagaria was an especially important to MacMaster's success and safety. Bagaria was a lesbian woman from Quebec who was interested in the Arab Spring and global LGBT+ rights. She encountered MacMaster posing as Amina on online forums in early 2011. Their interactions quickly turned flirtatious. She also communicated with what she thought were Amina's family members, including her cousin Rania, but MacMaster was controlling those accounts too.[4]

Although she did not bear the risks which MacMaster imposed on activists in Syria, Bagaria was the biggest individual victim of MacMaster's hoax. She was attracted to Amina, and rather than discourage her, MacMaster reciprocated until she considered herself Amina's partner. MacMaster would later try, unsuccessfully, to explained away the cruelty of deceiving Bagaria by telling her, "Amina has had flirty conversations with zillions of people."[5]

MacMaster exploited Bagaria to protect his hoax. Having Sandra Bagaria, a real human being, telling people online that Amina was her girlfriend provided a seemingly unimpeachable reference for Amina's existence. MacMaster had manufactured an online family for Amina by creating social media accounts that interacted with Amina's accounts, but they had limited online presence and were restricted to communicating with people through the written word. Indeed, the secondary accounts were even more vulnerable to being exposed than the primary Amina accounts because MacMaster could not invest enough time to create robust unconnected networks for them. Bagaria, however, was a real person with her own family, close friends, professional contacts, and history of interacting with people unrelated to MacMaster and his hoax. By 18 March Bagaria was calling Amina "my lover" online.[6] She also engaged with journalists who mentioned Amina or the blog on Twitter, sometimes identifying herself as Amina's girlfriend.[7] Bagaria's presence added to the assumption that Amina existed, because people assumed that a blogger with a lover who was easily verified as being who she said she was, must be a real human being. Pulling Bagaria into his hoax helped MacMaster sustain his performance at the price of making himself vulnerable to Bagaria if she became suspicious Amina was not real. Although MacMaster denied intentionally creating the relationship, his words should carry little weight. Encouraging the relationship was clearly in his interest, just as it was in his interest to deny having done so after being caught.

Without naming her, MacMaster began inserting references to Bagaria into the blog. In an entry, aptly titled "Selfish Wishes," he referred to plans he had made with Bagaria for her and Amina to finally meet in person. MacMaster told readers Amina had booked a vacation to Rome where she planned to see "my absolute dearests" and wanted to be "living la dolce vita, reenacting scenes from A

---

4 Sandra Bagaria, *Le Profil Amina.*
5 Thomas MacMaster, *Le Profil Amina.*
6 Sandra Bagaria, Twitter, https://twitter.com/sade_la_bag/status/48780443432128513.
7 Sandra Bagaria, Twitter, https://twitter.com/sade_la_bag/status/64667835770732544.

Room in Rome" with her.[8] These references emphasized to readers that Amina had an active romance, which could be verified online, and the post fed Bagaria's belief that Amina reciprocated her feelings. MacMaster's treatment of Bagaria was cruel and, in the short term, tactically brilliant.

Being a heterosexual married man in a relationship with a lesbian woman who believed he was a lesbian woman created long term problems for MacMaster. He needed to keep making excuses why Amina and Bagaria could not meet or speak directly to each other, which Bagaria was understandably keen to do. Pressed for forms of contact he could not provide, MacMaster claimed that Amina could not use her cellphone anymore because of surveillance and could not get a good enough signal to video conference. He gave Bagaria what he claimed was Amina's home phone number but was really a random Syrian phone number. Bagaria tried calling and it turned out to belong to a Syrian pharmacy. MacMaster knew Bagaria did not speak Arabic and gambled that whoever answered would not speak English or French. If the person who answered the number had spoken either English or French, MacMaster's hoax would have been in grave danger. Bagaria's effort to speak to Amina coincided with escalating efforts by journalists to interview Amina directly, either in-person on through video or phone. These two pressures led MacMaster to announce that Amina was going into hiding. Going on the run allowed MacMaster to deflect Bagaria and journalists' efforts to meet or talk, temporarily making his hoax more secure.

By 11 May, MacMaster was planting the seeds for Amina's excuse for missing the meeting in Rome. He explained to readers that Amina was determined to see the revolution through to the end and feared that if she left Syria, she would not be able to return. Thus, Amina's plans to visit Italy in June to see Bagaria were in jeopardy, as were her plans to move to Britain where MacMaster revealed she had been accepted into a history graduate program.[9] Having Amina go on the run allowed him to explain why Amina could not make a meeting abroad and it reinforced the carefully constructed sense that she was absolutely dedicated to creating a free and democratic Syria, which is what his readers had come to expect of the fearless activist-blogger.

With Amina on the run, informing readers about real events in Syria built dramatic tension around Amina's fate and readers emotional connection to the character. MacMaster reposted a story written by the *Al Jazeera* reporter Dorothy Parvaz about her ordeal in Syrian custody, which reminded readers what awaited Amina if she were captured. Syrian security agents arrested Parvaz on arrival in Damascus

---

8 MacMaster, "Selfish Wishes."

9 MacMaster, "Hopefully not a Final Post."

and she spent days in a detention center. She described being held in a cell that contained "pools of smeared, sticky blood" and hearing the screams of men her captors tortured for information. Syrian authorities soon deported her to Iran, where she was detained in much better conditions before being released. Posting Parvaz's story fed MacMaster's audience's assumptions, themselves rooted in Orientalist images about Middle Eastern prisons, that Amina would experience filthy, brutal, and degrading conditions.[10]

MacMaster warned readers that Amina could be tortured if the regime captured her. He reminded readers that according to Amina's backstory, in 1976 the Syria police had arrested and tortured her uncle for being a Muslim Brother. A later arrest and more torture followed before the family fled to the United States. MacMaster explained that "I am lucky; I have never been tortured. Yet." Amina, however, was not out of danger, because unless the regime fell "this is what awaits us all." The combination of reminders foreshadowed a possible arrest and return to the West for Amina.[11]

As Amina's media profile grew MacMaster found it increasingly difficult to satisfy readers' desire for more material while dealing with deflecting journalists' requests to speak to Amina. In early June, his personal life intruded into his hoax because he and Britta Froelicher were going on vacation to Istanbul after Edinburgh and St. Andrews's spring terms ended. The vacation would leave him with little time to tend to his hoax, especially if he needed to hide it from Froelicher. His solution was to try to unwind the project by ending the blog and having Amina fade away.

When the Syrian government interrupted internet access in the country on 3 June, MacMaster integrated it into his escape plan by posting about the outage as Rania, who lived in the United States. The post noted that Amina could not update the blog because of the interruption. Posting as Rania established that Rania would be able to access the blog to post updates if something happened to Amina.[12]

Soon after the outage ended, MacMaster posted a general political analysis of the situation in Syria. Ironically, MacMaster argued Syrians needed to control their own revolution without foreign meddling of any kind "whether Persian or Israeli, Russian or American." He tried to explain the revolution one last time, rooting it in the expansion of information access in Syria created by the internet. He argued that

10 Thomas MacMaster, "Dorothy Parvaz is Free," *A Gay Girl in Damascus*, 19 May 2011.

11 Thomas MacMaster, "Why We Fight," *A Gay Girl in Damascus*, 18 May 2011.

12 Elizabeth Flock, "Syria internet services shut down as protesters fill streets" Washington Post, 3 June 2011. https://www.washingtonpost.com/blogs/blogpost/post/syria-internet-services-shut-down-as-protesters-fill-streets/2011/06/03/AGtLwxHH_blog.html; Thomas MacMaster, "Internet Down in Syria" *A Gay Girl in Damascus*, 3 June 2011.

the regime's loss of control over access to information undermined its legitimacy as people discovered there were better political and social options than what their government was willing to give them. Over time pressure built up until the fear dissipated enough for people to say publicly what they had long thought privately. He predicted that if the revolution remained nonviolent it would eventually triumph over Assad's repression, but also warned that the regime was becoming more violent and that everyone who resisted was knowingly risking their lives. It was a chilling warning from what readers thought was a woman on the run.[13]

On 6 June 2011 MacMaster began what he hoped would be his hoax's triumphant climax. He posted on Israel's occupation of the Golan Heights and Palestinian land, comparing it to Assad's repression of the Syrian people. He predicted that Israel would have to give way because the "Arab people are asleep no more and the Arab people, not the regimes, are making their own history now." That history, he promised, would include "Millions of Arabs chanting, Thawra hat'n Nasr! [Revolution until Victory!]" on every Israeli frontier.[14] MacMaster's decision to include a post on the Israeli-Palestinian conflict as part of his escape plan reflected the centrality of that conflict to his analysis of the Middle East. MacMaster was trying to convince his readers that their sympathy for the Arab Spring should include embracing the Palestinian cause by drawing parallels between Israel and the Arab dictatorships that dominated the region.

Three hours later he posted about Amina's faith. In the post MacMaster cast Amina's Islam in explicitly progressive terms which he implicitly contrasted to conservative Christians in America. He praised the diversity of Sunni Islam and what he viewed as its warm compassionate concept of God. Amina's God cared "not just for certain people in certain places, but for all humanity." Another section asserted Islam's acceptance of science and Amina's belief that God intended humans to use reason to understand natural creation. MacMaster's Amina rejected the concept of original sin and an array of beliefs and practices of various Christian groups, including predestination and ecclesiastical hierarchies. He ended it by asserting that Amina was a Sunni because "I am a rational person" who believed in human freedom and "the equality of all people before God and in the difference between Good and Evil."[15]

Having summed up a version of Sunni Islam that fit comfortably within the contemporary Western progressive tradition, MacMaster ended with a poem, "Bird Songs." In it, he exalted freedom from a bird's perspective, remarking that

---

13 MacMaster, "Another Day in Damascus," *A Gay Girl in Damascus*, 3 June 2011.

14 Thomas MacMaster, "Jaulan is in Our Hearts," *A Gay Girl in Damascus*, 6 June 2011.

15 Thomas MacMaster, "Still Sunni After All These Years," *A Gay Girl in Damascus*, 6 June 2011.

"Borders mean nothing/When you have wings." "Bird Songs" reinforced MacMaster's construction of Amina as a universal agent before shifting to a darker tone in which Amina's wings vanished and she was "wrapped in a sheet" and "weighed down by dirtcods." Foreshadowing Amina's death reminded readers that she was in constant danger and that her aspirations for freedom and universality conflicted with her daily experience. MacMaster ended the poem imagining the "wind on my wings" and promising that "Freedom is coming." Its ambiguous dualism left it for readers to decide if the poem predicted victory and freedom or the release of death. Given MacMaster's penchant for straight-line foreshadowing, the poem should be read as a roadmap of the hoax's final act in which Amina would be caught, face potential death, and escape to freedom.[16]

#FreeAmina: Readers Mobilize

On the morning of 6 June, Quebec time, Sandra Bagaria received an email from MacMaster passing as Rania. The subject line read "Please read this sitting down" and told her that Amina had been kidnapped earlier that day in Damascus. MacMaster then shared a draft of a blog post announcing the kidnapping and asked Bagaria for advice on refining it.[17] In the post, Rania announced that at around 6:00 PM that evening, Damascus time, Amina and a friend had gone to the Abbassiyeen bus station to meet a member of the Local Coordinating Committee, the group that organized protests. MacMaster reported that as Amina recognized the activist, three young men grabbed her. Amina fought back, hitting one of the men and yelling for her friend to run and find her father. The men then dragged her into a waiting red Dacia Logan emblazoned with a Bassel al-Assad window sticker. Bassel was Bashar al-Assad's older brother who had been their father's chosen successor until his death in a car accident in 1994.[18]

Writing as Rania, MacMaster told readers that Amina's father, Abdallah, did not know which militia or security service had Amina or where she was and asked readers to contact Rania or Abdallah if they had any information to share. MacMaster closed the dramatic post by "hoping she is simply in jail and nothing worse has happened to her." He also told readers that Amina had sent Rania texts to post should something happen to her, but that she would wait until they knew more before posting Amina's final message to her readers.[19]

---

16 MacMaster, "Still Sunni After All These Years."
17 Sandra Bagaria, *Le Profil Amina.*
18 MacMaster, "Amina."
19 MacMaster, "Amina."

Two hours later MacMaster posted a short update to shape his readers' expectations about what would happen next. In it he said that the family was still trying to track down Amina, but that the vast array of government and party-based police services and militias made it hard to find her. He held out hope that she was alive, claiming that if they had intended to kill her, they would have done it in the station instead of abducting her. Writing as Rania, MacMaster speculated that based on the experience of other family members who had been arrested Amina would probably be released "fairly soon." It was also possible, MacMaster teased, that "they are forcibly deporting her."[20]

MacMaster later claimed that he intended Amina's arrest to force readers to face the "moral crisis" of repression in Syria.[21] It is possible that was true but having her arrested fit into the blog's Orientalist and progressive contexts. MacMaster's foreshadowing was rarely subtle, he had consistently signaled major plot twists in advance. Most likely, he expected that he could have Amina disappear for a week or so before reappearing – perhaps in the United States. Her reappearance, conveniently timed to coincide with the end of his vacation, would allow him to end the story by describing her imprisonment and release, escape, or deportation. In a post-exposure interview, MacMaster claimed that he had intended to end the blog by having Amina arrested, escape detention, and make her way to safely in the West.[22] An escape or deportation to the West would have fit with the Orientalist tropes that MacMaster had used to build his propaganda campaign.

Through Amina, MacMaster presented his readers with the impression that the Syrian Revolution offered two choices, remaining mired in superstition and bigotry, or shaking off the past by embracing a socially inclusive and cosmopolitan mentality. MacMaster's framing of that choice marked the blog as simultaneously Orientalist and progressive. If he had been able to complete the project by depicting Amina's escape from Assad's henchmen and her flight to freedom in the West, the symbolism of the blog's Progressive Orientalism would have been even clearer because Amina, the Western-born symbol of the East, would have achieved freedom through finding refuge in the progressive West, validating it as a universal ideology and society.

Ending the blog by having Amina deported from Syria would have been symbolically powerful to American progressives in 2011 because of the ongoing debate over immigration and calls from conservatives to deport millions of migrants. It would also have fit MacMaster's pattern of subordinating Syrian realities to American

---

20 Thomas MacMaster, "Update on Amina" *A Gay Girl in Damascus*, 6 June 2011.

21 Nana Queiroz, "'Eu sou o messias das lésbicas na Síria', diz autor de blog" *Veja*, 14 June 2011, https://veja.abril.com.br/mundo/eu-sou-o-messias-das-lesbicas-na-siria-diz-autor-de-blog/.

22 Flock and Bell 'Tom MacMaster, the man behind "A Gay Girl in Damascus"'.

politics. MacMaster could have leveraged his readers' sympathy for Amina to increase their opposition to the United States government's deportation of unauthorized migrants and failed asylum seekers.

MacMaster likely intended to cite Amina's traumatic experience to justify her refusing interviews as the blog faded away. However, MacMaster badly miscalculated his audience's reaction to the fictious abduction. His deception had gotten too successful for him to control the fallout. By the time he tried to pull the plug Amina was already, in the words of the journalist Andy Carvin, "the poster child of the Arab Spring blogosphere" and her "stock was rising faster than any blogger in the Middle East."[23]

Within hours of MacMaster's post, real people mobilized to save a nonexistent woman. Rami Nakhla, a Syrian activist, took up the call to save Amina, sharing the blog post on Twitter. Nakhla, who had fled to Lebanon earlier in the revolution, was an established spokesperson for Syrian groups and so had wide contacts with journalists. Posts from people like him quickly got attention from Western journalists including Andy Carvin. Other activists, including the transfeminist queer filmmaker Leil-Zahra Mortada, who was born in Lebanon but was living in Western Europe, urged people "at home" to "start making noise" and to contact Syrian embassies demanding her release.[24] When Elizabeth Tsurkov, an Israeli journalist and Palestinian rights activist who counted Amina as a friend, read about the kidnapping she started organizing a response among her contacts. She thought it was imperative to get Amina released quickly because her sexual orientation was known and could provide "an opening for even more abuse" than was normal.[25]

Sandra Bagaria began her own campaign to save her girlfriend by posting links to the blog's announcement and pleading "Please #FreeAmina" on Twitter.[26] Bagaria was not a professional organizer, but she reached out to activists and other users who were willing to help. Because she was in Canada, MacMaster's email reached Bagaria during the day, giving her much of 6 June to raise the alarm. During that day she posted at least thirty tweets and re-tweets about Amina's kidnapping.[27] By 7 June, Bagaria was in contact with journalists and gave interviews in a desperate attempt to create enough pressure on the Syrian government to get Amina released,

---

23 Carvin, *Distant Witness*, 188.

24 Leil-Zahra Mortada, Twitter, https://twitter.com/LeilZahra/status/77826348235767808.

25 Elizabeth Tsurkov, *Le Profil Amina*.

26 Carvin, *Distant Witness* 188; Andy Carvin, Twitter, https://twitter.com/acarvin/status/77804332778 659841; Leil-Zahra Mortada, Twitter, https://twitter.com/LeilZahra/status/77818945863811072; Sandra Bagaria, Twitter https://twitter.com/sade_la_bag/status/77816306669330433

27 Sandra Bagaria, Twitter, https://twitter.com/sade_la_bag.

least her captors casually kill her without realizing her connections. By 8:30 AM on 7 June she had done five interviews, including one that aired on *BBC Radio 4*'s *World Tonight* that evening in Britain.[28] Her efforts added credibility to the campaign, and initially slowed the emergence of doubts about Amina's identity and story.

By the end of 7 June 2011, reporters all over the world were writing about the case and for the first time in the West, the Syrian Revolution had a face, Amina's face. The news sources that had covered Amina's blog quickly piled into the campaign to save her. MacMaster's branding of Amina was strong enough that it shaped the coverage of the kidnapping. *The Guardian* reported Amina's kidnapping in a piece written by a journalist using the pseudonym Nidaa Hassan. Hassan's first line emphasized Amina's lesbianism, telling readers that her "frank and witty thoughts on Syria's uprising, politics and being a lesbian in the country shot her to prominence" and that she had "capture[ed] the imagination of the Syrian opposition as the protest movement struggled in the face of the government crackdown." Hassan did not provide any evidence that Amina or the blog were having any effect inside of Syria but instead was effectively speaking based on the reaction people like *The Guardian*'s readers had to the blog.[29]

The *Washington Post*'s veteran Middle East correspondent Liz Sly began her report on the kidnapping by identifying Amina as gay in the title and first line of the article before uncritically recounting the events of "My Father, the Hero." She praised Amina for fighting back against her capturers during the kidnapping, claiming that it "fit with the feisty, passionate and defiant personality that emerges from her blog." Sly provided a solitary note of caution, explaining that "some skeptics questioned whether someone who had grown up in the United States and returned to Syria only last summer could truly be said to speak for the Syrians battling to overthrow their regime." She did not, however, identify the sceptics or endorse their position, let alone question Amina's existence or biography.[30]

Al Jazeera's report frankly acknowledged that Amina's nationality and sexual orientation had drawn attention to the blog and her kidnapping. The unnamed author noted that previous arrests of bloggers in Syria, including Tal al-Mallouhi, Ahmad Abu al-Khair, Khaled El-Ekhetyar, and the Egyptian government's arrest of the Egyptian-American blogger Muhammed Radwan, had produced little reaction outside of the region. This time however was different, "probably because of the

---

28 Sandra Bagaria, Twitter, https://twitter.com/sade_la_bag/status/78121143260815360; https://twitter.com/sade_la_bag/status/78147159190544384.

29 Nidaa Hassan [pseudonym] 'Syrian blogger Amina Abdallah kidnapped by armed men' *Guardian*, 6 June 2011, https://www.theguardian.com/world/2011/jun/07/syrian-blogger-amina-abdallah-kidnapped.

30 Sly, 'Syrian American blogger'

unusual circumstances: She is a Syrian-American dual citizen, and an openly gay woman living in Damascus." *Al Jazeera* noted that Amina had become increasingly critical of the government over the spring and had narrowly escaped arrest in the past. The report included an interview with Bagaria who, taking her cues from previous electronic conversations she thought were with Amina, pushed MacMaster's line that Amina had not been arrested because she was gay, but because "she's trying to tell the truth about what's happening in Syria . . . this had to happen eventually."[31] It was important to MacMaster's goals that people believe it was Amina's activism, not her homosexuality, that led to her arrest because if she was arrested for being gay, it would undermine his claim that Arab societies and Islam were accepting of sexual diversity.

The coverage of the kidnapping brought a new wave of people into contact with the hoax. Driven in part by the uniformly sympathetic initial media coverage, social media users wanted to help Amina. By the afternoon of 9 June, the Free Amina Facebook page, which was written in English, had over 15,000 supporters. In contrast, when the Syrian police arrested the nineteen-year-old blogger Tal al-Mallouhi, a Facebook group demanding her release gathered 650 signatures. Ryan Gerety, an American digital researcher and activist who had worked in Damascus, created an iconic graphic featuring a drawing of Amina based on her profile picture and the phrase "borders mean nothing when you have wings," a quote from "Bird Songs," the poem MacMaster posted hours before he announced Amina's kidnapping. Overall 61 percent of all social media discussions about Amina took place in English and another 15 percent were in French. The language users post in does not necessarily correlate to their native language or culture, but the preponderance of English and French strongly suggests that the Amina's audience was mainly English-speakers and people living in Western countries.[32]

Those conversations were overwhelmingly supportive. 62 percent of social media posts about Amina explicitly indicated support for her. Another 12 percent reposted stories about the abduction or calls for her release without any comment, which suggests support for Amina. Only 26 percent made negative or neutral comments, most "neutral" comments noted her arrest and were implicitly supportive of freeing her. Even the critical comments rarely attacked Amina. The negative commenters generally followed *Al Jazeera*'s line and criticized journalists for

---

31 "This had to happen eventually' A close friend of detained Syrian blogger, Amina Abdallah Arraf, talks about her friend's arrest and work" *Al Jazeera*, 6 June 2011, updated 13 June 2011, https://www.aljazeera.com/blogs/middleeast/2011/06/43171.html.
32 'Buzz Report: Free Amina' *Social Eye*, 13 June 2011. https://social-eyez.com/2011/06/; Syria Cracks down on Bloggers" Instittue for War and Peace Reporting, 13 April 2010. https://iwpr.net/global-voices/syria-cracks-down-bloggers.

having ignored thousands of other arrested activists rather than questioning Amina's existence or honesty.[33]

Searching for the Real Amina

Although criticism of Amina and *A Gay Girl in Damascus* was absent from Western media, the friendly stories rung false to some observers. The skeptics had kept quiet before because it was not worth engaging, even if they were right. Because they supported the protest movement, discrediting the blog was of little value to them. In addition, if they were wrong it would be time wasted fighting an ally instead of working for their cause. That changed when Amina became the face of the Syrian Revolution. Until then, the only people with an incentive to dig into the blog and expose it were supporters of the Assad Regime. However, Amina's arrest and the media's focus on her case changed the situation. If she existed, she needed help, but if she did not exist, opposition activists in Syria were being asked to needlessly risk their lives.

Over the course of 6 and 7 June 2011 doubts emerged, though at first fear of being wrong kept sceptics quiet. Andy Carvin had built a vast network of social media contacts which allowed him to observe Arab social media and dissident conversations and report on them in the West. When he saw the first reports on Twitter of Amina's abduction, he announced the news to his followers, magnifying the #FreeAmina movement.

Several people, mainly Arab activists living in the Middle East, contacted Carvin to warn him to be cautious. One message, from Ahmad Danny Ramadan, a gay Syrian man Carvin had met in Egypt, warned him that he had it "from a good source that she is a fictional character."[34] Ramadan had already started digging into the hoax. He convinced a friend who was gay and worked inside the regime to find out who arrested her. The man was reluctant to do it because if he was caught, he risked arrest himself. Ramadan persuaded him to risk his life out of solidarity, but he found no record of Amina Arraf or anyone resembling her being detained. Ramadan contacted lesbian women he knew who lived in Damascus and found none of them had met Amina.[35] When Carvin responded that he had it from a "good source" [Bayaria] that Amina was real, Ramadan remained unconvinced. He pointed out details that did not make sense, like Amina using Blogspot to host her blog, even

33 'Buzz Report: Free Amina' *Social Eye.*
34 Carvin, *Distant Witness*, 191.
35 Ahmed Danny Ramadan, *Le Profil Amina.*

though it was blocked in Syria (there were ways to get around the block). He insisted that "My Father, the Hero" could not be true because he knew "from experience" that you cannot talk the secret police out of arresting somebody, "no matter who her father is. It's as simple as that." If she lied about that, he asked, how could anyone be sure she was not making up her own arrest?[36]

An anonymous Syrian activist reached out to Carvin saying the blog did not reflect real life in Syria. Besides being "wayyy too dramatic" the author clearly did not understand how arrests worked. Amina could not have debated why the militiamen were arresting her because they would neither have known nor cared, they just had lists of names and arrested their targets. Her father's grandstanding would have been impossible "security comes and gets you then moves on. No moving father's speech will stop that." He then cut off contact and deleted his messages, minutes after Carvin had saved them. Another Syrian posted, and then deleted, the comment "This isn't going to end well for us."[37]

Carvin, was already familiar with the blog and had not questioned Amina's veracity before the abduction but was worried about the warnings. He knew several of Amina's Facebook friends and contacted them privately asking if they had met or skyped with her and none of them had. Then he took to Twitter asking people if anyone had met, spoken with, or video conferenced with Amina.[38] Carvin contacted Sandra Bagaria, looking for confirmation that Amina's pictures were really Amina. Bagaria replied quickly via Twitter that they were.[39] He reached out to *The Guardian*'s managing editor, asking if its undercover reporter in Damascus who had interviewed Amina could confirm her identity. *Lez Get Real*'s owner contacted Carvin and offered to help with the investigation by tracing the IP addresses Amina used when she posted to *Lez Get Real*.[40]

While journalists started asking questions about Amina, one woman knew immediately that something was wrong about Amina when she saw the news on 7 June 2011. Jelena Lecic, a Croatian woman living in London, awoke to find that *The Guardian*, and then other outlets, had published pictures of her which they claimed were pictures of an abducted Syrian blogger named Amina Arraf. Lecic contacted *The Guardian* but initially got no response.[41]

---

36 Carvin, *Distant Witness*, 191.

37 Carvin, *Distant Witness*, 192–93.

38 Carvin, *Distant Witness*, 191–92.

39 Sandra Bagaria, Twitter, https://twitter.com/sade_la_bag/status/77841623639261184.

40 Carvin, *Distant Witness*, 194.

41 Jelena Lecic, *BBC Newsnight*, 8 June 2011. http://news.bbc.co.uk/2/hi/programmes/newsnight/9509289.stm; "Syrian mystery of Amina Arraf: 'A gay girl in Damascus'" *BBC News*, 9 June 2011. http://www.bbc.co.uk/news/world-middle-east-13719131.

Liz Henry, a San Francisco-based technology executive, blogger, and long-time progressive activist already knew about Amina and *A Gay Girl in Damascus* before the kidnapping. She discovered Amina following "My Father, the Hero" and had, unintentionally, been part of MacMaster's support system by pushing back against some of the small number of people who questioned whether it was possible to be as out in Damascus as Amina claimed to be. Henry had silenced them by saying that she "would not doubt someone based on their identity," implicitly warning them that they should not challenge an account from somebody with Amina's positionality.[42] When Henry first read that Amina had been kidnapped, she felt compelled to act, saying that "I was horrified and felt like it was an emergency."[43] As 7 June wore on, Henry started asking why none of Amina's family had been interviewed and why most of the coverage was having to cite the blog itself. Even if her friends and family in Syria were justifiably too afraid to appear on television, according to the blog Amina had family and friends in the United States; somebody should have been talking to the media.[44]

In a thoughtful post, which was clearly painful for her to write, Henry explored different possibilities. Amina could, she thought, have been who she appeared to be, "a talented writer living in Syria" who might have changed her name and obscured personal details to protect herself and her family. She could also have been another person in Syria, or even from another place entirely. Henry raised the possibility that Sandra Bagaria, the only clearly identifiable person journalists had found to talk about Amina, could have concocted Amina and created the blog herself. MacMaster's propaganda continued to color Henry's response even as she noticed warning signs that Amina was a hoax. It was only after noticing Amina's obviously and suspiciously deficient real-world presence, that Henry began noticing flaws in MacMaster's presentation of Amina in the blog. Henry, who had silenced people for questioning Amina before the kidnapping, continued to praise Amina's writing but now "detected patterns of storytelling that made me suspicious that she was a fiction."[45] Henry ended her post by pleading with readers to prove her doubts wrong, writing that "If I'm wrong then I am being very rude to Amina and I am terribly sorry for that" and suggesting that "Someone must have known her in Atlanta . . . meanwhile, I hope she is safe."[46]

---

42 Liz Henry, "Painful doubts about Amina," *Composite*, 7 June 2011, http://bookmaniac.org/2011/06/07/painful-doubts-about-amina/.

43 Liz Henry, *Le Profil Amina.*

44 Henry, "Painful doubts about Amina."

45 Henry, *Le Profil Amina.*

46 Henry, "Painful doubts about Amina."

Over the course of 7 and 8 June U.S. State Department officials too were hunting for Amina. If Amina was a real American citizen who had been arrested by the Assad Regime, the U.S. government had a duty to try to help her. The case was strange because no member of the Arraf or McClure families contacted the State Department. Journalists however did, asking the State Department's spokesperson about what it, Secretary of State Hilary Rodham Clinton, and rest of the Obama Administration were doing to protect Amina. The department's investigation found no evidence Amina Arraf was an American citizen. The State Department should have had a record of Amina's passport, but its staff could not find one. Moreover, investigators could not find her Virginia birth certificate.[47] They even tried emailing Bagaria and Rania asking for more information on Amina, Bagaria responded but Rania never did. Unable to find any proof of her citizenship or existence, U.S. diplomats resorted to posting a comment on *A Gay Girl in Damascus* asking Amina's family to contact the U.S. embassy in Damascus.[48]

The State Department's public silence was an ominous sign that few observers immediately noticed because if Amina Arraf had existed and had a U.S. passport, the department would have immediately made clear public statements to push the Assad regime to find her and protect her as an asset to trade and somebody too dangerous to accidentally kill. When asked why they had not yet intervened to protect Amina, an embassy official in Damascus told *The Guardian* that they could not "make a consular representation to the Syrian authorities on Ms. Arraf's behalf without first determining that she is a US citizen."[49]

By the evening on 7 June, word was spreading that people had doubts about the story. That evening Robert Mackey, a *New York Times* reporter, announced publicly what others had realized privately, nobody could prove Amina Arraf was a real person. He explained that none of the journalists who quoted Amina had spoken to her in person, via telephone, or via video conference. They had all interviewed her via email and texting. He also exposed the existence of MacMaster's 2007 blog which contained similar biographical material to *A Gay Girl in Damascus*, explaining that the 2007 blog presented Amina as "a mix of fact and fiction." Implicitly raising questions about Bagaria's integrity, he noted that she was the only person publicly saying she was a close friend of Amina's and that *The Times*, the *BBC*, and *Al Jazeera* had all relied on her to vouch for Amina's existence. He

---

47 Robert Mackey, "Sifting Syrian Fact From Syrian" *The Lede*, 8 June 2011, https://thelede.blogs. nytimes.com/2011/06/08/sifting-syrian-fact-from-syrian-fiction.
48 *Le Profil Amina.*
49 Ester Addley and Nidaa Hassan, "Syria: Mystery surrounds 'Gay Girl in Damascus' blogger abduction," *The Guardian*, 8 June 2011. https://www.theguardian.com/world/2011/jun/08/syria-gay-girl-damascus-abduction.

did not say Amina did not exist nor that the blog was a hoax, and explicitly wrote it was possible that story was all true, but his doubts accelerated the process of deconstructing MacMaster's hoax.[50]

The watershed moment came when journalists belatedly discovered that the photographs of Amina were stolen. Although *The Guardian* ignored Jelena Lecic's first attempt to reclaim ownership of her image, she later found journalists willing to listen and ended up talking to *BBC Newsnight* on the evening of 8 June 2011. In her interview, she told Jeremy Paxman that she had never heard of Amina until the kidnapping story and had no idea who she really was. She said that "if she's a real person, it's awful she has been kidnapped" but that "It's absolutely astonishing that someone has been using my picture and obviously campaigning with my face." All the over two hundred pictures MacMaster had posted of Amina on Facebook and the blog had, she believed, been downloaded from her Facebook account. The most prominently used ones, which MacMaster claimed had been taken in Damascus, were really pictures of Lecic in Paris.[51]

Despite the mounting evidence against Amina, *Newsnight* did not declare it a hoax and interviewed a sympathetic activist who defended the blog as essentially real, even if the author was probably not named Amina Arraf and was using Jelena Lecic's pictures. Mahmoud Hamad, a London-based activist, explained that Middle Eastern bloggers often wrote using false names and partially fictionalized biographies to escape government repression. He urged viewers to withhold judgment and vouched for the authenticity of Amina's message, even if he could not prove who the blogger really was, including whether she was really a woman or even a single person. However, Hamad believed the blog's messages were real because "Her level of writing, her sophistication, her intricate knowledge of Syrian society and what's happening – right now politically in Syria – compels you to believe that this person is actually a genuine political activist and homosexual."[52]

After the *Newsnight* report aired, a clearly frustrated Carvin posted that Amina was "a mystery wrapped in a riddle inside an enigma packaged into a blog" but allowed that "for her sake, I hope not in a jail cell as well."[53] Like Carvin and Henry, Hamad and *Newsnight*'s staff were willing to admit doubts, but continued to believe

---

50 Robert Mackey and Liam Stack, "After Report of Disappearance, Questions About Syrian-American Blogger" *The Lede*, 7 June 2011, https://thelede.blogs.nytimes.com/2011/06/07/syrian-american-blogger-detained/.

51 Jelena Lecic, *BBC Newsnight*; Syrian mystery of Amina Arraf: "A gay girl in Damascus'" *BBC News*, 9 June 2011. http://www.bbc.co.uk/news/world-middle-east-13719131.

52 Syrian mystery of Amina Arraf: "A gay girl in Damascus'" *BBC News*, 9 June 2011. http://www.bbc.co.uk/news/world-middle-east-13719131.

53 Andy Carvin, Twitter, https://twitter.com/acarvin/status/78626319855927296.

in parts of the exoticized and eroticized hoax that should have themselves been evidence that the blog was not real, including the projection of Western politics into the Middle East and the writing of Middle Eastern and Western politics onto Amina's body and sexuality. They were, however, all educated politically engaged and generally progressive people living in the West, and thus MacMaster's target audience. Even as his character unraveled, the propaganda messages still had power over his targets.

Carvin clung to the possibility that Amina was a real Syrian activist even after receiving an email from *The Guardian*'s editor admitting that the anonymous reporter in Syria never actually met Amina. Worse, Amina had sent the reporter a picture of Jelena Lecic to help her recognize Amina for the interview, proving that whoever Amina was, she was lying directly to reporters and never intended to meet Marsh.[54] On Friday 10 June, as he was tracking Amina's electronic paper trail from one dead-end to another, Carvin gave an interview to Jian Ghomeshi on CBC's *Q*. In response to Ghomeshi's question about Amina's identity, Carvin explained the doubts that existed and even mentioned theories that Amina was a Syrian or Israeli intelligence operation, but he argued she was probably more real than not. Citing Amina's long online paper trail, he suggested she could be exactly who she said she was and everybody was misunderstanding, or that "she is a person who had been writing under a pen name and does happen to be a lesbian woman in the Middle East and she's doing it to protect herself." He also theorized that Amina could be a closeted Middle Eastern woman who was writing about herself as if she could live as openly as Amina did in the blog.[55]

In retrospect, Carvin explained why he hesitated to call the hoax a hoax for so long. He claimed he was worried that if he expressed any public doubts about Amina and there was a real Syrian behind the blog, even one who had run a fake online identity for years, he could derail pressure to win her release. Carvin expressed his fear using Orientalist images that erotized torture in ways reminiscent of MacMaster's own work. He imagined Amina "strapped down on a cold, damp gurney . . . with that monster breathing against her cheek, gently caressing her face with the end of a jumper cable." Carvin recalled that, "for a moment I could hear his voice" asking Amina "'where shall we begin, *ya habibti?*'"[56] Carvin's explanation used the same long established Orientalist tropes equating the Middle East with brutality, torture, and the sexual enslavement of, in this case semi-white, women that MacMaster used to orchestrate the hoax.

---

54 Carvin, *Distant Witness*, 198–99.
55 Andy Carvin, *Q*, *CBC*, 10 June 2011.
56 Carvin, *Distant Witness*, 193.

Despite many journalists and activists' desire to believe in Amina, there were too many problems with the story for them not to investigate it. Journalists and activists wanted to know Amina's real identity because even though Amina was clearly not a Syrian American lesbian woman named Amina Arraf, most of them believed it remained possible that there was a real imprisoned activist who needed help but whose support network was either unaware of it because she was using a false identity or had been scared off by the revelations. There were also other possibilities, if the whole thing was a hoax there was a good story available for journalists and if Amina was a front for a Syrian security agency, then activists needed to know that their networks were compromised and that everything that had ever been viewable by Amina's accounts had been seen by the regime's agents. If so, real lives were at risk. A week before nobody but the Syrian government had a compelling reason to investigate Amina, now people all over the world did.

As the investigations into Amina intensified, digital technology went from protecting MacMaster to making exposing him easier. For almost a decade the relative anonymity of blogging and discussion groups had protected MacMaster and facilitated his hoax, but after people became suspicious, the electronic media MacMaster had used became a threat. MacMaster's old digital communications still existed on the internet, or more accurately on the hard drives of computers connected to the internet. This included metadata about when accounts were created, where Amina's internet connections originated, and what he posted online. The survival of traceable information made it easier to investigate Amina and to trace her back to MacMaster through following the digital breadcrumbs he had been leaving behind while passing as Amina. The most important of these enduring traces were the accounts he had created in Amina's name years before and the IP (Internet Protocol) addresses associated with Amina.

IP addresses exist to allow computers to locate and communicate with each other. The addresses contain information on the network a computer is attached to and its location to allow other computers to send it data. As a result, investigators could recover what networks Amina had used and approximately where they were located. This allowed investigators to track Amina's past locations at the city level and to compile a list of websites that computers using the same network as Amina had accessed. The lists made it possible to identify online activity potentially linked to the user behind Amina which would provide additional context to help identify the person. Ironically, the technologies that made the hoax possible made it unsustainable as soon as the audience questioned Amina's authenticity.

By 10 June, at least two groups of investigators had traced Amina's recent IP address to an unexpected place, Scotland. In response to the growing doubts about

Amina, *Lez Get Real* issued an apology on June 10 in which Managing Editor Linda Carbonell clung to her belief that Amina was deceptive but well intentioned and generally who she claimed to be. Carbonell apologized to readers for being duped by Amina who, she and her colleagues believed "apparently is a 35 year-old lesbian living in Edinburgh." She went on to defend Amina, even as both the kidnapping and the identity unraveled, explaining that "'Amina' didn't say anything that wasn't the truth" and that "the situation in Syria is no less horrific just because she wasn't there." She also presented a theory the person behind Amina had created the abduction story out of frustration that the Western press and public opinion had ignored the murder of a ten-year-old boy in Syria the previous week. She thus framed Amina as "trying to make people care about her country and make the United Nations get involved." Carbonell's theory demonstrated that MacMaster's deception remained deeply convincing for her and her colleagues. Despite having to admit that Amina was not who she said she was, she did not question that Amina was a Syrian lesbian woman and defended the blog's overall reliability.[57]

Andy Carvin's posts asking if anybody knew Amina offline led to a participant in an online group who thought he had known Amina for five years. While the man admitted that he had only communicated with her via email, he put Carvin in touch with another member who had sent her physical mail, which held out the hope of finding an address that could be checked. The second man, who asked Carvin to keep his name secret, gave him the address he sent Amina cards and a wedding gift. The address was in Stone Mountain, Georgia, near Atlanta, which matched details in the blog, though the timing of the gift did not match the blog's chronology of Amina's marriage which allegedly happened in the 1990s, not the mid–2000s. The incongruity was a result of MacMaster's rewriting of Amina's backstory when he launched *A Gay Girl in Damascus*. The man assured Carvin that none of the mail had been returned and Amina had acknowledged the gift. Rather than proving Amina' existence though, it led to more questions because a records search turned up no evidence anyone named Arraf, or anyone else with an Arab name had owned the home. Staff members at the local high school had never heard of Amina or a family resembling hers.[58]

As the investigators dug deeper, they eventually tripped MacMaster's notice. The same informant who swore to Carvin he had known Amina for five years told him about a listserv, TheCrescentLand, that Amina helped run. After joining

57 Linda S. Carbonell "An Apology to Our Readers About Amina Abdallah" *Lez Get Real*, 10 June 2011. http://lezgetreal.com/2011/06/an-apology-to-our-readers-about-amina-abdallah/comment-page-1/. Accessed via https://web.archive.org/web/20110612062742/http://lezgetreal.com/2011/06/an-apology-to-our-readers-about-amina-abdallah/comment-page1/#comment-166648.
58 Carvin, *Distant Witness*, 201–202.

the list, Carvin posted to it, explaining he was a journalist who wanted to talk about Amina's disappearance. Within minutes Carvin got his response, an administrator deleted the group, its public profile, its member list, and its message archive. There were only two people who were supposed to be able to do that, one was the administrator who had just admitted Carvin to the group, the other was Amina, though she had allegedly shared her password with Rania. Immediately afterward Rania's Facebook profile vanished as did a page promoting the blog and Amina's online dating profiles. MacMaster was belatedly trying to cover his tracks.[59] Carvin's post probably tipped MacMaster off, but he could have been reacting to queries coming from others, because Carvin was not the only person probing toward MacMaster at that moment.

At roughly the same time, *Electronic Intifada* was publishing the results of its investigation into the blog. Ali Abunimah and Benjamin Doherty wrote that they had traced Amina Arraf's electronic trail to two people "Thomas (Tom) J MacMaster and Britta Froelicher who are married to each other." They too had contacted TheCresentland members and found the Georgia address. Their research showed that MacMaster had owned it for years and gave Froelicher a share of ownership in it in 2007. They still owned it and, according to Facebook posts, had lived there until they moved to Britain in the fall of 2010. Abunimah and Doherty matched pictures in the blog to photos in Froelicher's Picasa account. They concluded that they were not simply stolen from the account because the photos on Picasa had been sharpened and cropped while the ones on the blog seemed to be the original image the Picasa photos were based on, meaning the blogger had access to the same original photos Froelicher had started with, but critically did not post, years before the blog used them. Finally, Abunimah and Doherty traced the IP addresses associated with Amina. In addition to *A Gay Girl in Damascus*, Amina had posted blog entries on *Lez Get Real*. Its director gave them access to the blog's metadata which showed that Amina had posted her blog entries from addresses associated with the University of Edinburgh, which was where MacMaster studied. They traced a series of edits on *Wikipedia* to the same address, all on pages about topics MacMaster or Froelicher wrote about or studied.[60]

Ali Abunimah and Benjamin Doherty contacted MacMaster who tersely responded that "I am not the blogger in question." He dismissed any connections between him, his wife, and the blogger as "unusual coincidences."[61] At around

---

59 Carvin, *Distant Witness*, 202–203.

60 Ali Abunimah, 'New evidence about Amina, the "Gay Girl in Damascus" hoax', *Electronic Intifada*, 12 June 2011. https://electronicintifada.net/comment/364.

61 Abunimah, 'New evidence about Amina, the "Gay Girl in Damascus" hoax.'

the same time Abunimah and Doherty confronted MacMaster, and shortly before Carvin's post on TheCresentLand, MacMaster was fending off questions from *Washington Post* reporters Elizabeth Flock and Melissa Bell. Froelicher too denied writing the blog or knowing anything about its author. MacMaster and Froelicher's situation was untenable, journalists had narrowed the list of suspects down to the two of them, the evidence was strong, and the story was too big to go away. After Abunimah and Doherty named them, either MacMaster or Froelicher needed to confess, rebut the evidence, or accept they would both be presumed guilty. Tom MacMaster answered on *A Gay Girl in Damascus* where he could issue a statement without being immediately interrogated.

Exposed

On 12 June, six days after he had announced Amina's kidnapping, MacMaster posted a confession in which he claimed he was "the sole author of all posts on this blog." Although titled "Apology to readers" MacMaster never expressed remorse and denied that he had truly deceived anyone, claiming that although "the narrative voice may have been fictional, the facts on this blog are true and not misleading as to the situation on the ground." Suggesting his efforts were not just benign but beneficial, he spun them as creating "an important voice for issues that I feel strongly about" and claimed that he "only tried to illuminate them for a western audience." Rather than ending by asking for forgiveness, he denied harming anyone, thanked his readers for their support, and most ironically of all, attacked the "superficial coverage of the Middle East and the pervasiveness of new forms of liberal Orientalism."[62]

After reading a torrent of denunciations of his failure to apologize in his apology, MacMaster posted a second apology on 13 June. The second effort combined admitting he harmed people with a continuing effort to explain away his actions. He named four people he had wronged, including Jelena Lecic, Sandra Bagaria, the founder of *Lez Get Real*, and Scott Palter, a game designer and fellow alternate history fan who MacMaster had interacted with while posing as Amina for years. Palter may have been the anonymous informant who gave Andy Carvin Amina's address and who had sent Amina gifts.[63]

---

62 Thomas MacMaster "Apology to Readers," *A Gay Girl in Damascus*, 12 June 2011. https://web.archive.org/web/20110613142248/http://damascusgaygirl.blogspot.com/.

63 Thomas MacMaster, "Apology to Readers," *A Gay Girl in Damascus*, 13 June 2011. accessed via https://web.archive.org/web/20110613161818/http://damascusgaygirl.blogspot.com.

In his apology, MacMaster used echoes of the same tactics he deployed within the hoax to justify his actions. He asserted an organic tie to the Middle East based on his mother's time teaching English in Turkey, his father's work with Middle Eastern refugees, and his own support for the Palestinian cause. As a result, he explained, "since my childhood I had felt very connected to the cultures and peoples of the Middle East. It's something that I came by naturally." MacMaster cast posing as Amina as a tactic designed to counter the "incredibly ignorant and stupid positions repeated on the Middle East," effectively claiming it was an extension of his engagement with the Iraq and Palestine peace movements. He rooted his fraud in his speculation about identity and positionality, claiming he had wondered if interlocutors would respond differently to his arguments if they came from a Middle Eastern Muslim woman. As a result, he wrote, "I decided to create her."[64]

MacMaster justified his long-term performance of Amina as an authentic artistic act because, he claimed, it was him responding to the character "coming alive." Examining that he could "hear her 'voice'" he described her as "funny and smart and equal parts infuriating and flirtatious." It was, he wrote, "almost as though she were dictating to me." He described his persona as if it was a drug, saying he stepped away repeatedly over the years and "meant to stop her" but then he would see a news report or hear something that he felt Amina would want to respond to and he would "find myself fighting the urge to respond as Amina . . . and occasionally giving in."[65] MacMaster's apology functioned within the same kind of world his blog did, an Orientalist rendering of reality in which fact and fiction could be blurred if it validated his own identity formation and political and social needs.

In the first couple of days after admitting he was the author of *A Gay Girl in Damascus*, MacMaster gave interviews to journalists from all over the world. He began by talking to *Washington Post* reporters Elizabeth Flock and Melissa Bell who had been the first journalists to contact him. In his interviews, first with Flock and Bell and then with a legion of other journalists, MacMaster presented contradictory explanations of his actions, none of which should be accepted at face value. MacMaster couched passing Amina as a creative writing experiment gone awry. Although acknowledging that he started pretending to be Amina Arraf for political reasons, he presented the hoax as a literary challenge that got out of control. According to MacMaster, after creating a simple character to use in chat

---

64 MacMaster, "Apology to Readers," 13 June 2011.
65 MacMaster, "Apology to Readers," 13 June 2011.

rooms and listservs he began fleshing out her and Amina "sprang into play with a clear voice."[66]

For years before starting *A Gay Girl in Damascus* he would image Amina's reactions to political and cultural events and add it to his performance. He later told Bagaria that he would hear Amina's voice in his daily life. He would know how she would respond to the news, what dress she would buy in a store, and what question she would ask at a lecture. When Bagaria asked him in 2012 if he still heard Amina, he swore he did not, though there was little reason to believe him.[67] Claiming that he relished the "challenge of being someone who wasn't me," be kept continuing the hoax.[68] MacMaster's claims indicated he misunderstood his own hoax. Instead of mastering the mental world of a real version of Amina as he believed he had, MacMaster merely projected his own worldview and politics onto the façade of a gay Middle Eastern woman.

Redefining the hoax as creative writing was also an attempt to defuse questions about the erotic themes in the blog. Although acknowledging that he mistreated Bagaria and owed her an apology, MacMaster sidestepped the implications of their relationship when speaking to journalists. When confronted about his sexually charged messages and Bagaria's characterization of Amina as being her lover, MacMaster blamed Bagaria. Using language that harkened to his character Lori blaming Amina after they had sex to avoid admitting she was a lesbian, MacMaster claimed "I was just going along with it. I hadn't thought it out. Suddenly it got more complicated than I expected."[69] When pressed by interviewers about why he engaged in a person-to-person relationship, he deflected questions by hiding behind claims he was suffering emotional distress. He told NPR that he was "feeling a lot of contrition and depression" and felt "really guilty and bad about it."[70] MacMaster's use of his emotions to avoid directly discussing his exploitative behavior reflected the emotionally charged defensive behavior, white fragility, which Robin DiAngelo argues self-consciously anti-racist white Americans use to avoid scrutiny for their own complicity in racist systems.[71]

His tactic proved less successful when Bagaria confronted him in person as part of an ambush interview for a documentary film about the hoax. He tried to

66 Flock and Bell, "Tom MacMaster, the man behind 'A Gay Girl in Damascus.'"

67 Thomas MacMaster, *Le profil Amina*.

68 Flock and Bell, "Tom MacMaster."

69 Flock and Bell, "Tom MacMaster."

70 Eyder Peralta, "Man Behind Syrian Blogger Hoax: 'Something 'Innocent . . . Got Out Of Hand'" *The Two-Way* NPR, 13 June, 2011, https://www.npr.org/sections/thetwo-way/2011/06/14/137148644/man-behind-syrian-blogger-hoax-something-innocent-got-out-of-hand.

71 DiAngelo, *White Fragility*.

frame his performance of Amina as accidental, assuring her "the love story was not intentional." When that did not convince her, he shifted to blaming Amina, telling Bagaria he only kept interacting with her and deepening their relationship because "Amina doesn't want you to leave." He also implied Bagaria was herself to blame because "I was expecting this woman in Quebec would get bored of emailing" but continued the relationship because Bagaria remained interested in Amina. He then tried hiding behind undiagnosed mental health issues, saying that "I don't know if I'm a sociopath or if I'm schizophrenic."[72]

Pride and vanity played a role in MacMaster's hoax. He had tried and failed to publish fantasy novels in the past and having people believe what he wrote was thrilling. He admitted that the act of deception made him feel powerful, telling Flock and Bell he remembered thinking "I'm good. I'm smart. These journalists don't realize I'm punking them.[73] He later told Bagaria that he felt satisfaction and pride when journalists printed his ideas and took his analysis of Syrian politics seriously, even though they attributed it all to Amina.[74]

While saying he wanted to "come clean" and apologize for actions that made him "feel terrible," MacMaster kept justifying himself. He told journalists that he designed Amina as a tool to educate people who did not understand the Middle East.[75] He sometimes defended his work, claiming the blog reflected "real stories of thousands of people" that he "fused into a single fictional character."[76] When the blog garnered press attention, he initially saw it as "an opportunity to put forward some things I thought were important: issues around Middle East conflict, religious subjects" which he believed Westerners were failing to understand.[77] MacMaster told the journalist Nana Queiroz that his project was successful and beneficial because he "got people to discuss the subject."[78]

MacMaster believed that his blog had educated readers about the existence and struggles of LGBT+ Arabs, and corrected pinkwashing-induced stereotypes painting Islam as especially intolerant of sexual diversity. MacMaster adopted a multiple discourse strategy, saying different things to different audiences. In English he tried to come across as chastened and contrite, but he was not always so careful when talking to journalists for non-English language publications. He told the conservative Brazilian magazine *Veja* that the blog had been beneficial to

---

72 MacMaster, *Le profil Amina.*
73 Flock and Bell, "Tom MacMaster."
74 MacMaster, *Le profil Amina.*
75 Flock and Bell, "Tom MacMaster.".
76 Queiroz, "'Eu sou o messias das lésbicas na Síria.'"
77 Flock and Bell, "Tom MacMaster."
78 Queiroz, "'Eu sou o messias das lésbicas na Síria.'"

LGBT+ people in Syria because it raised global awareness about them, making him "like a messiah to Syrian lesbians."[79]

He admitted knowing that his hoax could harm the Syrian democracy movement but spun that as another excuse for sustaining his impersonation. According to him, he feared the Syrian government would use his unmasking to smear its opponents as foreign dupes and agents. But he hoped that if he "continued with the masquerade, I could keep from creating that situation for them."[80] Although his claim was probably merely an effort to deflect blame for his actions, he was right that the Assad Regime pounced on the propaganda opportunity he provided. The regime-controlled Syrian Arab News Agency aggressively promoted the hoax's collapse describing it as part of a "misleading media campaign against Syria." It declared that MacMaster's blog had been a propaganda operation "aimed at enhancing continuous fabrications and lies against Syria in term of kidnapping bloggers and activists."[81]

When pressed about why he made Amina a lesbian, MacMaster claimed it was primarily because of the challenge of convincing people he was somebody so different from himself. He also believed it would give him more opportunities to, in his mind, correct misconceptions about the Middle East and Islam and show that "in Syria, too, there are people who are all different, gay, straight, people of every possible permutation." Under questioning he acknowledged that making Amina gay was a tactic designed to make her even more of an outsider and thus more interesting and sympathetic to readers like himself. Outsiders appealed to MacMaster because he fetishized oppression as a moral marker and sign of authenticity, or as he succinctly put it, "someone marginalized is more interesting."[82]

Collateral Damage: Another Impersonator

The story of the hoax kept evolving even as journalists wrestled with the questions it raised about journalistic methods and ethics. MacMaster's exposure triggered a second outing of a prominent online lesbian as a straight white male progressive activist. While investigating Amina, a lengthy list of journalists and bloggers including Elizabeth Flock, Melissa Bell, Andy Carvin, Ali Abunimah and Benjamin Doherty collaborated with the founder and senior editor of *Lez Get Real*, who identified

---

79 Queiroz, "'Eu sou o messias das lésbicas na Síria.'"
80 Peralta, "Man Behind Syrian Blogger Hoax."
81 R. Raslan and H. Sabbagh, "*The Guardian* Reveals Mystery of Syrian Lesbian Blogger as Part of Misleading Media Campaign against Syria" *Syrian Arab News Agency*, 13 June 2011, https://web.archive.org/web/20110616195346/https://www.sana.sy/eng/337/2011/06/13/352331.htm
82 Flock and Bell, "Tom MacMaster."

herself as Paula Brooks. She had cooperated with the investigations, but parts of her story raised investigators' suspicions as well. She had run *Lez Get Real* since 2008 and claimed to be a middle-aged deaf lesbian woman living in North Carolina's Outer Banks. Paula's backstory, like the one MacMaster built for Amina, piled sympathetic and unlikely elements on top of each other. Paula claimed to have two Ph.Ds. and to have had her children using medical assistance after her partner's tragic death from breast cancer.[83]

While Liz Henry expressed her worries about Amina's lack of real-world presence, she also noted the thinness of Paula's presence.[84] Investigating journalists communicated with Paula via email and text messages, but *Lez Get Real*'s staff told them they could not speak directly to Paula because she needed a human translator for telephone conversations. After investigators found that there were no records of any of Paula's degrees or her partner's death and nobody had met her in person, they questioned her identity as well. *Lez Get Real*'s writers fired back, charging the investigators with ableism. Linda Carbonell claimed it was unfair to expect a deaf woman to conduct telephone interviews without her translator. Even questioning Paula's identity was unfair and ablest, Carbonell explained, because "Paula cannot respond to [the] accusation because of her disability."[85]

Despite *Lez Get Real*'s writers attempt to frame Paula as the victim of discrimination and persecution, journalists kept probing until Bill Graber confessed that he was Paula Brooks. Graber was married straight white man and progressive activist who claimed he created his persona and founded the site after a local hospital mistreated a lesbian couple he knew. Graber also claimed his passion for supporting LGBT+ equality and opposing religious zealotry was an outgrowth of being a survivor of sexual abuse by a Catholic priest.[86] He thought that the "mainstream media" did a poor job of covering LGBT+ issues and hoped that a site dedicated to lesbian issues would help address that. He organized it as a blog because he "thought that the best way to do it was to have people who were in the life, living the life, tell the story."[87] His comments should, however, be read lightly

---

83 Suzanne Goldenberg and Ester Addley, "Outrage in US as 'lesbian' bloggers revealed to be men," *The Guardian*, 14 June 2011. https://www.theguardian.com/world/2011/jun/14/lesbian-blog gers-revealed-men.

84 Henry, "Painful doubts about Amina."

85 Carbonell, "Apology to Our Readers."

86 Elizabeth Flock, "Bill Graber's full interview: 'I'm not gay, but I want gay people to be equal'" *Washington Post*, 14 June 2011. https://www.washingtonpost.com/blogs/blogpost/post/bill-grabers-full-interview-im-not-gay-but-i-want-gay-people-to-be-equal/2011/06/14/AGNLlpUH_blog.html.

87 Goldenberg and Addley, "Outrage in US as 'lesbian' bloggers revealed to be men."

because he continued to lie as part of his confession and the details of his explanation shifted from interview to interview. Even his military service proved challenging for investigators to pin down.[88]

In interviews with journalists, including the *Washington Post*'s Elizabeth Flock, Graber curated his biography in ways reminiscent of MacMaster's crafting of Amina. Graber claimed to be a blue-collar progressive who served in the Air Force and then worked in construction. However, instead of being a cultural conservative he was committed to LGBT+ equality because of having seen the effects of Don't Ask Don't Tell inside the Air Force. He railed against the, then still existent, policy as "the stupidest story I ever saw." He also claimed a Catholic priest had raped him as a child and blamed the Catholic Church for spreading hate, saying he wanted to show that "Gays are not demonic monsters like the bishop tells you they are."[89]

Graber bristled against the suggestion that he had tried to manipulate the journalists investigating Amina and that he had done the same thing as MacMaster. He insisted that he had worked with, not against, investigators, telling *The Guardian* that "what I wanted you guys to do was catch the sonofabitch" because he was "doing damage to my site, damage to the Syrian people. Damage to gays." Graber desperately tried to distinguish his own impersonation from MacMaster's, claiming he wanted "actual news" and not "some fantasy" and complaining that MacMaster "took this into a whole different realm of fantasy" by creating "something that didn't exist." Unsurprisingly, others were not as forgiving to Graber as he was to himself, with one former collaborator noting that the lesbian blogsphere was a small world in which Graber had wielded tremendous power through fraud. After Graber's exposure, former employees and collaborators came forward to claim he had used his forged positionality to bully and exploit lesbian women who disagreed with his views or who wanted fairer collaboration terms.[90]

In the wake of Graber's unmasking, skeptics dug into his story and raised questions about his confession. Graber refused to communicate with journalists via video leaving them reliant on a single picture he sent to multiple outlets that may or may not have been him and did not appear to be a recent photo of him based on his alleged age. He offered no proof of his military service or confirmable details about it and did not provide evidence or details related to his claims to have suffered sexual abuse from a Catholic priest. Further, his confession

---

88 Henry, *Profil Amina.*
89 Flock, "Bill Graber's full."
90 Goldenberg and Addley, "Outrage in US as 'lesbian' bloggers revealed to be men."

interviews contained contradictory information about when he would stop working with *Lez Get Real*, including later disproven claims that he would be locked
out of the system within hours of an interview. He also veered between claiming
that his wife, friends, and associates at *Lez Get Real* did and did not know that he
was passing himself off as Paula Brooks, which was his wife's name. Although the
name Paula Brooks was itself suspect, since it was the name of an animal print
leotard wearing DC comics villain (aka The Huntress) originally created in the
1940s, court records revealed that a Paula Brooks had appeared in court to testify
against Graber in a domestic violence case.[91]

The accidental revelation of Graber's fraud added a degree of farce to the
overall affair. Many commentators were amused by imagining the two fraudsters
chatting and flirting with each other while posing as lesbians. The 2013 play *Sour
Lips* even included a scene in which MacMaster and Brooks sexted each other
while pretending to be Amina and Paula.[92] There was, however, a darker side to
these fantasies. They reflect a residual homophobic and sexist belief that the
worst thing that can happen to a heterosexual man is to lose his manhood by
being seen as either gay or resembling a woman. Many of MacMaster and Graber's retrospective critics deployed these ideas despite knowing that their use per-
petuated homophobia and sexism because they saw MacMaster and Graber as
fair game because of their transgressions.

The absurdity of the double revelation created a comforting scene of unreality in which the wrongdoers deflated each other, but that merely obscured the
more uncomfortable parts of the hoaxes. In both cases straight white men had
successfully appropriated a discriminated-against identity to speak and act with
added credibility on a public stage based on forged positionality. They exploited
predispositions to accept marginalized people's testimony and self-identification,
predispositions painstakingly created to prevent privileged gatekeepers from
choking off authentic critiques of power. In the process MacMaster and Graber
satisfied their desire to feel like champions of the oppressed and to be accepted
as experts and leaders despite never having experienced the discrimination and
oppression which was part of the identities they performed.

---

91 Adam Polaski "The Unreliable World of Bill Graber from 'Lez Get Real'" *The Bilerico Report
on LGBTQ Nation*, 16 June 2011. https://bilerico.lgbtqnation.com/2011/06/the_unreliable_world_of_
bill_grabers_lez_get_real.php.; Liz Henry, "Bill Graber and Paula Brooks: Open Question," *The
Composite*, 16 June 2011. https://bookmaniac.org/2011/06/.
92 El-Khoury, *Sour Lips*.

Fallout

Initially journalists and commentators focused on what the hoax said about the state of journalism and the problems it highlighted in using internet sources for reporting. These interrelated issues seemed especially important because of the perceived centrality of social media in fueling the Arab Spring. Some journalists, including Andy Carvin, remained committed to using social media as a source and reporting medium, but reflected on the vulnerabilities MacMaster exposed. The Amina hoax grew in the spring of 2011 based on journalists assuming previous authors had vetted Amina. Carvin believed that *The Guardian*'s interview with Amina, had played a crucial role in deflecting skepticism because although *The Guardian*'s reporter never explicitly wrote that she had met Amina, the story referred to an interview without saying it was conducted only via email. Most journalists assumed that *The Guardian*'s correspondent had met Amina and based on the paper's reputation as an extremely credible news organization, they did not doubt Amina was real.[93]

Irem Köker, a Turkish journalist, was one such reporter. She reported on *A Gay Girl in Damascus* and Amina's narrow escape from the secret police after reading American press coverage, which itself relied on *The Guardian*'s work. She interviewed MacMaster via email, believing he was Amina, and later interviewed him in person in Istanbul after he admitted he was the blog's author.[94] Carvin's analysis helped explain why people who encountered the blog after the initial media reports came out assumed Amina was a real person, but it obscured other more important questions. It did not explain why people believed in Amina before the first news reports about the blog and it totally ignored the larger question of why nobody in the media challenged the blog's outlandish stories.

Arab bloggers and journalists worried that the increased skepticism engendered by the hoax would damage their credibility. Mustapha Hamoui, who ran BeruitSpring.com, feared MacMaster's hoax could get a real blogger killed because, "if I'm kidnapped by my government, many readers won't care because I could turn out to be another Amina." He warned that MacMaster had "forever tarnished the reputation of bloggers in this region who chose to write in English." If English-language Middle Eastern blogs lost credibility, it would choke off groups' ability to speak directly to Western audiences and get information to the Western media quickly. Losing those quick connections would make it harder to organize international pressure on repressive regimes.

---

93 Andy Carvin, *Le profil Amina*.
94 İrem Köker, "'Şam'daki eşcinsel kız' erkek çıktı, dünyada ilk kez hurriyet.com.tr'ye konuştu" *Hürriyet*, 14 June 2011, http://www.hurriyet.com.tr/gundem/samdaki-escinsel-kiz-erkek-cikti-du nyada-ilk-kez-hurriyet-com-trye-konustu-18021813.

Hamoui condemned MacMaster as a "prick" who distracted people from trying to help real arrested activists. He also cast doubt on MacMaster's claims that he never expected media attention, "a damsel in distress who's easy on the eyes and fights tyranny in her country, only in the end to be kidnapped by regime goons? Can there be a more effective attention grabbing device?"[95] Writing in *Foreign Policy*, David Kenner too focused on MacMaster's role in shaping coverage. Kenner argued that although there was a lot of information flowing out of Syria about the protest movement, even in English, it was largely unprocessed: fragments of information on Twitter and unedited and often confusing *YouTube* videos. However, MacMaster's blog was polished, written in "flawless English" and provided easily coopted social and political analysis. That made it easier for journalists to parrot MacMaster's propaganda than to sift through the mass of information coming out of Syria themselves.[96]

Depoliticizing Amina

In the wake of MacMaster's unmasking, journalists and other commentators focused on the absurdity of the revelation which pushed it from a political or current events story to a human-interest account. My emphasizing MacMaster's personal deception, accounts of the hoax stripped the politics out of the hoax, allowing the participants to avoid serious self-reflection. Privatizing the fraud and using MacMaster's abusive romance with Bagaria as a framing device thus became a form of collective self-defense.

Subsequent artistic and scholarly treatments have framed it as an example of catfishing. The term has first appeared in a 2010 documentary about an online relationship between Nev Schulman and "Megan" who Schulman believed was a 19-yearold woman but was really Angela Wesselman, a married woman in her forties. Schulman went on to host a 2012–2018 television series that featured the stories of people who thought they were being "catfished."[97]

---

95 Mustapha Hamoui, "*Thank you Tom MacMaster," *BeirutSpring.com*, 12 June 2011, https://bei rutspring.com/thank-you-tom-macmaster-586118aef15a. Also quoted in Carvin, *Distant Witness*, 209–210.

96 David Kenner, "Straight Guy in Scotland" *Foreign Policy*, 13 June 2011, http://www.foreignpo licy.com/articles/2011/06/13/straight_guy_in_scotland.

97 Thomas Berman, Gail Deutsch and Lauren Sher "Exclusive: 'Catfish's' Angela Wesselman Speaks Out" *ABC News* 8 October 2010. https://abcnews.go.com/2020/catfish-woman-angela-wessel man-twisted-cyber-romance-abc/story?id=11831583.

The term achieved cultural resonance in the United States early 2013 when reports emerged that Manti Te'o, Notre Dame's star linebacker, had fallen victim to a similar hoax amid leading the team to an undefeated regular season. On 11 September 2012, Te'o learned that this girlfriend Lennay Kekua, who he had talked with on the phone and via text but never met in person or via video, had died of leukemia. Her death became a national story when it was covered during the Notre Dame-Michigan State game that weekend. In January it was revealed that Lennay contacted Te'o again in December and eventually Ronaiah Tuiaso-sopo admitted he had masquerade as Lennay, including in phone conversations. Coverage of the event described it as an example of catfishing.[98]

The widespread later use of catfishing to describe MacMaster's hoax rein-forced its depoliticization by trivializing it as private wrongdoing. As a political act it invited analysis to explain how and why it was effective and why the people MacMaster interacted with were so willing to believe him. Framing the hoax as a personal fraud spared the journalists, activists, and other readers who had ea-gerly accepted what Amina was telling them from asking why they had so easily bought into MacMaster's improbable but ideologically laden stories. As a form of personal and romantic identity fraud, however, it could be pigeonholed in a polit-ically neutral frame in which those taken in become victims. They might be la-belled as naïve or foolish, but they were not morally complicit and certainly not part of an unconscious common enterprise with the perpetrator.

Conclusion

In May and June 2011, *A Gay Girl in Damascus*'s success made it increasingly hard for MacMaster to sustain the illusion that Amina existed and overtime managing the connections that buttressed his hoax became increasingly fraught. As the real world intruded into his hoax, MacMaster sought a way out and began having to tailor his blog posts to explain why Amina could not speak directly to anybody. MacMaster's escape plan drew on elements that had worked for him before: ratchet-up the tension, eroticize the hunt for Amina, assert her fearlessness and ideological commitment, and then have her manage a narrow escape from a crisis. MacMaster's interlocutors too responded according to the same model they had before. Putting Amina in distress rallied readers and journalists whose responses

---

98 Timothy Burke and Jack Dickey "Manti Te'o's Dead Girlfriend, The Most Heartbreaking and Inspirational Story of The College Football Season, Is A Hoax," *Deadspin*, 16 January 2013. https://deadspin.com/manti-teos-dead-girlfriend-the-most-heartbreaking-an-5976517.

were permeated by the same Orientalism MacMaster baked into the blog and his escape plan. This time however, he could not control events. The blog had gotten too popular, and Amina's kidnapping touched off a race to save her.

Initially Western journalists and activists pushed aside doubts raised by Arab activists, especially LGBT+ Arabs, but it soon proved impossible to ignore all the problems surrounding Amina, especially after Jelena Lecic reclaimed her image from MacMaster. MacMaster's manipulation of the unacknowledged Orientalism latent within liberating theory and Western progressive politics allowed him to make an otherwise mediocre hoax into a successful propaganda operation. Nowhere was this more evident than in the reaction of Western skeptics themselves. Even when confronted with unambiguous evidence that the blog could not be true as written and that there was no objective reason to believe that the blog's creator was a lesbian pro-democracy activist in Syria or had been kidnapped, journalists and activists were desperate to find a way to avoid accepting the blog was a lie. The propaganda message was so well implanted that even as journalists and activists exposed MacMaster's lies, they kept praising Amina as a talented and courageous writer. The enduring power of MacMaster's implausible character and narrative combined with the relative ease with which basic research unraveled his fraud emphasized the critical role readers and journalists' desire to believe in Amina played in the hoax's success.

Chapter IV
Academics, Ideology, and Identity

The *Gay Girl in Damascus* hoax existed at an intersection of culture, politics, activism, and the academy and can be understood within multiple contexts. However, this projects' use of fraud and Orientalism to expose the political and ideological background that allowed MacMaster to succeed makes situating the *Gay Girl in Damascus* hoax within overlapping academic and ideologically progressive frameworks especially productive. It explains how and why the hoax worked, reveals that McMaster's actions are not unprecedented, before or after, and emphasizes liberating theories' vulnerability to Orientalism, racism, and other ideas they exist to combat. In the process, it highlights a substantial subset of academic activists who struggle to reconcile their lives and activism with the theory they believe in, and which some of them help to create and expand.

When belatedly skeptical activists and journalists exposed MacMaster's hoax in June 2011, commentators viewed the *Gay Girl in Damascus* affair as a bizarre outlier. They contextualized it within previous examples of white people who pretended to be Native Americans, but overall, it was seen as such an extreme example that few lessons could be drawn from it beyond being a cautionary tale for journalists relying on anonymous internet sources. Viewed with hindsight though MacMaster's fraud no longer looks like an outlier. In the decade following MacMaster's exposure, a steady stream of related frauds came to light within the overlap between academic and activist circles that magnified the *Gay Girl in Damascus* hoax's significance.

Academic Activism and Identity Passing

The media attention generated around Rachel Dolezal in 2015 sparked a discussion about identity appropriation and created a popular archetype for white people passing as Black that made it easier for skeptics to question a person's claimed identity. Before national media outlets picked up stories about Rachel Dolezal, a white woman who had publicly passed as a Black woman for years, she had no national profile. While attending Howard University she earned an MFA and unsuccessfully sued the school for discriminating against her for being white. Later she began self-identifying as Black, was elected president of the NAACP chapter in Spokane in 2014, and received a political appointment in Spokane. Media attention focused on Dolezal's use of her assumed identity, which included darkening her

https://doi.org/10.1515/9783111057231-005

skin, to achieve credibility as a Black activist leader, but in retrospect her academic connections were also important. Dolezal had been teaching college classes at two public universities in eastern Washington for a decade before she was exposed, and her family included a brother who was a tenured professor. In the wake of her unmasking, Eastern Washington University, where she taught in its Africana Education program, ended its relationship with Dolezal. Activism and the academy formed an overlapping lattice of ideas in Dolezal's life because they drew from the same theoretical sources, including critical race theory.[1]

The academic-activist nexus was even clearer in the case of BethAnn McLaughlin. On 31 July 2020 McLaughlin, a former assistant professor of neurology at Vanderbilt and co-founder of the website MeTooStem.com, announced that a friend of hers who was a bisexual Native American woman and anthropology professor at Arizona State University had died of Covid-19. The anonymous woman had been tweeting for years as @Sciencing_bi. McLaughlin claimed @Sciencing_bi contracted Covid because Arizona State University had forced her to teach in-person into April 2020 despite the pandemic. McLaughlin organized a virtual memorial service which accidentally raised concerns when attendees noticed the lack of colleagues or family members at the event. They also noted that Arizona State had not made any statement about her death and there was no indication of a death in the school's Anthropology Department. Moreover, professors and administrators at Arizona State insisted it had not offered any in-person classes in April 2020. When participants began asking for details about who @Sciencing_bi was – such as her name – and how McLaughlin knew her fate, McLaughlin admitted that @Sciencing_bi was a persona she created.[2]

McLaughlin's construction of @Sciencing_bi reflected many of the processes MacMaster used and had similar ideological implications, although in McLaughlin's case her hoax focused on race, gender, and sexual orientation inside the United States. She created an online alter ego to intervene in debates that mattered to her. In 2016 McLaughlin crafted a biography for @Sciencing_bi that was attuned to academics, activists, and journalists' focus on gender equity and sexual violence which was magnified by Donald Trump's sexist attacks on Hilary Clinton and other women during the 2016 presidential election. She made her character a bisexual woman because she wanted added credibility when speaking about violence against LGBT+ women and to emphasize that that character, who she had

---

1 Leah Sottile and Abby Phillip "How Rachel Dolezal created a new image and made a black community believe" *Washington Post*, 15 June 2015. https://www.washingtonpost.com/national/amid-con troversy-rachel-dolezal-resigns-as-head-of-spokanes-naacp-chapter/2015/06/15/b0ca8690-129c-11e5-9ddc-e3353542100c_story.html.

2 Jonah Engel Bromwich and Ezra Marcus "The Anonymous Professor Who Wasn't" *New York Times*, 4 August 2020. https://www.nytimes.com/2020/08/04/style/college-coronavirus-hoax.html.

not yet made a Native American, was authentically Othered in American society. Like MacMaster, McLaughlin slowly evolved her persona's biography to keep it at the cutting edge of activist and media focus.[3]

In 2016 McLaughlin was an assistant professor of neurology at Vanderbilt and was in the middle of a struggle to secure tenure and keep her job. She used @Sciencing_bi to tweet praise for her accomplishments and her political posts. She also used the account to support her campaign for tenure in the face of an institutional investigation into allegations she had electronically harassed colleagues.

In 2015 Vanderbilt postponed its decision on whether to tenure McLaughlin because she had been accused of using (different) anonymous Twitter accounts to harass colleagues. She denied the allegations at the time – though she subsequently admitted to in legal documents – and alleged she was being discriminated against because she had tried to expose sexual harassment against women by male colleagues at Vanderbilt and had campaigned against sexual harassers being granted honors within STEM organizations. McLaughlin leveraged @Sciencing_bi's curated identity in the hope it would add credibility to her defense against the allegations against her. Even though she failed to get tenure, she was successful enough at creating a sympathetic version of her situation that she leveraged the controversy to set up MeTooSTEM.com, which provided her with an income stream and led her to win awards for her activism.[4]

Overtime, McLaughlin evolved @Sciencing_bi's biography to maximize the persona's credibility as progressives shifted their political attention. This manifested itself in her elaboration of a marginalized racial identity for the persona. Initially @Sciencing_bi' focused on women's equality and LGBT+ issues while McLaughlin was unsuccessfully fighting to overcome Vanderbilt's decision to deny her tenure. She explained that @Sciencing_bi had been raised in Alabama but had "fled the south because of their oppression of queer folk." McLaughlin later layered race on top of gender by telling readers about @Sciencing_bi's indigenous background before ultimately identifying the account as a Hopi woman.[5] The account's growing emphasis on racial justice issues tracked with intensifying popular discussion about the Black Live Matter movement and racial justice in the United States just as the account's initial focus on gender equality paralleled McLaughlin's investment in the MeToo movement against sexual harassment and assault which was energized by the 2016 elections.

---

3 Bromwich and Marcus "The Anonymous Professor Who Wasn't."

4 Bromwich and Marcus "The Anonymous Professor Who Wasn't."

5 Bromwich and Marcus "The Anonymous Professor Who Wasn't."

McLaughlin was undone by her constant search for added relevance. In 2020, she integrated the Covid-19 pandemic into her impersonation. During the late spring and summer of 2020 President Donald Trump was pushing for an immediate lifting of Covid-19 related health restrictions, including the full and immediate reopening of restaurants, shops, and offices. Trump repeatedly railed against schools moving to online classes and demanded immediate returns to in-person classes. Trump's desires ran counter to the advice of most epidemiologists who warned a full reopening before widespread vaccination was achieved would lead to a catastrophic rise in infections that could overwhelm hospital resources and would kill people. Trump's interventions polarized the public, turning the debate into a political struggle and caused many people to strongly identify with their positions on Covid mitigation, integrating it into their ideological identity.

In April 2020 McLaughlin tweeted that @Sciencing_bi had contracted Covid because Arizona State had forced her to keep teaching in-person classes in violation of the Center for Disease Control's advice. Between April and July new tweets chronicled her losing struggle with the virus. @Sciencing_bi's slow death positioned her as a victim of Donald Trump and Arizona's conservative Republican-led state government. McLaughlin may have been looking for a way to end the account or she may have felt compelled to kill her character off because having her recover from Covid would have been less ideologically validating than blaming the death of a queer indigenous woman on the Trump Administration and its Republican supporters. Regardless, McLaughlin inability to provide real world evidence of @Sciencing_bi's death led to her unmasking.[6]

Although less common than progressive impersonators, conservative academics have exploited the internet's partial anonymity to pass as marginalized people. Two months after McLaughlin was outed, reports emerged that Craig Chapman, a conservative male professor at the University of New Hampshire had been running a Twitter account under the label "the Science Femme, Woman in STEM." Chapman claimed to be an immigrant Black woman who had been born into poverty but had, through diligence and personal initiative, earned a Ph.D. and become a professor. He created the account in 2019 and used it to criticize what he viewed as out-of-control "wokeness" in universities.[7]

Science Femme's persona reflected Chapman's contradictory relationship to the academic and activist ideas he was exploiting. Chapman made Science Femme a woman of color and an immigrant to give himself access to the credibility that

---

6 Bromwich and Marcus "The Anonymous Professor Who Wasn't."
7 Colleen Flaherty, "Unmasking a Troll," *Inside Higher Ed*, 6 October 2020. https://www.inside highered.com/news/2020/10/06/university-new-hampshire-suspends-professor-amid-investigation-online-persona.

resistance identities carried, but he neither agreed with nor fully understood the ideology he exploited. Chapman used his fabricated identity to confront other scientists, including people of color, who pushed for greater awareness of structural disparities of opportunity and power within the sciences. He exploited Science Femme's claimed background to make progressive scientists uncomfortable. His goal was to chill progressive scientists' speech by exploiting their ideology instead of persuading them. Chapman wielded Science Femme's background more clumsily than other impersonators and his performance of Science Femme involved sustained and repetitious aggression. Chapman was outed when scholars noticed that some of Science Femme's posts were identical to posts on Chapman's personally branded account.[8]

Chapman's performance of Science Femme reflected his own ideological self-construction even as he tailored the persona to intimidate progressives. Science Femme emphasized a bootstrap narrative that celebrated hard work, personal responsibility, and American exceptionalism. Chapman's Science Femme grew up sleeping on a dirt floor in Africa and was able to rise to the middle-class respectability after her family immigrated to the United States, giving her access to American education and the chance to rise in a meritocracy. Through hard work and self-sacrifice, she succeeded in school and became a science professor. His narrative reflected deeply in-grained American conservative themes present in Barry Goldwater and Ronald Reagan's presidential campaigns and repeated in contemporary conservative media. It also give hints about how a version of MacMaster's hoax aimed at conservative Americans could succeed.[9]

Whole Life Impostors

The internet facilitated academic-activist identity appropriation, but it did not create the phenomenon. Andrea Smith, currently a professor of ethnic studies at the University of California Riverside, began portraying herself as a Cherokee woman in the early 1990s when she founded a Chicago chapter of Women of All Red Nations and led anti-Columbus Day protests. Her appropriation of Native American identity coincided with the emergence of indigeneity as a powerful marker of authenticity in academic and activist circles and continued after she

---

8 Kamilah Newton, "White male professor caught posing as Black woman on Twitter is just the latest in a bizarre trend: 'Identity tourism'" *Yahoo!*, 20 October 2020. https://www.yahoo.com/now/white-male-professor-caught-posing-as-black-woman-on-twitter-is-just-the-in-a-bizarre-trend-identity-tourism-153355043.html.
9 Flaherty, "Unmasking a Troll."

became an ethnic studies scholar. To impersonate a Native American Smith had to overwrite her own life by publicly living her claimed identity. That involved significant personal costs and risks because it left her vulnerable to people from her past, including family, friends, and former colleagues emerging to expose her reinvented biography.[10]

Andrea Smith benefited repeatedly from her impersonation. Posing as a Native American helped her gain admission to UC Santa Cruz's History of Consciousness graduate program. She might have been admitted if she applied as a white woman, but the intersection of her forged indigenous identity and her scholarship made her especially attractive to some admissions committee members and led J. Kēhaulani Kauanui to champion her admission. Smith was later able to leverage her claim to be a Cherokee to gain respect and attention for herself and her work. Smith's hoax has been publicly exposed several times, but she has consistently denied the allegations and has retained her academic jobs, in part because she has steadfastly refused to admit any wrongdoing.[11]

Smith is far from the only white academic to successfully pass as a person of color in the academy. The case of Jessica Krug, formerly an associate professor of history at George Washington University, illustrated the close connections between impersonation, activism, and academic scholarship. Krug's case bears a strong resemblance to MacMaster's fraud despite Krug living her identity instead of merely performing it on the internet. Krug was born into a white Jewish American family in Kansas City where she was educated at an elite private high school. She began telling people she was Black while earning a degree in Black studies and history at Portland State University. She earned a Ph.D. in African/African American diaspora history from the University of Wisconsin in 2012. Her advisor at Wisconsin, James H. Sweet, later became president of the American Historical Association. After graduation, Krug became an assistant professor of history at George Washington University in Washington D.C.. She secured prestigious funding for her project on the emergence of new identities among people fleeing slavery in the Kisama region of Angola including a Hayes-Fulbright Dissertation Fellowship and an Andrew Carnegie Fellowship. In 2013–2014 she was a postdoc-

---

10 Sarah Viren "The Native Scholar Who Wasn't" *New York Times*, 25 May 2021. https://www.ny times.com/2021/05/25/magazine/cherokee-native-american-andrea-smith.html. Jung, *Moral Force of Indigenous Politics*, 70–71.
11 Viren "The Native Scholar Who Wasn't."

toral fellow at the Schomburg Center for Research in Black Culture in New York, the premier center for studying Black culture in the United States.[12]

Krug summarized the connection between her appropriation of Black identity and her personal worldview by claiming to have "operated with a radical sense of ethics, of right and wrong, and with rage, rooted in Black Power." Krug's desire to live what she believed was a virtuous and radical life ran up against the reality that she believed white women's identities were hopelessly contaminated with the benefits of racism. Krug took this to an extreme. After being exposed she explained the challenge she believed she faced, to live as a white woman she had to "figure out how to be a person that I don't believe should exist." Masquerading as a woman of color had given her a way to, dishonestly, feel like she could be fully moral within her worldview.[13]

Like MacMaster and McLaughlin's performances of Amina and @Sciencing_bi, Krug's impersonation was sensitive to changes in American culture and current events. She repeatedly repositioned herself to the forefront of activist attention while also taking advantage of professional opportunities like scholarships or increased interest which often accompany academic and cultural focus on a region or a group of people. In the 2000s and early 2010s she claimed North African Blackness, giving her a connection to the Arabic-speaking world while American activists, like MacMaster, were focused on opposing the Iraq War and excited about the Arab Spring. At times she claimed American Blackness, but she chose Caribbean Blackness for her academic career, allowing her to identify with Spanish-speaking immigrant communities targeted by conservative immigration restrictionists while retaining her claim to be Black. It also reflected academic interest in global and transnational history which let her align her performed identity with her scholarship and activism.[14]

Like MacMaster, Krug relied on her audiences' sympathy, which was rooted in the interplay of ideology and identity, to ignore the limits of her impersonations. Krug's appearance was at odds with her claims, leading her to lean on ideological sympathy and activism to stabilize her impersonation. Unless she kept her hair rigorously dyed, her natural blond hues emerged and some people who knew her harbored doubts she was Black. Krug silenced many of those doubters by aggressively embracing the language and ideology of antiracist activism. For example, the scholar Akissi Britton admitted she had had doubts about Krug since meeting her in 2007 but chose not to "police" her Blackness in part because of her activism. Britton explained that Krug "mimicked a militant, pro-Black

---

12 Viren "The Native Scholar Who Wasn't"; https://jameshsweet.com/teaching/.
13 Jessica Krug, "The Truth, and the Anti-Black Violence of My Lies" *Medium*, 3 September 2020 https://medium.com/@jessakrug/the-truth-and-the-anti-black-violence-of-my-lies-9a9621401f85.
14 Krug, "The Truth, and the Anti-Black Violence of My Lies."

politic to get people on her side."[15] Writing on Twitter, Britton elaborated on Krug's ability to use ideology to get people to self-censor their doubts about her, claiming that "No one, or at least I didn't, 'look' at her and accept unquestionably that she was Black. She went HAAARRRDDD to portray an identity and politic that aligned with the anti-racist work we were all doing."[16]

Krug's exploitation of stereotypes and assumptions began with her own name. Drawing on long discredited immigration tropes, she insisted that her family name was pronounced "Cruz" because the spelling had been changed from Cruz to Krug at Ellis Island. She made her claim despite Ellis Island having closed before her non-existent Puerto Rican family would have moved to New York and even though Puerto Ricans, as United States citizens, were not subject to immigration controls and so did not pass-through Ellis Island when it was open. She performed a stereotyped version of Black Puerto Rican, or Boricua, identity including adopting an exaggerated Bronx Puerto Rican accent characterized by intentional mispronunciations and thick rolling Rs, wearing caricatured clothing, and using the nickname "Jess La Bombalera" while engaged in activism in New York.[17] The nickname may have been an inside joke for Krug. It harkened to the New York-born Puerto Rican American actress Olga San Juan's 1945 role of Rosie "La Bomba" Perez in the Oscar-nominated short *La Bombalera*. In her online author biography for UNC Press, Krug framed herself as "an unrepentant and unreformed child of the hood" whose life was "consumed in the struggle for her community in El Barrio and worldwide." She identified police violence and "the encroaching colonialism of gentrification" as the major threats "her community" faced.[18]

The exoticization of nonwhite cultural and racial groups in the United States is powerful enough that white Americans and Americans of color can believe flamboyant stereotypes of marginalized groups' cultures. Krug's ability to pass as a Black Afra-Latina while performing a stereotype drenched caricature of the identity that, in retrospect, resembled a modern minstrel show revealed the

---

15 Marisa Kashino "The True Story of Jess Krug, the White Professor Who Posed as Black for Years – Until It All Blew Up Last Fall" *Washingtonian*, 27 January 2021. https://www.washingtonian.com/2021/01/27/the-true-story-of-jessica-krug-the-white-professor-who-posed-as-black-for-years-until-it-all-blew-up-last-fall/.

16 Akissi Britton, Twitter, 3 September 2020. https://twitter.com/kinkyintellect/status/1301624743989260292.

17 Lauren Michele Jackson, "The Layered Deceptions of Jessica Krug, the Black-Studies Professor Who Hid That She Is White" *The New Yorker*, 12 September 2020. https://www.newyorker.com/culture/cultural-comment/the-layered-deceptions-of-jessica-krug-the-black-studies-professor-who-hid-that-she-is-white.

18 Graham Starr, Image of Jessica Krug's Author Biography, Twitter, 3 September 2020. https://twitter.com/GrahamStarr/status/1301567380313829381/photo/1.

existence and power of domestic American Progressive Orientalism. Strikingly, when buttressed by political affinity, Krug's veneer of Black and Puerto Rican identity was sufficient to let her live an Orientalist stereotype for two decades of encounters with self-consciously antiracist white Americans and Americans of color in academic and activist circles. Like MacMaster's hoax, Krug's story emphasizes that American culture's exoticization of nonwhite cultural and racial groups crosses racial, cultural, educational, and ideological boundaries and so is not limited to white, conservative, or poorly educated Americans. The exoticization of marginalized lives by people who think of themselves as supporters of equality is more than a failure of egalitarianism, it subverts antiracism, antisexism, and antihomophobia to the point that they can be coopted into forms of the very oppression they are intended to end.

In the summer of 2020 Krug appeared to have achieved long term success within her assumed identity. Duke University Press published her book *Fugitive Modernities: Kisama and the Politics of Freedom.* The book had earned her tenure and promotion at George Washington, and she had all the hallmarks of a rising star. In addition to her scholarship, Krug was trying to assert an identity as a public intellectual by publishing essays on activist sites like RaceBaitr. Then it all came crashing down when she found out that Yomaira Figueroa, a professor of global afro-Diaspora studies in Michigan State's English Department was asking people in their field about Krug's racial identity.

Realizing that even minimal research would turn up unexplainable inconsistencies in her biography and evidence she had repeatedly changed her backstory, Krug tried to shape events with a preemptive confession. In a letter published on *Medium,* Krug admitted she was a white Jewish woman from Kansas City and had pretended to be part of different Black communities over the previous two decades. Like MacMaster, Krug blamed unspecified traumas and mental illness for her actions while claiming to take full responsibility for her deception. Falling into a caricatured version of the activist language she had long deployed to sustain her impersonation, she wrote that her actions were "unethical, immoral, anti-Black, colonial" and declared "you should absolutely cancel me, I absolutely cancel myself."[19] Krug couched her confession in antiracist language and academic jargon, but, like MacMaster's first apology, she never said she was sorry for her actions. The centrality of ideology in her confession inadvertently emphasized that her impersonation was about her own political identity. Within days George Washington University's History Department published a collective letter calling for her resignation on the grounds that fabricating the past is antithetical

---

19 Krug, "The Truth, and the Anti-Black Violence of My Lies."

to the historical profession's goals.[20] Facing possible firing and heavy pressure from the university administration, Krug resigned her position.

It is impossible to know how many people successfully assume a dishonest cultural or racial identity because the public record only includes those who are exposed. Another George Washington professor, the writer H.G. Carrillo, provides an example of a scholar who succeeded in living his impersonation until his death. Carrillo was unusual in another way as well, rather than a white person passing as a person of color, Carrillo was a gay Black American man who re-shaped his life to perform Afro-Cuban identity. Born Herman Glenn Carroll[21] in Detroit in 1960, he renamed himself Hermán G. Carrillo in the 1990s when he began publishing as an Afro-Cuban. He later went by Hache, the Spanish pronunciation of H. He won awards for his writing which was praised for exposing the complexity of Latin American immigrants' experience by integrating homosexuality and working-class experiences with religiosity and religious education. His success as a writer secured him a position as assistant professor of English at George Washington University. His impersonation predated his writing career or higher education and even his husband, who he married in 2015, was unaware that he was not a Cuban exile.[22]

In April 2020 Carrillo died of complications related to Covid-19. His death led his family in Detroit to reveal he had been living a lie. It was only after the revelation that scholars and literary critics noticed that although his Cuban American fiction had won awards, it was almost completely unknown in the Cuban American diaspora. The white, Black, and Hispanic – but not Cuban – literary experts who had awarded him prizes and praised his scholarship had not noticed linguistic tells that his Spanish was not Cuban Spanish nor cultural mistakes such as placing Puerto Rican dishes into Cuban homes and using Mexican instead of Cuban versions of names.[23]

---

20 "Our Statement on Jessica Krug," George Washington University Department of History, 4 September 2020, https://web.archive.org/web/20200905111900/https://history.columbian.gwu.edu/our-statement-jessica-krug.
21 This work uses the name H.G. Carrillo instead of Herman Glen Carroll because although the backstory Carrillo claimed for himself was fraudulent, he lived, married, and died using the name H.G. Carrillo. Calling him Carrol would not recreate the identity erasure of deadnaming, but it would deny the reality that he was known to others and chose to be called Carrillo, which is a historical fact even though he chose the name to perpetuate a fraud.
22 Paul Mejia, "The Secret Life of H.G. Carrillo" *Rolling Stone*, 21 February 2021, https://www.rollingstone.com/culture/culture-features/h-g-carrillo-hache-identity-herman-glenn-carroll-afro-cuban-1120491/.
23 Paul Duggan, "Novelist H.G. Carrillo, who explored themes of cultural alienation, dies after developing covid–19" *Washington Post*, 23 May 2021. https://www.washingtonpost.com/local/

Carrillo's passing as a Black Cuban was exceptional in terms of who was passing but typical in terms of how he pulled it off. He deployed stereotypes and generalized markers of Cuban and Latin American identity which, however inaccurate they were, fit within non-Cubans limited knowledge about Cuban and Cuban American culture. Like MacMaster, Carrillo drew heavily on exoticized stereotypes that were passively held even by educated Americans to sustain the illusion that he was Cuban. He would not have thought he was spreading stereotypes because, like most impostors, he built his fraud on the assumption that he was an expert in the culture he appropriated even as he subordinated it to his own goals and relied on exoticized stereotypes including writing about swashbuckling pirates and Columbus seducing Queen Isabella of Castille.[24]

Impersonation vs. Deconstruction: The Sokal Hoax and its Descendants

Until the unmasking of McLaughlin, Krug, and Chapman, the Sokal Hoax was the best-known academic hoax. Named for Alan Sokal, then a professor of physics at New York University, the hoax was an attack by Sokal against postmodernism. In 1995, Sokal submitted an article to a 1996 special edition of *Social Text* titled "Transgressing the Boundaries: Towards a Transformative Hermeneutics of Quantum Gravity." *Social Text* was a collectively run journal with a reputation for fostering postmodern, postcolonial, and queer studies research. Sokal's article was an artful parody. He used the language of postmodernism to apply concepts drawn from postmodern, feminist, and postcolonial critiques to gravity. In the paper, Sokal argued that gravity was a social construct built on gendered assumptions that subordinated women and foreclosed alternate feminist constructions of physical forces.[25]

Sokal couched his article in a blend of pseudo-scientific jargon and postmodern linguistic analysis to produce a scientifically farcical argument, implying that gravitational forces were socially constructed through a morphogenic field. Its

—————

cuban-american-author-hg-carrillo-who-explored-themes-of-cultural-alienation-died-after-con
tracting-covid-19/2020/05/21/35478894-97d8-11ea-91d7-cf4423d47683_story.html; F. Lennox Campello, "The curious and disgusting case of H.G. Carrillo" *DC Art News*, 13 September 2020. https://dcartnews.blogspot.com/2020_09_13_archive.html.

24 Asombra, "'Cuban' by appropriation: The strange case of H. G. Carrillo" Babalú Blog 3 November 2020, https://babalublog.com/2020/11/03/cuban-by-approprriation-the-strange-case-of-h-g-carrillo/; Campello, "The curious and disgusting case of H.G. Carrillo."

25 Alan Sokal, "Transgressing the Boundaries: Toward a Transformative Hermeneutics of Quantum Gravity." *Social Text* (1996): 217–252.

acceptance by the journal's editors – who reviewed it in-house and did not send it to a scientist to review, revealed weaknesses in peer review. Like MacMaster's hoax it also showed that academically derived theory was vulnerable to universalist assumptions embedded in cultural studies, especially if the speech in question was couched within a sympathetic ideological framework.

There was however a stark difference between Sokal's hoax and MacMaster's. Both used fraud, but the form and intent were radically different. Whereas MacMaster created a fraudulent persona and used a mix of real and untrue information to present a message he believed was true, Sokal had two different audiences: *Social Text*'s editors and a larger educated readership. When trying to deceive the editors he used a mix of their ideology and fraudulent analysis to present a message be knew to be false. His major goal was to speak to a broader audience by using irony to undermine postmodern, feminist, and postcolonial scholarship through exposing the disjuncture created by leading theorists' accepting an article that relied on cutting-edge theory to make scientifically farcical claims.

Sokal's hoax laid the groundwork for how later commentators reacted to MacMaster and sometimes led those commentators astray. The partial overlap between the two highlighted process failures. In Sokal's case, the failure of rigorous peer-review and in MacMaster's case journalists' assumptions that Amina was who MacMaster claimed she was without backchecking sources. It is not necessary to accept Sokal's dismissive view of the theory he abused to recognize that it remains vulnerable to distortions that exploit the ideological sympathies of people who broadly share the assumptions embedded in the theory. To do otherwise is to depoliticize the inherently political processes of social and political change.

Social Media vs. Whole Life Impersonation

The growth of social media expanded the range of identities a person could plausibly pass as (it would have been impossible for MacMaster to pass himself off as an Arab lesbian woman if he had to do it face-to-face) while lowering the cost of passing by allowing impersonators to conserve their own identity. Because social media is inherently networked, it provides a medium to disseminate the impersonators views. This is true regardless of the audience's size. At the height of *A Gay Girl in Damascus*'s popularity MacMaster used Amina to communicate with hundreds of thousands of people through his blog and social media accounts, but social media is also effective when used on a smaller scale. BethAnn McLaughlin used her @Sciencing_bi persona to engage with people she already knew and build a larger audience within the confines of academic Twitter.

Limiting an impersonation to social media creates problems for an impersonator should their actions draw too much attention. While living the lie imposes significant personal costs, it leaves a verifiable trail. Andrea Smith really founded a chapter of Women of All Red Nations, and a skeptical researcher could confirm that she earned a Ph.D. from the University of California, Santa Cruz and has an extensive array of publications. Through living her professional and personal life she naturally accumulated networks of people she knew, legal records showing where she lived, and an employment history. Attempts to research her background would turn up all the records of modern American life that firmly establish her existence and history, but which would be missing for a purely social media-based character like Amina or @Sciencing_bi. The lack of such corroboration, especially in circumstances where it should be readily available, is often noticed soon after a social media fraud's targets first begin to question the hoax.

When impostors choose to live their assumed identity, they gain the advantage of accruing evidence of their identity and proof of their existence, but at the price of jettisoning their pre-existing identity and often curtailing and cutting ties with family, friends, and networks. That sacrifice is however, often embraced as a benefit by impostors who want to escape from aspects of their lives and identity that they find embarrassing, inconvenient, or simply uninteresting compared to their vision of the alternate identity. This escape into exoticism that impersonators like MacMaster, Carrillo, and Krug exhibited reflects the Orientalist strands that coexist with liberating theory. Impostors also leverage their forged identity for material benefits. Jessica Krug benefited from research funding, workshops, and greater attention repeatedly in her career, but she was far from alone and BethAnn McLaughlin used @Sciencing_bi as part of her campaign to pressure Vanderbilt to tenure her.

Jessica Krug and Andrea Smith also emphasized the range of effects of being exposed. Smith has been repeatedly exposed but has doggedly refused to concede that she fabricated her indigenous ancestry. The revelations have damaged her professional life and destroyed friendships in her private life, but she has retained her job as a tenured professor. Krug, on the other hand, suffered national humiliation and lost her position. Krug's admission and string of discarded identities made it impossible for any observer to believe that she believed the contradictory identity claims she had made. In contrast Smith's consistent backstory may have helped her to professionally survive being exposed.

Fraud and Identity: Not Limited to the Academy

People exploiting hierarchies by assuming false identities is not new and has long been used by political actors and fiction writers. At its most extreme this has involved royal frauds who have attempted to foment rebellions or usurp political power through assuming the identity of a dead royal heir. There are many examples of this but the most famous are Russian. For examples, after the death of Tsar Ivan IV's son Dmitry in 1591 a string of impostors claimed to be Dimitry, and one even managed to briefly assume the Russian throne with Polish-Lithuanian aid in 1605. The women who claimed to be Grand Duchess Anastasia, daughter of Nicholas II, are more recent examples of this phenomenon. However more quotidian forms of assuming a false identity or background are often motivated by social or economic gain, including evading discrimination based on gender or race.

Scholars have long used the history of Black people passing as white in Europe and its settler colonies, including the United States, as evidence for the power and fragility of the racial categories created by the slave trade.[26] There is also a long history of women writers passing as male by using a pseudonym or signing their works using artfully designed versions of their name. Amantine Lucile Aurore Dupin became famous under the name George Sand because she found it easier to publish under a male name. Even in the contemporary period, author Joanne Rowling adopted the gender obscuring signature J.K. Rowling for her Harry Potter books because her publisher believed boys were less likely to buy books written by women.[27]

Dupin and Rowlings sought to sidestep discrimination, which is different from seeking to leverage an assumed identity to exact an active advantage. There are, however, examples of people falsifying discriminated-against identities for economic gain. In October 2021 Grupo Planeta awarded Carmen Mola the coveted Premio Planeta de Novela prize, worth 1 million Euros, for the novel *Bestia*. The author had acknowledged that "Carmen Mola" was a pen name and identified herself only as a female professor in Spain and mother of three who wrote crime novels in her spare time. Carmen had given interviews, but always through non-visional or voice means, and the publisher posted a picture of a woman with her back to the camera that it claimed was Carmen. Journalists and literary critics had praised Carmen's work as pathbreaking for female crime authors and as expanding the field by integrating women's voices into a male-dominated subfield.

---

26 See Allyson Hobbs, *A Chosen Exile: A History of Racial Passing in American Life* (Harvard: Harvard University Press, 2016).

27 Connie Ann Kirk, *J. K. Rowling: A Biography* (Westport CT: Greenwood, 2003), 76.

The Instituto de la Mujer de Castilla-La Mancha included *Bestia* on its feminist reading list because the compilers believed it reflected a specifically feminine voice diversifying a traditionally male-dominated field.[28] However when Carmen Mola's win was announced, three male writers, Jorge Diaz, Agustin Martinez, and Antonio Mercero, accepted the award and the million Euro prize.

Diaz, Martinez and Mercero's fraud exploited the desire of scholars and literary critics to diversify literature. Clearly, however the positive value literary elites placed on combatting long term marginalization was not paired with the ability to correctly detect the voices they valued. The differences between Carmen and Amina's creators' goals show that the power of ideology to dull observers' suspicions is not limited to overtly political acts but operates in many different facets of life.

Impostors, Gatekeeping, and Social Violence

The appropriation of marginalized identities by the relatively secure is an inherent act of social aggression because it allows impostors to overwrite the lives of real human beings. In addition to generalized violence, impostors often engage in aggressive bullying aimed at cowing opponents or intimidating people who might unmask them. In the process, impostors publicly entrench their own identity claims.

During her impersonation of a Black woman, Krug used the perceived credibility of her appropriated identity to sit in judgment of women of colors' identities if they did not conform to her ideal of intersectional Blackness. Krug's view of authentic Black identity was soaked with stereotypes that distorted her progressive antiracist ideology. The simplicity of her stereotypes sat uneasily beside her sophisticated scholarship, but the dissonance did not stop the impersonation. Women of color she interacted with described being challenged for not sharing Krug's views or engaging with activism in the same ways she did. She challenged Akissi Britton, who is not from a Spanish-speaking cultural background, for not being engaged enough with Latinx culture.[29] As a student, she demeaned middle-class Black graduate students for not conforming to her standards of authentic Black identity. One member of Krug's graduate school cohort described Krug calling her a "bougie" because of her middle-class background and, in Krug's view,

---

28 https://www.castillalamancha.es/actualidad/notasdeprensa/el-instituto-de-la-mujer-reco mienda-50-t%C3%ADtulos-para-disfrutar-del-cine-y-la-lectura-feminista-y-con.
29 Akissi Britton, Twitter, 3 September 2020. https://twitter.com/kinkyintellect/status/130162474 3989260292.

insufficiently radical politics. Krug tried to establish emotional dominance by claiming to have been raised in "the ghetto" by a drug addicted mother who got pregnant after being raped by a white man. That story was itself cast from a previous claim that she was the child of a Black Algerian woman raped by a white German man. Even as a professor, Krug used racist abuse to assert dominance over women of color and silence potential critics. She repeatedly harassed her African American colleague Erin Chapman, accusing her of "trying to be white" and mocking her for "not wanting to get too dark" if she saw Chapman sitting in the shade.[30] It was not a coincidence that Krug resorted to racist abuse and emotionally laden ideological constructions to preemptively silence Black woman.

As a young activist in Chicago's Native American community Andrea Smith took an active role in policing the movement and deciding who was "legit" in ways that resonated with Krug and MacMaster's gatekeeping. Katie Jones, a Cherokee activist, described Smith's tactics during an interview with Sarah Vixen. She recalled Smith targeting women and accusing them of faking their heritage based on little more than her own intuition. In one instance she attacked a woman, saying, "She is Portuguese, she is Black, but she's not one of us; she's lying, she's a fake."[31]

Krug's violence was far from unique. MacMaster wielded Amina's forged positionality against a wide variety of people. He targeted other white progressives if they disagreed with him. His confrontational tactics were often successful. Posing as Amina he accused Linda Carbonell and other women writing for *Lez Get Real* of being Israeli apologists and dupes of American imperialism because they did not cast the Israeli occupation of Palestinian land as a major driver of the Arab Spring and were not challenging neoliberal capitalism enough. Faced with Amina's identity-based credibility within her own worldview, Carbonell adopted MacMaster's analysis and became an enthusiastic online support of Amina's blog and activism. MacMaster's subsequent praise for Carbonell solidified her support for Amina by allowing Carbonell to use Amina's approval as proof that she was on the right side of history.[32]

MacMaster's bullying of Carbonell was disturbing, but his attacks on Sami Hamwi, Haider Ala Hamoudi, and Catriona Davies were especially dangerous and brutal. Hamwi and Hamoudi's analysis of the prospects for LGBT+ rights and equality in the Muslim Middle East directly challenged MacMaster's view of the Arab Spring. Hamwi also represented a potential threat to MacMaster's hoax. As

---

30 Kashino "The True Story of Jess Krug, the White Professor Who Posed as Black for Years."
31 Viren "The Native Scholar Who Wasn't."
32 Linda S. Carbonell, "Syria Protests Story Apology" *Lez Get Real*, 7 February 2011.

a well-connected gay Arab journalist and activist, he had the positionality to risk challenging Amina's biography based on the inaccurate version of LGBT+ life in the Middle East MacMaster was claiming as reality. The scatological attacks on Hamwi, including comparing him to a genocide perpetrator and implying he was an Israeli stodge should be read as a preemptive assault on Hamwi's credibility as well as an act of personal bullying.[33] Craig Chapman too used Science Femme's positionality to bully people into silence.[34]

Krug's bullying of Black women and Smith's attacks on indigenous women fit with MacMaster's attack on LGBT+ Arabs, they were acts of preemptive self-defense. By putting people who legitimately held the identities the impostors were merely passing as on the defensive the impostors hoped to silence potential critics. By preemptively challenging a potential threat's own authenticity MacMaster, Krug, Smith, and Chapman sought to establish their dominance and make any challenge to their passing look like petty retaliation. The victims were faced with a challenging dilemma: if they wanted to challenge an impostor's identity, the mere act of questioning their tormentor could make them look, and perhaps even feel, like they were exactly what they were being attacked as: inauthentic traitors. In context, these intimidation attacks embodied the social violence aimed at marginalized people, whether collectively or individually, inherent in the act of fraudulently claiming a resistance identity.

The Academic-Activist Nexus

Impostors are more likely to convince other people their personas are real if the stereotypes are believable to the observers. A successful passing thus reveals how the impostor and the audience construct the people and places that are part of the performance. Examples such as a *Gay Girl in Damascus* can thus reveal unacknowledged ideological and cultural baggage that survives within people's minds and groups' collective culture. The academy is an especially fertile example to investigate because it has been an important generative site for antiracist and anti-imperialist activism. Many academics view themselves as helping to expose and remedy inequity. The relative absence of overt conservatism among substantial portions of the academy also helps to focus on progressive forms of Orientalism by making it easier to connect the role of common progressive ideological elements in the creation and reception of Orientalized identities.

---

33 MacMaster, "Pinkwahsing Assad?"
34 Flaherty, "Unmasking a Troll."

Most white academics who pass as marginalized people claim to believe that systemic racism, sexism, colonialism, and homophobia have created durable hierarchies of power and exclusion that define access to wealth and power in the modern world and assigned greater weight to privileged people's opinions. This is not universally true, but conservative impostors like Chapman or systemic critics like Sokol approach hoaxing from differently than progressive scholars-activists. These progressive and activist scholars often believe that the power structures of modern life need to be amended and that one way to do this is for the privileged to voluntarily step back, decentering themselves, and allow the marginalized to have the space and platform to articulate critiques of their own oppression. This is true both for those like Smith and Krug who lived the lie and for those like MacMaster and McLaughlin who created limited personas. Their passing was their attempt to bridge the gap between their belief that confronting racism, sexism, and homophobia requires decentering privileged voices and their unwillingness to limit their actions. It was an emotional acting out against the imposition of limits, even self-imposed limits, on their freedom to perform their political identity.

It is common for academics to feel a strong connection to the people and places they study. That perceived connection can make it easier for academics to convince themselves that they can transcend social and historical boundaries to present the reality of racism, sexism, and homophobia to other privileged people. As they do so they believe they are helping rectify discrimination and marginalization by changing other privileged people's perspective to take account of structural discrimination. However, scholars have argued that claiming to transcend racism is a form of personal escapism, which allows people making the claim to exempt themselves from responsibility for benefiting from the oppressive systems they believe permeate national and global societies.

Ironically, one impostor, Andrea Smith, wrote an early and influential popular article highlighting the appropriation of non-white identities by progressive whites. Smith's work focused on the appropriation of Native American identity, but her analysis has been generalized. Published in *Ms. Magazine* and *Women of Power* in 1991 the article theorized that white feminists struggle to accept white women's historical complicity with racism led some to retreat into an imaginary non-white identity. Smith postulated that, "They do this by opting to 'become Indian.' In this way, they can escape responsibility and accountability for white racism." Smith condemned white feminists for reducing Native American culture to a collection of "romanticized gurus who exist only to meet their consumerist needs" and warned white feminists seeking to escape "white racism by becoming 'Indian,' [that] they are, in fact, continuing the same genocidal practices of their forefathers/foremothers"[35] Smith's work, written when she was an activist but not yet an academic, became an important theoretical work included in many indigenous history and ethnic studies classes.

Passing provides a way for impostors to see themselves as fighters for egalitarianism without having to impose limits on themselves. Masquerading as disadvantaged people is an emotional acting out which redirects the privileged impostors' attention away from their advantageous places in racialized, gendered, and heteronormalized hierarchies and is a radical form of white fragility that functions as erasure. It reflects a seizure of marginalized people's identities to forestall any criticism of the impostor's own role as a beneficiary of systems of power and exclusion. White progressive academics and activists who root their conception of themselves in antiracism and egalitarianism are especially vulnerable to this process because it is difficult for some to reconcile their ideals with the reality that they benefit as much as their political opponents from the discrimination they campaign against.

Weaponizing the Accusations of Imposture: *The Bright Ages*, Progressive Orientalism and Academic Fragility

Progressive ideas' vulnerability to narratives that comfort and reinforce privileged progressives' egalitarian self-identification is visible beyond imposture. The acrimonious debates among academics and activists over Matthew Gabriele and David Perry's 2021 book *The Bright Ages: A New History of Medieval Europe* illustrates this process. Gabriele and Perry, who both had public profiles as supporters of social justice campaigns in the academy, wrote a general history of Medieval Europe for a popular audience with the avowed goal of disrupting white supremacist renderings that exclude people of color from Europe's history and consciously or subconsciously rooted Europeans' later conquest and colonization of large parts of the world in their cultural or racial superiority. Their much-anticipated book received extensive praise from popular commentators before becoming the catalyst for a conflict over antiracist identity and alleged imposture.

Sarah Bond, a professor of history at the University of Iowa and an editor of the *Los Angeles Review of Books* (LARB) solicited Mary Rambaran-Olm to review *The Bright Ages* for the LARB. Rambaran-Olm is a mixed-race woman of Afro-Indo Caribbean decent well-known among late-classical and early medieval scholars as a scholar-activist whose well-reviewed research focused on disrupting

---

35 Andrea Smith, "For All Those Who Were Indian in a Former Life" *Ms Magazine* November/December 1991, 44–45.

white nationalist narratives of early English literature and as a social justice advocate. Bond likely assumed Rambaran-Olm would write a positive review given that she was thanked in the book's acknowledgements. However, Rambaran-Olm had objected to major parts of the text she had been shown.[36]

Rambaran-Olm critiqued Gabriele and Perry work for adopting the form of antiracism while sustaining white normativity by repackaging whiteness instead of deconstructing it.[37] In a linguistic analysis that could have been deployed against MacMaster's language when passing as Amina, Rambaran-Olm argued that "The book's diction and phrasing signal its 'white-centricism' throughout." It used exoticism to define Otherness in ways that marked the normativity of whiteness though deploying stereotyped language like the phrase "coconuts, ginger, and parrots" to mark "the brown skin on the faces of the North Africans who always lived in Britain." In turn, she pointed out, they "never mark white skin." Rambaran-Olm criticized Gabriele and Perry for catering to mainly white "readers who want to believe they are progressive and demand superficial fixes to complex problems and issues." She denounced Gabriele and Perry and their supporters as white people "eager to become more recognized as 'antiracist,'" but who are unwilling to meaningfully disrupt their sense of themselves or undermine their own privilege.[38]

Rambaran-Olm's critique of Gabriele and Perry and their supporters as people who "believe they are progressive" reflects another perspective from which to see Progressive Orientalism at play. Rambaran-Olm went on to dismiss the authors and their supportive readers as "neoliberals" because they did not live up to her standards of antiracism.[39] An alternate construction would view them as progressives who, at least in her view, failed to live up to their ideological commitments. Regardless, in either case the basic elements of Progressive Orientalism remain visible: relatively elite Westerners' project their views onto an Other (in this case Medieval Europe instead of the Middle East) and use the projection to validate their own politics and identity.

Bond asked Rambaran-Olm to remove her most pointed criticisms and when Rambaran-Olm offered minor revisions, Bond pulled the review. One of the

---

36 Mary Rambaran-Olm, "Sounds About White: Review of Matthew Gabriele & David M. Perry's "The Bright Ages," *Medium*, 27 April 2022. https://mrambaranolm.medium.com/sounds-about-white-333d0c0fd201.
37 Rambaran-Olm, "Sounds About White."
38 Rambaran-Olm, "Sounds About White."
39 Rambaran-Olm, "Sounds About White."

LARB's other editors then solicited and published a review by Eleanor Janega, a white academic and public intellectual who had already praised the book in a *Slate* article. In Janega's hands *The Bright Ages* became an antidote to white supremacy and imperialism that showed "The world can be beautiful without centralized and brutal imperial power. Trade, commerce, even travel for interest, can exist without requiring violent organized military intervention."[40] After the LARB published Janega's review, Rambaran-Olm posted her review online at *Medium*. During the resulting furor, Ana Lucia Araujo, a Brazilian-born professor at Howard University and antiracist academic activist who studies the trans-Atlantic slave trade, challenged Rambaran-Olm's background, implying that she was lying about being Black to buttress her authority.[41]

Araujo believed that she was being attacked by "impostors" who she identified as "people with zero training in history" who use "profile pictures of black persons (celebs, cartoon versions, etc) and fake names when they are not black." Her comments were a pointed attack on Rambaran-Olm, who holds a Ph.D. in English (i.e. not history) and whose Twitter profile used a photograph of Eddie Murphy and the name "Axel Folio, Ph.D." (playing off Murphy's character in *Beverly Hills Cop*, Axel Foley and the word folio, which refers to the most common format of early medieval sources). Unlike impostors though, Rambaran-Olm publicly owned her account and used it to speak as herself, even linking to it in public-facing articles she wrote. Araujo's claims that Rambaran-Olm was an impostor reflected Araujo's attempt to protect her conception of herself as a progressive antiracist. Araujo, who most Americans would view as a woman of color, reacted to her view of herself being challenged, by lashing out defensively and casting herself as a victim in ways clearly analogous to Robin DiAngelo's concept of White Fragility. Her weaponization of accusations of imposture highlighted the corrosive effects real impostors have on the people whose identity they appropriate.[42]

The Bright Ages controversy was not unique in demonstrating the potential power of weaponizing accusations of imposture. Partisan politics had already shown the potential for ideologically motivated and self-interested actors to exploit

---

40 Elenor Janega, "Shedding Light in the Darkness of Our Historical Imaginations" *Los Angeles Review of Books*, 24 April 2022. https://lareviewofbooks.org/article/shedding-light-in-the-darkness-of-our-historical-imaginations/.

41 Jennifer Schuessler, "Medieval Scholars Spar on a Modern Battlefield: Twitter" *New York Times*, 6 May 2022. https://www.nytimes.com/2022/05/06/arts/medieval-race-twitter.html.

42 Ana Lucia Araujo Twitter 30 April 2022 quoted at https://twitter.com/DrSid_S/status/1521304490061795328; For an example of Araujo's antiracist engagement see Ana Lucia Araujo, "Museums as Monuments to White Supremacy" *Public Books*, 2 February 2021. https://www.publicbooks.org/museums-as-monuments-to-white-supremacy/.

claims an opponent was lying about their identity. In 2012 Republican Senator Scott Brown was running for re-election against Harvard Law School Professor Elizabeth Warren when conservative activists and the Brown campaign accused Warren of falsely claiming indigenous ancestry. Brown's campaign argued that Warren, who Harvard had listed as a Native American until 1995, had falsely claimed to be a Cherokee to exploit affirmative action policies. Warren denounced the claims as a smear, claimed she did not know Harvard was publicly identifying her as non-white and defended her claim to native ancestry by citing family stories including examples of her grandparents enduring anti-Indian prejudice.[43] Harvard administrators who were involved with her hiring stated that they did not consider race in her hiring and that she was hired based on her outstanding scholarly record. Despite Brown's attacks, Warren defeated him in the 2012 senate election.[44]

In 2018, after years of being taunted with racial slurs by President Donald Trump who promised to donate a million dollars to charity if she proved she was a Native American, Warren announced she would publish the results of a DNA heritage test. The test estimated that she was between 1/64 and $1/1,042^{nd}$ Native American, suggesting her most recent purely indigenous ancestor was six to ten generations behind her in her family tree. The implication of the test was that her small indigenous heritage came from long before her family had moved to Oklahoma and so was unlikely to be Cherokee. Following continued criticism, in 2019 she formally apologized for having claimed Cherokee ancestry.[45] Public debate about Warren's ancestry led to a limited reckoning with the long history of Europeans and Euro-Americans claiming indigenous ancestry for professional or emotional gain, but the benefits of the reckoning were balanced against the negative effects of the stream of anti-indigenous rhetoric it sparked. President Trump's normalization of anti-Indian racial slurs against Warren reinforced the continued marginality of indigenous Americans.

Similarly, Jacqueline Keeler, an activist of Navajo and Yankton Dakota ancestry accused former Colorado Senator Ben Nighthorse Campbell of falsely claiming to be Cheyanne. Keeler has campaigned against cultural appropriation and founded

---

43 Hilary Chabot, "Warren: I used Minority Listing to Share Heritage" *Boston Herald*, 2 May 2012. https://web.archive.org/web/20120503200317/http://bostonherald.com/news/politics/view/20220502warren_i_used_minority_listing_to_make_friends.

44 Josh Hicks, "Did Elizabeth Warren check the Native American box when she 'applied' to Harvard and Penn?" *Washington Post*, 28 September 2012. https://www.washingtonpost.com/blogs/fact-checker/post/everything-you-need-to-know-about-the-controversy-over-elizabeth-warrens-claimed-native-american-heritage/2012/09/27/d0b7f568-08a5-11e2-a10c-fa5a255a9258_blog.html.

45 Asma Khalid, "Warren Apologizes to Cherokee Nation For DNA Test," *NPR*, 1 February 2019. https://www.npr.org/2019/02/01/690806434/warren-apologizes-to-cherokee-nation-for-dna-test.

Eradicating Offensive Native Mascotry, a group that seeks to end the use of Native American nations and symbols as sports mascots. Using the space created by well-known impostors, Keeler claimed Campbell lied about his ancestry. Emphasizing that his mother was a Portuguese immigrant, Keeler denied that Campbell's father was really a Cheyanne and included the senator in a list of "pretendians" she posted publicly. Journalists cited her claims, though many were skeptical because Campbell was an enrolled member of the Cheyenne nation and a recognized Cheyenne chief.[46]

Ben Nighthorse Campbell made an inviting target for Keeler because he represented the antithesis of her self-construction of Native American identity. He was a moderate Democrat who eventually became a conservative Republican after being elected to the Senate in 1992. His social and economic conservativism were at odds with Keeler's progressive vision of Native American identity. Campbell's public support of Donald Trump's use of memorial preservation legislation, which Campbell had authored, to protect statues of Andrew Jackson and other slave holders and supporters of violence against Native Americans during the 2020 Black Lives Matter protests may also have angered Keeler, encouraging her to selectively interpret Campbell's biography to expel him from her own identity group.[47]

Conclusion

Following the identity-ideology nexus from MacMaster's hoax back along its activist and academic roots emphasizes the critical role ideological constructions of the self play in shaping how people interact with the world. Comparing different forms of academic fraud shows the centrality of ideology in motivating academic impostors. Even the differences between progressive and conservative impersonators emphasize the centrality of ideological self-conception to privileged people's identities. It is powerful enough that it makes people blind to the limits of their own understanding.

A comparative perspective reveals that ideologically grounded identities function actively and passively. Actively, progressive and antiracist self-identification helps impostors justify their actions to themselves by believing that they understand

46 Anne Branigin and Kelsey Ables, "Sacheen Littlefeather May Have Lied About Her Identity. Does it Matter?" *Washington Post*, 1 November 2022. https://www.washingtonpost.com/lifestyle/2022/11/01/sacheen-littlefeather-identity-controversy-indigenous/.
47 Namrata Tripathi, "Indigenous ex-senator who brought monument protection laws defends Andrew Jackson statue despite gory history" *MEAWW*, 27 June, 2020. https://meaww.com/native-american-senator-who-introduced-moument-protection-law-defends-andrew-jackson-statue.

the effects of racism and inequality enough to speak for historically marginalized people. Active self-defense also involves lashing out against threats to the sense of self. Passively, it shields people from recognizing the limits of their understanding of the lives of less privileged people. These processes make people vulnerable to appeals that reinforce their preferred sense of themselves, even if it leads them to take actions that undermine the goals they seek to advance.

The exoticization of marginalized lives by people who think of themselves as supporters of equality is more than a failure of egalitarianism, it risks turning anti racism, antisexism, and antihomophobia into engines of the very forms of oppression they seek to end. Theorists of Orientalism have labored to force Westerners to recognize and tear down power structures that justify Western domination of the Middle East just as antiracist activists and scholars have sought to challenge the structures of white supremacy, but neither group can succeed unless Western progressives examine their own assumptions, power structures, and behavior with the same critical lenses they apply to their societies as a whole.

Conclusion

After being exposed, Tom MacMaster claimed that his blog was like a work of fiction, not completely true but still capable of communicating truth. Fiction can, of course, communicate truth. Arthur Miller's 1953 play *The Crucible* was fiction, but it spoke directly to the dangers of political paranoia and the abuse of power during the McCarthy era. Similarly, *Uncle Tom's Cabin* was immediately understood as a powerful indictment of slavery despite being a novel and containing what modern readers realize were pernicious stereotypes about enslaved African Americans. However, MacMaster's work passed itself off as a day-to-day account of what was happening and not as an exploration of underlying values. In addition, Miller and Stowe's works were masterfully written while MacMaster's hoax relied on the audience's complicity to coverup its weaknesses; it would have failed as fiction because without ideology to shroud its weaknesses, readers would have quickly seen through it.

Writing years after the hoax, Kevin Young devastatingly summarized MacMaster's reliance on stereotypes and readers' suspension of disbelief. Although journalists and activists in 2011 had believed the clichéd sex stories were real and praised MacMaster's writing as compelling and bold, Young explained that "having read what I could, I can report it's a hot mess." He characterized MacMaster's "Middle East as a place of secret sexuality, white slavery as white fantasy that would do the Circassian Beauty proud." Young summarized it as being "as tasteless as it is talentless."[1] Young's summary is irrefutable as a literary judgment, but the hoax worked on so many people that there was clearly some talent behind it. Seeing that talent requires changing the framework of analysis from literature to political propaganda.

When understood as an attempt to influence the political opinions of educated progressive Westerners, *A Gay Girl in Damascus* is a useful example through which to understand modern online political persuasion. Political propaganda can be masterful literature, Aleksandr Solzhenitsyn wrote with the aim of persuading people the Soviet system was unjust and inhumane, but propaganda need not be good literature to be effective. The *Protocols of the Elders of Zion* was no classic of Russian literature, but the stereotype-ridden forgery has fed antisemitism for more than a century. Political persuasion is judged by its effect, not its artistry. By that standard, *A Gay Girl in Damascus* was, at least temporarily, successful. It was impressive and ominous that a single individual without the financial or personnel resources of a

---

1 Young, *Bunk*, 144.

https://doi.org/10.1515/9783111057231-006

state or other large organization was able to have so much effect on news coverage and activists' views.

Efficient persuasion does not try to completely transform its targets' beliefs and values. MacMaster worked with the grain of his targets' existing beliefs to shape how they reconciled their general beliefs with what was happening around them. His messaging was well targeted to his intended audience because he aimed it at the people he best understood, people like himself. Although he imagined that he was merely helping them see the Middle East accurately, he was performing an Orientalized version of their common ideology in ways that reinforced their views of themselves. In the process he leveraged his audience's preexisting political beliefs to encourage them to adapt his own interpretation of the Arab Spring by marking it as an extension of the domestic politics and cultural values that helped define his audience members' sense of themselves.

MacMaster's process was simple, which is why it worked. He built Amina's backstory with a series of identity markers which his educated and generally progressive Western readers were used to seeing associated with themselves and their political allies, including Amina's overall politics, sexual orientation, gender, race, and foreign policy views. Posing as Amina, he made it clear to readers that she embraced progressive positions on abortion, economics, and the rights of religious and ethnic minorities while also opposing Western military intervention in the Middle East. He reinforced this by equating Amina's experience with homophobia and Islamophobia with anti-Black racism. These signals encouraged readers to see Amina as one of them and thus to see themselves as being naturally on her side. Amina validated MacMaster's readers by assuring them that Syrian activists shared their core values. Through Amina, MacMaster framed the Syrian Revolution using markers of domestic American politics which let his progressive audience read themselves into the action in Syria while seeing the Syrian Revolutions' existence as an affirmation of their own beliefs and politics. Reading the Syrian Revolution as a Western-style progressive social movement let Western progressives believe that they had transcended their place in global hierarchies and were functionally universal change agents – which ironically was a core colonialist and Orientalist delusion and a clear marker of white and Western power within their own worldview. In the process, MacMaster help foreclose the possibility his progressive Western readers would have to confront a liberation movement that looked different from their own politics and challenged even a few of their core beliefs about how the world should work.

MacMaster's writing was not subtle, which meant that it was hard for readers to miss his intent and he often needed their goodwill to look past the deficiencies Young identified. Having Amina freed from fear through having self-consciously lesbian sex for the first time following a massage-seduction scene enabled by the September 11 terrorist attacks was a clear red flag that readers should have objected to, but the story worked with the grain of their biases, allow MacMaster to lean on their sympathy. The story was poorly written and improbable, but like the descriptions of Amina's family's stereotypical experience with Islamophobic violence, it exploited his target audience's preexisting desire to show solidarity with marginalized and oppressed people and disinclination to interrogate their testimony. Whether they believed it or wrote it off as an amusing flourish, his readers looked past it and accepted the story and its implications without questioning the blog's truthfulness.

A *Gay Girl in Damascus* invited its readers to assimilate Amina's views on Syrian politics as their own because it was what people like them should believe about Syria. MacMaster never had Amina challenge his readers' core beliefs, instead he worked outward from their common ideological and cultural ground to try to change their derivative belief structure by shifting sympathy to the Palestinians and by encouraging readers to see Islam as a progressive religion to reduce their fear of Islamists.

Above all MacMaster made sure Amina had the right enemies: his readers' enemies. He positioned her as being afraid of racist rural whites ("big guys howling for my blood"), neoconservatives, the Bush Administration, American homophobes, and the Republican Party. His conflation of the Assad regime with Western cultural conservatives, including George W. Bush's Administration, Evangelical Protestants, and the Tea Party combined with his identification of Amina as a living symbol of the Syrian Revolution established a two-way connection between Syrian and American politics. He demonized progressives' domestic opponents while using domestic politics to show readers how they should view events in Syria. This reduced Syria to a venue where Western progressives reenacted stylized versions of their own politics to build up their identities as engaged and progressive citizens.

It is impossible to measure how many people's views changed because of Mac-Master's hoax, but it is possible to demonstrate his success in affecting the way journalists were covering the Syrian Revolution. Every time a journalist mentioned the blog without challenging its veracity was a tacit endorsement of Amina's existence and the value of MacMaster's views. In addition to being mentioned in articles, *CNN, BBC, Al Jazeera, CBS*, and the *Guardian* all interviewed MacMaster posing as Amina, giving him the ability to speak directly to their readers. When those outlets, and the legion of others that never engaged MacMaster directly, reported on the kidnapping, they echoed the messages in *A Gay Girl in Damascus*, allowing MacMaster to influence millions of people, an audience vastly larger than the blog's readership.

Journalism

The *Gay Girl in Damascus* hoax emphasized the importance of holistic diversity in journalism and the academy, and by extension other kinds of organizations and professions. MacMaster exploited his audience's blinders by feeding them messages wrapped in their own biases. By giving them emotional and ideological incentives to accept Amina and exploiting their lack of contextual information that would have highlighted the inconsistencies between MacMaster's assertions and Amina's claimed environment, MacMaster was able to pass as Amina. The people who were most likely to detect MacMaster's fraud were people largely excluded from Western journalism: LGBT+ Middle Easterners.

The vast majority of the Western media outlets that covered the *Gay Girl in Damascus* relied on white reporters based in the United States or Western Europe. They were engaged in an honest version of what MacMaster was doing, trying to explain events in Syria while living and working elsewhere. Even when white Western journalists called on people from the Middle East or Middle Eastern backgrounds to comment on Amina, they usually relied on people who were well educated and living in the West. They were thus also from the same broad milieu as MacMaster, especially if they were left-of-center activists.

A more diverse group of journalists and commentators would have made it harder for MacMaster's hoax to succeed. The closure of Western media bureaus in the non-Western world because of budget cuts and Western media groups' failure to create robust reporting relationships with Middle Eastern journalists hampered them from identifying MacMaster's fraud before he pushed it to the point of self-destruction. Middle Eastern bureaus would have meant there were more reporters with personal networks they could call on in the Middle East to comment on Amina's blog, which would have raised the likelihood of detecting MacMaster's fraud. Greater diversity in sexuality and race in Western newsrooms might also have complicated MacMaster's efforts. Although no substitute for engaging Middle Eastern-based Arab journalists, even greater ideological diversity would have made newsrooms more resilient against MacMaster's exploitation of progressive ideology. A robust array of ideologies in newsrooms could have led to pushback against MacMaster's narratives from journalists whose did not share MacMaster's ideological framework.

Failed Analysis

The same factors that made *A Gay Girl in Damascus* good propaganda undermined MacMaster's analysis of the Syrian Revolution. By forcing Syrian politics into the mold of American progressive politics, he had to, knowingly or unknowingly, misrepresent Syrian politics through a combination of outright inaccuracies and smothering assumptions. Strikingly, MacMaster overwrote the Syrian Revolution despite believing that his overall analysis was true. MacMaster's analysis of two critical issues was especially distorted: the likely efficacy of nonviolent protests and Syria's religious politics. In both key areas MacMaster's analysis was almost entirely off base, in the former case so badly that by the end of the blog he was struggling to integrate the regime's increasingly violent repression into the blog without compromising the sense that the movement would naturally win through nonviolent protest without outside help.

MacMaster's rhetoric and policy recommendations were designed to convince readers that the Syrian Revolution was likely to succeed. He assured readers that the Syrian people had awoken and would not tolerate the regime anymore so many times it became a refrain. He never explained how protests would force the regime from power, but the idea that they would was at least credible given the events in Tunisia and Egypt. However, the Assad regime resorted to deadly force and mass repression early in the uprising, which should have raised questions about whether protests alone could bring it down. By late May, MacMaster had to acknowledge the rising violence and fear of civil war, but his only answer was to assure readers that Amina would keep working for peaceful change and that nobody in Syria wanted a civil war.

If the Assad regime retained control of its security forces and got them to use sustained deadly force against civilians, protests alone were extremely unlikely to force a change of regime. Indeed, in such a circumstance only outside intervention or military revolt could force Assad from power. There were good reasons for observers to oppose a military intervention by the United States or Western European powers but opposing outside intervention required honest observers to accept that the protest movement could well fail in the face of the regime's relentless violence. MacMaster was unwilling to admit failure was possible but could not explain how success was possible without outside intervention or internal military force, which might have contributed to his decision to wrap up the blog.

Although it is impossible to know for sure what would have happened in Syria if Assad had quickly stepped down, subsequent events have undermined MacMaster's claims about the Syrian opposition's ideological makeup. He confidently assured Western progressives they could embrace Syrian Islamists without fear of compromising their support for LGBT+ equality, women's rights, or democracy because Syrian Islamists were closer to the Turkish Justice and Development Party than the Saudi version of Islamism. Neither half of his prediction stood the test of time well. The rise of Islamist groups like Islamic State in Syria and the authoritarian drift of Turkey under the Justice and Development Party's rule have eroded MacMaster's claims.

Technological and Ideological Determinism

A Gay Girl in Damascus exemplified a technological determinist mindset that permeated media and expert opinion on the Arab Spring in the West. Because his blog did not go live until after the technology-driven narrative of the Tunisian Revolution had taken root, MacMaster was able to blend seamlessly with what was already becoming received opinion. He exploited the assumption that protest movements in the Middle East were driven and enabled by social media to cloak the ideological assumptions that underwrote his preferred narrative.

MacMaster argued that easy individual access to social media meant that ordinary Syrians were able to connect with each other and sidestep the state-controlled media. This alternate method of disseminating news and holding discussions catalyzed preexisting discontent and propelled people into the streets. He assumed that such a movement was naturally progressive because he viewed progressivism as a universal ideology. According to MacMaster's narrative, social media exposed users to a diverse group of fellow Syrians who shared a common desire for greater control over their lives and government. The process of connecting with people of diverse backgrounds and beliefs naturally transformed Syrians' political and social views, making them more egalitarian and accepting of ethnic, religious, and sexual diversity as well as more favorably disposed to democracy. Western progressivism thus did not need to be explained historically because it was the natural ideology for modern people, only deviations from Western progressivism needed historically contingent explanations.

By allying his technological determinism to assumptions that social media favored egalitarian movements and that the West represented the vanguard of human progress, MacMaster was able to give the impression that Amina had proof the Syrian protest movement was egalitarian. He could rely on his fabricated claims of personal experience, which were unverifiable even if they had been true, as evidence of the Syrian Revolution's progressive trajectory. Western journalists uncritically accepted MacMaster's assumptions, despite his lack of verifiable evidence for them, and incorporated them into their coverage in major media outlets because they fit easily with journalists' own personal and professional identities.

The successful fusion of technological determinism and the assumption that progressive change was intrinsically tied to technological modernization created the perception that Western progressives would naturally and inevitably triumph over their political and cultural opponents all over the world. That assumption fit with a broad swath of political opinion in the United States that theorized that demographic change was moving the country to the economic and social left and would transform American politics and culture. MacMaster's assumptions colored his view of the Arab Spring and formed part of his larger Orientalist reduction of Syria to a site on which he performed his American political identity. The ease with which commentators, whether journalists or activists, embraced MacMaster's assumptions showed that they either shared his assumptions or shared enough of his worldview to be vulnerable to them.

Possibilities and Limits of Social Media-Based Impersonation

The networked structure of social media helped MacMaster create and sustain the illusion that Amina Arraf existed. Facebook provided mechanisms for people to encounter and connect with Amina while both Facebook and Twitter provided ways for blog readers to spread links to the blog to people who would never have gone looking for it on their own. Because social media users and blog readers were used to consuming information from and interacting with people they had not met and whose identities they accepted on trust, social media was a fertile ground for MacMaster's style of hoax.

Blogs and Facebook provided ways to display information that created the impression that readers could see a window into the poster's life even as they limited the nature and amount of information readers could access. This combination of apparent transparency and strictly limited information helped sustain MacMaster's hoax. Because there was an effective ceiling on the forms of interaction users could expect from blogs and Facebook accounts, an engaged impostor like MacMaster could come very close to matching the profile of an authentic person. The limits of social media thus combined with its natural ability to disseminate information to make it a convenient and practical medium for MacMaster's form of propaganda and imposture. It would have been possible to run a form of MacMaster's hoax without social media, but it would have been extremely difficult to match its scope if he had been limited to publishing in print media under an assumed name. Social media gave MacMaster the ability to very cheaply self-publish his work which greatly accelerated his propaganda's spread.

MacMaster's hoax unraveled in part because he could not sustain his own success. The hoax's success gave him the power to affect the world while making it harder to hide the limits of his ability to perform Amina's identity. Although he could and did download hundreds of images of Jelena Lecic, he could not create custom images to validate Amina's presence at key events or even pictures clearly establishing when they were taken. And most obviously, he could not interact with people via voice or video as Amina. Within those limits, MacMaster had to manage Amina's online presence and interactions to make it seem like she existed. This included maintaining the accounts and the blog in her name as well as the entire ecosystem of fake accounts that filled out Amina's backstory while also living his own life. That all took time, and the more successful the hoax was the more time it took because Amina needed to interact with more people.

The fact that MacMaster ran an intricate and successful hoax in his spare time with no budget showed social media's vulnerability to information operations designed to influence public opinion. An organization that had the time, staff, and money MacMaster lacked could have more effectively exploited the vulnerabilities he exposed. In 2011, commentators implicitly recognized the potential for a state to influence public opinion via this kind of hoax when some speculated that Amina was a front for Israeli or Syrian intelligence agencies, but after Mac-Master confessed they did not follow up on the implications of their concerns.

Even in 2011, state actors were well-positioned to use MacMaster's model. The human and financial resources of a state would allow it to manage online relationships and networks of accounts in ways impossible for MacMaster. It would also allow it to create seeming proof of existence that was more complex than MacMaster could muster. A robust organization could manipulate images or even have a real person model a character so that the model could appear on video or speak via telephone with journalists and others.

Since 2011, new technologies and software have made it easier to sustain persuasive fake online personas. The subsequent development of more advanced image, video, and voice manipulation software, including deepfake technology, has made it easier for a well-funded operation, and even individuals, to build on MacMaster's model.[2] For example the fifty-eight-year-old Chinese influencer Qiao Biluo used a commercial video filter to make herself look like a woman in her early twenties. She had accumulated over 100,000 followers on *DouYu* until her filter failed during a livestream on 25 July 2019, revealing her real appearance.[3]

In September 2022, unknown impostors, presumably Russian intelligence or military agents, took advantage of audio and visual deep fake technology to harass prominent Western opponents of the Russian invasion of Ukraine. On 30 September Michael McFaul – a former U.S. ambassador to Russia and a prominent critic

---

2 Marie-Helen Maras and Alex Alexandrou. "Determining Authenticity of Video Evidence in the Age of Artificial Intelligence and in the Wake of Deepfake Videos." *The International Journal of Evidence & Proof* (2018): https://doi.org/10.1177/1365712718807226. Web.
3 Dhruti Shah & Kerry Allen "Chinese vlogger who used filter to look younger caught in live-stream glitch" *BBC*, 30 July 2019. https://www.bbc.com/news/blogs-trending-49151042.

of Putin's regime – reported that a third party was using clone video conference accounts to call opinionmakers. When they answered they saw a deep fake video of him that, using a facsimile of his voice, was able to interact with them and asked questions designed to "undermine Ukraine's diplomatic and war efforts." The fraud was quickly exposed, but the hoax's connection to the ongoing Russo-Ukrainian War meant that its targets were unusually attentive to the possibility of being manipulated.[4]

The exposure of a US government social media-based influence operation aimed primarily at the Middle East in July and August 2022 provides useful illustrations of how technological and software developments have made recreating Mac-Master's hoax easier. When Twitter and Meta (the renamed parent company of Facebook) took down accounts linked to the operation, Twitter revealed that it had been operating since 2012 and included 146 different Twitter accounts. Meta identified 39 Facebook profiles, 16 pages, two groups, and 26 Instagram accounts linked to the operation. They relied on fake profiles much like those MacMaster used, but new software allowed them to create images. They used GANs (Generative Adversarial Networks) to make images using artificial intelligence. The resulting images looked real but were not of any real individual. The computer-generated models would be placed into pictures of real places to provide what looked like proof the account holder was an authentic person in the places the holder claimed to be.[5]

The US government operation revealed the limits of inauthentic social media influence operations, while illustrating how remarkable MacMaster's hoax's success was. 81% of the fake accounts tied to the US government operation generated less than 1000 followers. They generated almost no secondary media exposure and averaged 0.49 likes and .02 retweets per tweet. Strikingly the most successful accounts tied to the operation were authentic accounts that advertised their connection to the US military. They generated significantly more engagement than the inauthentic accounts. MacMaster's operation was vastly more successful in less than four months than a much larger decade-long US government equivalent.[6]

Confronting Progressive Orientalism

A Gay Girl in Damascus should not have been taken seriously by knowledgeable observers. MacMaster's stories were replete with problematic stereotypes and

---

4 Michael McFaul, Twitter, 30 September 2022. https://twitter.com/McFaul/status/1575911859609210880.
5 *Unheard Voice: Evaluating five years of pro-Western covert influence operations* (Grafica and Stanford Internet Observatory, 2022), 2–3. https://graphika.com/reports/unheard-voice.
6 *Unheard Voice.* 2–3.

piled unlikely scenarios on top of each other as he built his character. The sexualization of Amina and the integration of ideological tropes into her life and family history all should have alerted readers that something was amiss. The key to understanding why it worked is to take its apparent weaknesses, its eroticization of same-sex relationships and exoticization of Arab women, as important parts of its persuasive apparatus; it worked because it played on tropes that remain deeply embedded even in progressive Western narratives of the Middle East.

Although on one level the blog deconstructed Orientalism by challenging the traditional Orientalist tactic of differentiating the West from the East by "marking the East as lacking 'civil society,' 'individuality,' or 'secondary structures,'" on a deeper level, it reinforced Orientalism by reducing the Middle East to a stage Westerners use to talk about themselves.[7] MacMaster's Syria was a wish fulfillment for his readers. He promised them that a vibrant, diverse, and self-consciously egalitarian civil society composed of people suspiciously like themselves was asserting itself in Syria. All they had to do to see a positive result was to spread the word and oppose Western military intervention. Through selective reporting, exaggeration, and outright fabrication, MacMaster emphasized the Syrian opposition's unity and ethnic, religious, and gender diversity. Because MacMaster's Syria was a proxy for the United States and the West more broadly, he was promising his readers that they were destined to win in the Middle East and in their own countries.

Readers who generally shared MacMaster's politics and cultural values wanted to believe in Amina because she comforted and validated them. The Orientalist subtext of Western depictions of the non-Western world accustomed them to seeing exaggerated portraits of their own hopes and fears when they looked at the Middle East. Amina's open lesbianism was at odds with other descriptions of life in Damascus, but it helped MacMaster's readers see her as an authentic spokesperson for the oppressed by making her marginalized despite obviously being elite. The blog's focus on political issues that were salient to Western progressives in 2011, especially LGBT+ equality, manufactured a comforting sense that progressive values were sweeping across the world at the same moment that progressives feared progress at home was under threat from cultural conservatives like the Tea Party.

Ultimately, *A Gay Girl in Damascus* revealed little about Syria, but a lot about the Western political, academic, and activist milieus. Orientalism's potential to distort anti-imperialist, antiracist, and egalitarian goals does not mean that postcolonial theory, critical studies, and other critiques cannot be effective tools against injustice. Yet, because MacMaster's views were so easily espoused and furthered by an array of progressive Western journalists and activists, much work

---

7 Yeğenoğlu *Colonial Fantasies*, 6.

clearly remains to fully disentangle even self-consciously liberating and anti-imperialist ideas from Orientalism.

In some ways, Progressive Orientalism ought to be easier to combat than other forms of Orientalism because the people it most effects at least believe they are the most committed to rooting out Orientalism and other forms of racism. Critical and antiracist theory demand that their adherents examine their own place in power hierarchies and be willing to correct their own behaviors in light of their realizations. The theoretical foundations for a comprehensive attack on Progressive Orientalism thus already exist, but it requires overcoming barriers that are powerful because they are the least visible to the very people who should be most equipped to challenge them.

Confronting Progressive Orientalism is hard because it is rooted in the Western progressives' sense of self. Like other forms of Orientalism, it reassures Orientalists that they are forces for good in their own societies and around the world. Progressive Orientalism allows Westerners of different races and gender identities to see themselves as particularly enlightened and in solidarity with marginalized people around the world without having to painfully examine themselves. As Mary Rambaran-Olm's analysis suggested, it substitutes instant gratification for the hard and painful work of critical self-examination. Moreover, the progressive normativity it validates allows Western progressives to escape considering the limitations and failures of the progressive and antiracist ideologies that define their sense of self. Tom MacMaster and other academic impostors provide a way to bring Progressive Orientalism into relief, but its manifestations are usually less spectacular and entertaining the *A Gay Girl in Damascus*. Linda Carbonell's confidence that Latin Americans and Muslim Middle Easterners should or did celebrate Bill Clinton and Barack Obama as their liberators was a less theorized version of the same ideology.

To overcome Progressive Orientalism, the people who have been most likely to confront those with ideologies other than their own for their Orientalism must be willing to deconstruct their own relationship to Orientalism. Accepting that progressive and antiracist ideas are vulnerable to Orientalism is challenging for people whose view of themselves is tied up with confronting and unmaking marginalization. To succeed they must overcome the reflective tendency to expel critics or those they are compelled to confront from their own ideological family. Only by identifying the specifically progressive roots of Progressive Orientalism can it be effectively combatted. Relying on narrowing the definition of progressivism or antiracism merely protects the critic and observers from confronting their own role in Progressive Orientalist thought. Good intentions are important, and preferable to seeking to erase and dominate others, but they are not enough.

Final Word

MacMaster cloaked himself in noble motives, but his performance was about validating his view of himself and making other people reinforce it through accepting his performance. This book has not tried to recover what really happened in Syria during early 2011 because it is not a book about Syria, it is a book about how educated Westerners used the Syrian revolution for their own purposes, distorting other Westerners' view of the Middle East and the Arab Spring in the process. A lot of people were embarrassed or inconvenienced by the hoax, but the real victims were the Syrians whose speech and actions were overwritten by Western narratives, including MacMaster's hoax. After MacMaster was unmasked, Ahmed Danny Ramadan, a gay Syrian activist based in Lebanon, vented his anger with MacMaster's "holier than thou attitude" of claiming "'I'm just trying to bring attention to those poor people in Syria.'" He reminded MacMaster that "we have voices, thank you very much. We can talk. We know how to create blogs. We have plenty of blogs. We can talk . . . now back off. All you did was create shit for us."[8]

---

8 Ahmed Danny Ramadan, *Profil Amina*.

Bibliography

Abu-Lughod, Lila. *Do Muslim Women Need Saving*. Cambridge MA: Harvard University Press, 2015.

Abu-Lughod, Lila. "Review: 'Orientalism' and Middle East Feminist Studies." *Feminist Studies*. 27, no. 1 (Spring, 2001): 101–113.

Ahmed, Sara. *The Promise of Happiness*. Durham NC: Duke University Press, 2010.

Akou, Heather. "Interpreting Islam through the Internet: making sense of hijab." *Contemporary Islam* 4 no. 3 (2010): 331–346

Alcoff, Lina. "The Problem of Speaking for Others." *Cultural Critique* 5, no. 20 (1991): 5–32.

Gordon Alley-Young, "Co-opting Voice and Cultivating Fantasy: Contextualizing and critiquing the A Gay Girl in Damascus hoax blog" in *Ethic, Ethnocentrism and Social Science Research*, ed. Diya Sharma (New York: Routledge, 2021), 122–147.

Asenbaum, Hans. "Anonymity and Democracy: Absence as Presence in the Public Sphere." *American Political Science Review* 113, no 3 (2018): 459–472.

Abunimah, Ali. "New evidence about Amina, the 'Gay Girl in Damascus' hoax," *Electronic Intifada*, 12 June 2011. https://electronicintifada.net/comment/364

Axford, Barrie. "Talk about a revolution: Social media and the MENA uprisings." *Globalizations* 8, no 5 (2011): 681–686.

Ben Mhenni, Lina. *Tunisian Girl: Blogueuse pour un printemps arabe*. Barcelona: Indigène éditions, 2011.

Bhambra, Gurminder K. "Postcolonial and decolonial dialogues" *Postcolonial Studies* 17, no 2 (2014): 115–121.

Bollmer, Grant. "Demanding Connectivity: The Performance of 'True' Identity and the Politics of Social Media" *JOMEC Journal*. 0 no 1 (June 2012): 1–12.

Boone, Joseph A. *The Homoerotics of Orientalism*. New York: Columbia University Press, 2014.

Bromwich, Jonah Engel and Ezra Marcus. "The Anonymous Professor Who Wasn't," *New York Times*. 4 August 2020. https://www.nytimes.com/2020/08/04/style/college-coronavirus-hoax.html

Bruns, Axel, Tim Highfield, Jean Burgess. "The Arab Spring and Social Media Audiences: English and Arabic Twitter Users and Their Networks". *American Behavioral Scientist* 57, no 7 (2013): 871–98.

Butler, Judith. "Explanation and Exoneration, or What We Can Hear" *Grey Room* 7 (Spring 2002): 56–67.

Cardell, Kylie and Emma Maguire. "Hoax Politics: Blogging, Betrayal, and the Intimate Public of a Gay Girl in Damascus" *Biography*. 38 no. 2 (2015): 205–221.

Carbonell, Linda S. "Syria Protests Story Apology," *Lez Get Real*. 7 February 2011.

Carvin, Andy. *Distant Witness: Social Media, the Arab Spring, and a Journalism Revolution*. New York: CUNY Journalism Press, 2012.

Cassano, Graham. "'The Last of the World's Afflicted Race of Humans Who Believe in Freedom:' Race, Colonial Whiteness and Imperialism in John Ford and Dudley Nichols's The Hurricane (1937)." *Journal of American Studies* 44 (2010): 117–136.

Castells, Manuel. *The Power of Identity*. Oxford: Blackwell, 1997.

Caudill, Helen. "Tall, Dark, and Dangerous: Xena, the Quest, and the Wielding of Sexual Violence in *Xena* On-Line Fan Fiction." In *Athena's Daughters: Television's New Women Warriors*, edited by Frances Early and Kathleen Kennedy. 27–39, Syracuse University Press: Syracuse NY, 2003.

Cole, Juan. *The New Arabs: How the Millennial Generation is Changing the Middle East*. New York: Simon & Schuster; 2014.

https://doi.org/10.1515/9783111057231-007

Conklin, Alice. *A Mission to Civilize: The Republican Idea of Empire in France and West* Africa, *1895–1930*. Stanford: Stanford, University Press, 1997.

Dalacoura, Katerina. "Homosexuality as cultural battleground in the Middle East: culture and postcolonial international theory" *Third World Quarterly* 35, no 7 (2014): 1290–1306.

DiAngelo, Robin. *White Fragility: Why it's so Hard for White People to Talk About Racism*. Boston MA: Beacon Press, 2018.

El-Khairy, Omar. *Sour Lips*. London: Oberon, 2013.

El Feki, Shereen. *Sex and the Citadel: Intimate Life in a Changing Arab World*. New York: Anchor Books, 2014.

Eng, David. *The Feeling of Kinship Queer Liberalism and the Racialization of Intimacy*. Durham: Duke University Press, 2010.

Engel, Stephen and Timothy Lyle. *Disrupting Dignity: Rethinking Power and Progress in LGBTQ Lives*. Oxford: Oxford University Press, 2021.

Enright, Mairead. "Girl interrupted: citizenship and the Irish Hijab debate." *Social & Legal Studies* 20, no 4 (Dec, 2011): 463–480.

Epps, Brad. "Comparison, Competition, and Cross-Dressing: Cross-Cultural Analysis in a Contested World" in *Islamicate Sexualities: Translations across Temporal Geographies of Desire*. Edited by Kathryn Babayan and Afsaneh Najmabadi. Cambridge MA: Harvard University Press, 2008, 114–160.

Feinberg, Richard. *The Intemperate Zone: The Third World Challenge to U.S. Foreign Policy*. New York: W. W. Norton & Company, 1983.

Flock, Elizabeth and Melissa Bell "'A Gay Girl in Damascus' comes clean," *Washington Post*. 12 June 2011. https://www.washingtonpost.com/blogs/blogpost/post/tom-MacMaster-the-man-behind-a-gay-girl-in-damascus-i-didnt-expect-the-story-to-get-so-big/2011/06/13/AGhnHiSH_blog.html?utm_term=.b19b82dd2824.

Flock, Elizabeth and Melissa Bell, "Tom MacMaster, the man behind 'A Gay Girl in Damascus' 'I didn't expect the story to get so big,'" *Washington Post*. 12 June 2011. https://www.washingtonpost.com/blogs/blogpost/post/tom-macmaster-the-man-behind-a-gay-girl-in-damascus-i-didnt-expect-the-story-to-get-so-big/2011/06/13/AGhnHiSH_blog.html

Halperin, David. *What Do Gay Men Want? An Essay on Sex, Risk, and Subjectivity*. Ann Arbor: University of Michigan Press, 2007.

Haritaworn, Jin, Tamsila Tauqir, and Esra Erdem "Gay Imperialism: Gender and Sexuality Discourse in the 'War on Terror.'" In *Out of Place: Interrogating Silences in Queerness/Raciality*, edited by Adi Kuntsman and Esperanza Miyake. York: Raw Nerve Books, 2008 71–92.

Hassan, Oz. "Bush's Freedom Agenda: Ideology and the Democratization of the Middle East". *Democracy and Security* 4, no. 3 (2008): 268–89.

Hobbs, Allyson. *A Chosen Exile: A History of Racial Passing in American Life*. Cambridge MA: Harvard University Press, 2016.

Hollinger, David. *Postethnic America: Beyond Multiculturalism*. New York: Basic Books, 1995.

Hunt, Michael. *Ideology and Foreign Policy*. Cambridge MA: Harvard Universit Press, 1987; 2009.

Hunt, Michael. *The Making of a Special Relationship: The United States and China to 1914*. New York: Columbia University Press, 1983.

İlkkaracan, Pinar. 'Women, Sexuality, and Social Change in the Middle East and the Maghreb.' *Social Research*. 69, no 3 (Fall 2002): 753–779.

Iwamura, Jane Naomi. *Virtual Orientalism: Asian Religions and American Popular Culture*. New York: Oxford University Press, 2011.

Jung, Courtney. *The Moral Force of Indigenous Politics: Critical Liberalism and the Zapatistas*. New York: Cambridge University Press, 2008.

Kabbani, Rana. *Europe's Myths of the Orient*. Bloomington: Indiana University Press, 1986.

Kashino, Marisa. "The True Story of Jess Krug, the White Professor Who Posed as Black for Years – Until It All Blew Up Last Fall," *Washingtonian*. 27 January 2021. https://www.washingtonian.com/2021/01/27/the-true-story-of-jessica-krug-the-white-professor-who-posed-as-black-for-years-until-it-all-blew-up-last-fall/

Kawakibi, Salam. "Les médias privés en Syrie." *Maghreb-Machrek* 203 (2010): 59–71.

Khalidi, Rashid. "Preliminary Historical Observations on the Arab Revolutions of 2011" in *Dawn of the Arab Uprisings: End of an Old Order?* eds Bassam Haddad, Rosie Bsheer, and Zaid Abu-Rish. London: Pluto Press, 2012: 9–16.

Kirk, Connie Ann. *J. K. Rowling: A Biography*. Westport CT: Greenwood, 2003.

Krug, Jessica. "The Truth, and the Anti-Black Violence of My Lies," *Medium*. 3 September 2020. https://medium.com/@jessakrug/the-truth-and-the-anti-black-violence-of-my-lies-9a9621401f85

Kumar, Deepa. *Islamophobia and the Politics of Empire*. Chicago: Haymarket Books, 2012.

Le Profile Amina, Amazon Streaming Video, Directed by Sophie Deraspe Montreal: Esperamos and the National Film Board of Canada, 2015.

Lewis, Reina. *Gendering Orientalism: Race, Femininity and Representation*. Routledge: New York, 1995.

Liu, Petrus. *Marxism in the Two Chinas*. Durham NC: Duke University Press, 2015.

Loewenstein, Antony. *The Blogging Revolution*. Melbourne: Melbourne University Publishing, 2008.

MacMaster, Thomas. *A Gay Girl in Damascus: An out Syrian lesbian's thoughts on life, the universe and so on . . .* http://damascusgaygirl.blogspot.com; archived at http://www.minalhajratwala.com/wp-content/uploads/2011/06/damascusgaygirl.blogspot.com.zip.

MacMaster, Thomas. *Amina Arraf's Attempts At Art (and Alliteration)*, http://aminaarraf.blogspot.com. Archived as *Internet Archive: Wayback Machine*. https://archive.org/web/

MacMaster, Thomas. 'News from the East: The seventh century crises as reflected in western sources.' Master's Thesis, University of Edinburgh, 2012.

Majed, Ziad. *Syrie: La revolution orpheline*. trans Fifi Abou Dib and Ziad Majed. Sindbad/Actes sud L'Orient des livres, 2014.

Maras, Marie-Helen, and Alex Alexandrou. "Determining Authenticity of Video Evidence in the Age of Artificial Intelligence and in the Wake of Deepfake Videos". *The International Journal of Evidence & Proof* (2018): https://doi.org/10.1177/1365712718807226. Web.

Marhoefer, Laurie. *Racism and the Making of Gay Rights: A Sexologist, his Student, and the Empire of Queer Love*. Toronto, University of Toronto Press, 2022.

Marx, Anthony. *Making Race and Nation: A Comparison of the United States, South Africa, and Brazil*. Cambridge: Cambridge University Press, 1998.

McAdam, Doug, John McCarthy, and Mayer Zald. *Comparative Perspectives on Social Movements: Political Opportunities, Mobilizing Structures, and Cultural Framings*. Cambridge: Cambridge University Press, 1996.

McMaster, H.R. *Battlegrounds: The Fight to Defend the Free World*. New York: Harper, 2020.

Mejia, Paul. "The Secret Life of H.G. Carrillo," *Rolling Stone*. 21 February 2021. https://www.rollingstone.com/culture/culture-features/h-g-carrillo-hache-identity-herman-glenn-carroll-afro-cuban-1120491/

Morgenthau, Hans and Ethel Person. "The Roots of Narcissism." *The Partisan Review*, (Summer 1978): 337–347.

Najmabadi, Afsaneh. *Women and Mustaches and Men without Beards: Gender and Sexual Anxieties of Iranian Modernity*. Berkeley CA: University of California Press, 2005.

Nakamura, Lisa. "Cyberrace." *PMLA* 123, no 5 (October 2008):1673–1682.

Nye, David. *Technology Matters: Questions to Live With*. Cambridge MA: MIT Press, 2007.

Puar, Jasbir. "Citation and censure: Pinkwashing and the sexual politics of talking about Israel" in *The Imperial University: Academic Repression and Scholarly Dissent*. Edited by Piya Chatterjee and Sunaina Maira, 281–298. Minneapolis: University of Minnesota Press, 2014.

Puar, Jasbir. *Terrorist Assemblages: Homonationalism in Queer Times*. Durham NC: Duke University Press, 2007.

Pullen, Christopher. *Gay Identity, New Storytelling and the Media*. New York: Palgrave Macmillan, 2009.

Rambaran-Olm, Mary. "Sounds About White: Review of Matthew Gabriele & David M. Perry's "The Bright Ages,'" *Medium*. 27 April 2022. https://mrambaranolm.medium.com/sounds-about-white-333d0c0fd201

Reed, James. *The Missionary Mind and American East Asia Policy, 1911–1915*. Cambridge MA: Harvard University Press, 1983.

Rohy, Valerie. *Anachronism and Its Others: Sexuality, Race, Temporality*. Albany, NY: SUNY Press, 2009.

Rust, Paula. "'Coming out' in the age of social constructionism: Sexual identity formation among lesbian and bisexual women." *Gender & Society* 7, no 1 (March 1993): 50–77.

Ruti, Mari. *The Ethics of Opting Out: Queer Theory's Defiant Subjects*. New York: Columbia University Press, 2017.

Said, Edward. *Covering Islam: How the Media and the Experts Determine How We See the Rest of the World*. New York: Vintage Books; 1981; 1997.

Said, Edward. *Orientalism*. New York: Vintage Books, 1979; reprint 1994.

Said, Edward. *Power, Politics, and Culture: Interviews with Edward W. Said*. New York: Vintage Books, 2002.

Said, Edward. 'Representing the Colonized: Anthropology's Interlocutors.' *Critical Inquiry* 15 no. 2 (1989): 205–225.

Savcı, Evren. *Queer in Translation: Sexual Politics and Neoliberal Islam*. Durham NC: Duke University Press, 2021.

Scott, Joan Wallach. *The Fantasy of Feminist History*. Durham NC: Duke University Press, 2011.

Selim, Hebatullah. "Religionizing Politics: Salafis and Social Change in Egypt." PhD Diss. University of Birmingham, 2016.

Smith, Andrea. "For All Those Who Were Indian in a Former Life," *Ms Magazine*. November/December 1991: 44–45.

Smith, Julia Marie. "*A Gay Girl in Damascus*: A Multi-vocal Construction and Refutation of Authorial Ethos." In *Authorship Contested: Cultural Challenges to the Authentic, Autonomous Authors*, edited by Amy E. Robillard and Ron Fortune, 21–39. New York: Taylor & Francis, 2016.

Smith, Merritt Roe and Leo Marx, eds, *Does Technology Drive History? The Dilemma of Technological Determinism*, Cambridge MA: MIT Press, 1994.

Sokal, Alan. "Transgressing the Boundaries: Toward a Transformative Hermeneutics of Quantum Gravity." *Social Text* (1996): 217–252

Somerville, Siobhan. *Queering the Color Line: Race and the Invention of Homosexuality in American Culture*. Durham NC: Duke University Press, 2000.

Somerville, Siobhan. "Scientific Racism and the Emergence of the Homosexual Body" *Journal of the History of Sexuality*, 5, no 2 (1994): 243–66.

Spivak, Gayatri Chakravorty. "Can the Subaltern Speak?" In *Marxism and the Interpretation of Culture*, edited by Cary Nelson and Lawrence Grossberg, 271–316. Chicago: University of Illinois Press, 1988.

Spivak, Gayatri Chakravorty. "Post-structuralism, Marginality, Postcoloniality and Value." In *Literary Theory Today*, edited by Peter Collier and Helga Geyer-Ryan, 219–244. Cambridge: Polity Press, 1990.

Talhamy, Yvette. "The Fatwas and the Nusayri/Alawis of Syria." *Middle Eastern Studies* 46, no. 2 (2010): 175–194.

Trebilcot, Joyce. "Dyke Methods." *Hypatia* 3, no. 2 (1988): 1–13.

Unheard Voice: Evaluating five years of pro-Western covert influence operations Grafica and Stanford Internet Observatory, (2022) https://graphika.com/reports/unheard-voice.

Walters, Mary C. *Ethnic Options: Choosing Identities in America*. Berkeley CA: University of California Press, 1990.

Whitlock, Gillian. *Soft Weapons: Autobiography in Transit*. Chicago: University of Chicago Press, 2006.

Winter, Bronwyn. *Hijab & the republic uncovering the French headscarf debate*. Syracuse, NY: Syracuse University Press, 2008.

Yazbek, Samar. *A Woman in the crossfire: Diaries of the Syrian Revolution*. Translated by. Max Weiss. Haus Publishing: London, 2012.

Yeğenoğlu, Meyda. *Colonial Fantasies: Towards a feminist reading of Orientalism*. New York: Cambridge University Press, 1998.

Young, Kevin. *Bunk: The Rise of Hoaxes, Humbug, Plagiarists, Phonies, Post-Facts, and Fake News*. Minneapolis: Graywolf Press, 2017.

Viren, Sarah. "The Native Scholar Who Wasn't," *New York Times*. 25 May 2021. https://www.nytimes.com/2021/05/25/magazine/cherokee-native-american-andrea-smith.html

Zainal, Humairah and George Wong. "Voices behind the veil: Unravelling the hijab debate in Singapore through the lived experiences of hijab-wearing Malay-Muslim women." *South East Asia Research* 20, no 2 (June 2017): 107–121.

Major Press Sources

ABC News
Al-Jazeerah
BBC
CNN
HuffPost
Lez Get Real
Los Angeles Review of Books
Medium
New York Times
Rolling Stone
The Guardian
The Washington Post
Time
Washingtonian

Twitter Accounts

Bagaria, Sandra. Twitter. https://twitter.com/sade_la_bag
Britton, Akissi. Twitter. https://twitter.com/kinkyintellect
Carvin, Andy. Twitter. https://twitter.com/acarvin
McFaul, Michael. Twitter. https://twitter.com/McFaul
Mortada, Leil-Zahra. Twitter. https://twitter.com/LeilZahra
Starr, Graham. Twitter. https://twitter.com/GrahamStarr
Sudiacal, Sid. Twitter. https://twitter.com/DrSid_S

Index

https://doi.org/10.1515/9783111057231-008